1989

Jack C. Stewart

Counseling Parents
of Exceptional Children
Second Edition

Charles E. Merrill Publishing Company
A Bell & Howell Company
Columbus   Toronto   London   Sydney

Published by
Charles E. Merrill Publishing Co.
A Bell & Howell Company
Columbus, Ohio 43216

This book was set in Garamond.
Cover Designer: Cathy Watterson
Text Designer: Jeffrey Putnam
Production Coordination: Anne Daly

Photo credits: Dutchie S. Riggsby, pp. 3, 12, 30, 69,
111, 124, 140, 176, 187; David S. Strickler, p. 16;
Jean Greenwald/CEM, pp. 41, 59; Margaret Thomas, p. 57;
Harvey R. Phillips, p. 93; Marjorie McEachron/CEM, p. 150;
March of Dimes Birth Defects Foundation, p. 155.

Library of Congress Catalog Card Number: 85-72219
International Standard Book Number: 0-675-20510-7
Printed in the United States of America
  2   3   4   5   6   7   8   9   10—90   89   88   87

Acknowledgements

*A*s with any endeavor of this magnitude, preparation of this book involved the assistance of several people. I wish to thank the following administrators at Columbus College for being a constant source of support, encouragement, and understanding: Sue Dezendolet, Joe Johnson, Steve Halverson, and Carolyn Cartledge.

Dutchie Riggsby, a colleague and outstanding educator, merits my deepest appreciation for providing the splendid photography which adds much to this book's visual appeal. A debt of gratitude is extended to another colleague and friend, Tom Atkins, for his interest in this project and the loan of many reference and resource materials. In addition, thanks go to Dr. Kenneth Burk (Wichita State University), Dr. Daro Larsen (Mankato State University), and Dr. Ray Brewer (California State University at Fresno) for their helpful reviews of this manuscript. Special recognition is due to my secretary, Dianne Fredrick, for the dedication, enthusiasm, and skill with which she undertook the typing of the lengthy manuscript. Her help and tolerance are greatly appreciated.

The people at Charles E. Merrill who gave much care to the design and production of this book are to be commended. A special thanks to my administrative editor, Vicki Knight, who was instrumental in bringing about the second edition and in coordinating the helpful review process. Appreciation is also extended to Carol Huston Driver for her thoughtful editing of the manuscript which greatly improved the text readability and style.

Thanks also and a special note of appreciation to my mother, Joy C. Stewart, and mother-in-law, Ruth M. Scott, for their longstanding love, faith, and confidence. Finally, I am boundlessly grateful to my wife, Beverly, whose endless patience and tolerance with my work bolstered me in many trying hours.

Jack C. Stewart
Columbus College, Georgia

Contents

1 Overview of Special Education

After mastering the material in this chapter, you should be able to

1. Define and explain the following terms and concepts:

special education	PL 94–142
exceptional children	early identification
categories of impairment	and intervention
litigation	labeling
mainstreaming	

2. Discuss the importance of developing and practicing effective helping skills.

3. Briefly describe what the term *special education* means and discuss its implications for those who render helping services.

4. Give a definition and brief description of the term *exceptional children*.

5. Understand and cite specific examples of how litigation, legislation, mainstreaming, early intervention, and labeling are important issues affecting the education of exceptional children.

As Liza sang in 'My Fair Lady,' "wouldn't it be loverly" if it were common to see impaired children playing with their non-impaired friends in parks and in neighborhoods; to notice more quick smiles or welcomes by nonimpaired people when an impaired person comes into a room; to have an increased number of impaired employees in the work force but also increased numbers in the artistic community as well; to find fewer and fewer children functioning below their genetic potential because of lack of appropriate environmental stimulation. It is not only beautiful to think about, it is possible to achieve.

—Nicholas J. Anastasiow

*T*he primary objectives of this second edition are essentially unchanged from the previous one. This revision is designed to fulfill and accomplish three basic purposes. First, it was written for those about to enter into or are already engaged in a profession that assists parents of exceptional children. This includes, but is not limited to, people such as special education teachers, regular classroom teachers, mental health workers, guidance counselors, social workers, vocational rehabilitation counselors, school administrators, psychologists, and physicians. The primary intent of this book is to help the reader improve his or her ability to counsel parents of exceptional children.

Second, this revised edition has updated and expanded sections on recent trends and developments in parent counseling, and is recommended as a primary or supplementary text for graduate or undergraduate students pursuing a degree in one of the many fields of special education. It may be used as a supplementary text in a counselor education program. The subject matter and arrangement of material also make this book appropriate for preservice or inservice training in local school systems or various agencies and organizations.

Third, this edition is a substantial overall revision of *Counseling Parents of Exceptional Children.* The first edition (1978) was written to tie together two essential considerations for effective counseling of parents of exceptional children:

1. Counselors need to have both a practical and theoretical understanding of the purpose, nature, and function of counseling.
2. Counselors need to understand the educational, personal, social, and economic problems encountered by parents with exceptional children and appropriate counseling strategies and techniques to help these parents.

ORGANIZATION OF THE BOOK

This book is in three parts. Chapter One introduces the text and discusses some critical contemporary issues in the special education field. The six chapters in Part One explore counseling theory and practice for helping parents of exceptional children.

Part Two includes a new chapter (Seven): "The Family and the Exceptional Child—Overview and Impact." Chapters Eight and Nine deal with counseling parents of mildly to profoundly handicapped children.

Part Three discusses some important considerations and principles for helping parents cope with the challenges faced by their gifted, talented, and creative children.

A Word About Terminology

Throughout this edition, the terms *counselor* and *helper* are used interchangeably. The individual or persons receiving help may be referred to, again interchangeably, as clients, helpees, interviewees, parents, or parents of exceptional children. Regardless of the specific terminology, I will be referring to someone who functions as counselor, and parents who receive the counselor's assistance, services, skills, and professional knowledge.

SUGGESTIONS TO THE READER

This volume does not claim to be comprehensive; it by no means attempts to discuss (even if this were possible) every facet of counseling parents of exceptional children. The reader should not expect to find magic formulas or prescriptions covering the entire spectrum of parental concerns and problems. Neither does this text suggest cookbook techniques or simple recipes for the helper to apply in any given counseling situation. This revision *does* provide basic information and a review of relevant literature, enabling professionals to form a better conceptual framework of the nature and function of the helping relationship.

As stated later in this text, "advice-giving" is a risky business; however, to enable you to obtain the maximum benefit from this text, I suggest five supplementary activities that will provide a more beneficial and systematic approach toward your study of this material:

1. Use the list of objectives, including terms and concepts, at the beginning of each chapter to focus, direct, and guide your study. Review these both *before* and *after* you begin to study each chapter.
2. Take advantage of the discussion questions at the end of each chapter, and feel free to add questions of your own. You may want to apply this saying to your endeavor: People do not gain wisdom by seeking the right answers; they find it by asking the right questions.
3. Use the primary references at the end of each chapter to further broaden your knowledge and understanding of a specific topic.

4. The suggested supplementary references at the end of each chapter provide an excellent opportunity to expand your knowledge and explore topics of personal interest in greater depth.
5. You don't become an effective helper simply by reading a book—you must constantly be aware of and strive to improve your skills as a helper. Don't be hesitant or afraid to use role-playing activities and/or videotaping to record, identify, discuss, and improve your helping skills.

Johnson (1981) suggests that interpersonal skills are learned just as other skills are learned, through

1. understanding why a skill is important and how it will be of value to you.
2. understanding what the skill is and the component behaviors needed to perform the skill.
3. finding situations where you can practice the skill.
4. getting someone to critique your performance of the skill.
5. practicing!
6. setting up practice units that you can easily master.
7. getting friends to encourage you to use the skill.
8. practicing until it feels real.

Providing a stimulating early environment is critical to a child's development.

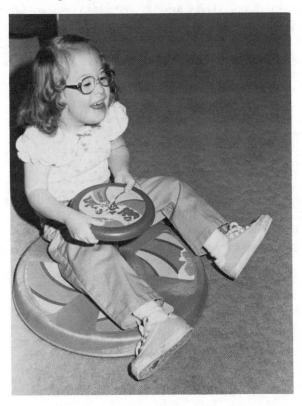

You must have confidence in yourself and say, "This is a learning situation and I'm perfectly willing to take risks and learn from my mistakes (and the mistakes of others)."

Finally, be willing to make a personal commitment and undertake your own additional study or research. If a topic or issue is not covered to your complete satisfaction, then venture out on your own. There may be a more efficient way! Thinking, learning, and discovering are your own prerogatives—nobody else can do these for you. Given this spirit of inquiry and optimism, I hope you will learn and discover more than you thought possible about counseling parents of exceptional children.

Before concluding Chapter One, two other topics require attention. First, it is appropriate to acquaint (or reacquaint) the reader with special education and to define the areas that comprise this field of study. Second, it is important to identify and discuss some of the contemporary issues related to educating exceptional children.

OVERVIEW OF SPECIAL EDUCATION

In his discussion of special education from past to present, Lilly (1979) suggests that special education history can be divided into four time periods:

☐ 1800–1900 Special education treatment begins; residential schooling is stressed

☐ 1900–1925 Many residential schools become custodial in nature; "new" handicaps are discovered

☐ 1925–1960 All types of special education undergo continuous, steady expansion

☐ 1960–1970 Controversy develops concerning nature and role of special education; federal influence increases

The subfield of education, or *special education,* evolved from these major movements. Although different terminology is used, there is general agreement about what constitutes special education. Heward and Orlansky (1984) offer a comprehensive view of special education by stating:

> In one sense, it is a profession, with its own tools, techniques, and research efforts, all focused on improving instructional arrangements and procedures for evaluating and meeting the learning needs of exceptional children and adults. At a more practical level, special education is the individually planned and systematically monitored arrangement of physical settings, special equipment and materials, teaching procedures and the other interventions designed to help exceptional children achieve the greatest possible personal self-sufficiency and academic success. (p. 18)

In light of this definition, one central question remains: Who are exceptional children? Kneedler (1984) offers this straightforward comment:

> Exceptional children are those whose characteristics are so different from most children's that the usual educational programs of the public schools are not appropriate for them. These children are extremely unlikely to achieve their full human potential without a special program designed to capitalize on their abilities and/or help them overcome their disabilities. (p. 7)

Many authors also point out the distinction between the terms *exceptional, disabled,* and *handicapped,* often used interchangeably to refer to the same individual. Mandell and Fiscus (1981) identified an exceptional child as one who is atypical and whose performance deviates from what is expected. (The term *exceptional children* would then include the intellectually gifted as well as the mentally retarded child because both deviate from the norm.) Disability refers to either a total or partial behavioral, mental, physical, or sensory loss of functioning. In other words, all disabled people are exceptional; the reverse is not true. A disability or exceptionality is within an individual; a handicap refers to a person's environmental restrictions because of his or her disability or impairment.

Exceptional children are frequently grouped into categories. This arbitrary grouping of students may be done for a number of reasons—certainly it facilitates communication among professionals and also serves to expedite the allocation of federal and state funds for exceptional children.

According to Kneedler (1984), the following groups are typically included as exceptional:

1. Mentally Retarded
2. Learning Disabled
3. Emotionally Disturbed
4. Physically Handicapped
5. Hearing Impaired
6. Visually Impaired
7. Speech and Language Disordered
8. Gifted and Talented

Kirk and Gallagher (1983) suggest a slightly different arrangement of groupings as typical:

1. Mental deviations, including children who are intellectually superior and slow in learning ability/mentally retarded;
2. Sensory handicaps, including children with auditory impairments and visual impairments;
3. Communication disorders, including learning disabilities and speech and language impairments;
4. Behavior disorders, including emotional disturbance and social maladjustment;
5. Multiple and severe handicaps, including various combinations of impairments: cerebral palsy and mental retardation, deaf-blind, severe physical and intellectual disabilities, and so forth.

In the Education for All Handicapped Children Act (Public Law 94–142*), impairments are established for handicapped children. According to this legislation, handicapped children must meet two criteria: The child must have one or more of the disabilities listed in the next section, and he or she must require special education and related services. In other words, not all children who have a disability require special education; many are able to and should attend school without any program modification. Some of the disabilities included in the PL 94–142 definition are

☐ Deaf
A hearing impairment so severe that the child cannot understand what is being said with or without a hearing aid.

☐ Deaf-blind
A combination of hearing and visual impairments causing such severe communication, developmental, and educational problems that the child cannot be accommodated in either a specific program for the deaf or one for the blind.

☐ Hard of hearing
A hearing impairment that adversely affects a child's educational performance but is not as severe as deafness.

☐ Mentally retarded
Subaverage intellectual functioning and deficits in adaptive behavior. These deficits should have been observable throughout the child's development.

☐ Multiple-handicapped
A combinationn of impairments, other than deaf-blindness, that causes such severe problems that the child cannot be accommodated in a special education program for any one impairment.

☐ Orthopedically impaired
A severe physical disability that adversely affects educational performance. The term includes impairments such as a club foot, absence of a limb, cerebral palsy, poliomyelitis, and bone tuberculosis.

☐ Other health impaired
Limited strength, vitality, or alertness due to chronic or acute health problems such as rheumatic fever, asthma, hemophilia, and leukemia, that adversely affect the child's educational development.

☐ Seriously emotionally disturbed
Children who have a marked degree of one or more of the following characteristics displayed over a long period of time:
An inability to learn that cannot be explained by intellectual, sensory, or health factors.
An inability to build or maintain satisfactory interpersonal relationships.
Inappropriate types of behavior or feelings under normal circumstances.

---

*Legislation is typically designated PL (for Public Law), followed by a hyphenated number. The first number signifies the number of the Congress that passed the bill; the second number indicates the exact number of the bill. PL 94–142, then, was the 142nd Public Law enacted by the 94th Congress.

A general pervasive mood of unhappiness or depression.
A tendency to develop physical symptoms or fears associated with personal or school problems.
This term does not include students who are socially maladjusted, unless they are also seriously emotionally disturbed.

☐ Specific learning disability
A disorder affecting the child's understanding or use of spoken or written language. The student's ability to listen, think, speak, read, write, spell, or do mathematical calculations may be affected. Conditions such as perceptual handicaps, brain injury, minimal brain dysfunction, dyslexia, and developmental aphasia are included in this category. This term does not include children who have learning problems that are primarily the result of visual, hearing, or motor handicaps; mental retardation; or environmental, cultural, or economic disadvantage.

☐ Speech impaired
A communication disorder such as stuttering or impaired articulation, a language impairment, or a voice impairment that adversely affects a child's educational performance.

☐ Visually handicapped
A visual impairment that, even with correction, adversely affects a child's educational performance. The term includes both partially seeing and blind children.

CONTEMPORARY ISSUES IN SPECIAL EDUCATION

Some of the critical issues in the education of exceptional children should be briefly discussed. These issues directly or indirectly affect not only professionals who work with exceptional children and youth, but also parents and their children. These issues are as follows:

1. Litigation
2. Legislation
3. Mainstreaming (Least Restrictive Environment)
4. Early Identification and Intervention
5. Labeling/Classification

The discussion that follows is not a complete listing and chronology of all major issues; it is an attempt to focus on selected issues relevant to the field of special education and to emphasize how these issues influence the education of exceptional children. Readers interested in a more detailed coverage should refer to the primary and supplemental references cited at the end of this chapter or consult any of the introductory texts in special education now available.

Litigation

Litigation comes from the word *litigate,* which, according to Webster's New Collegiate Dictionary, means "to carry on legal contest by judicial process." Weintraub and Abeson (1974) describe a quiet revolution that has been fought within American education during the past few years to protect the right to an education for all American children—particularly the handicapped, whose mental, physical, emotional, or learning problems require special education services. Weintraub and Abeson comment:

> This revolution to establish for the handicapped the same right to an education that already exists for the nonhandicapped has been occurring throughout the nation, in state and local school board rooms, state legislative chambers, and perhaps most importantly, in the nation's courts.
>
> The legality of denying a public education to handicapped children by exclusion, postponement, or any other means is increasingly being challenged. The basis for this challenge comes from the equal protection clause of the Fourteenth Amendment to the U.S. Constitution, which guarantees to all the people equal protection of the laws. (pp. 526–529)

Judicial action has undoubtedly been a primary vehicle in stopping inequity and suggesting procedural remedies and relief for our handicapped population. Schmid and Nagata (1983) remind us that the *Brown* v. *Board of Education* decision of 1954 had great impact on litigation for the handicapped. The Warren Court, in declaring school segregation illegal because it violated the equal protection clause of the Fourteenth Amendment, provided the legal base for subsequent right to education litigation. A landmark decision in securing rights for the mentally retarded was *Pennsylvania Association for Retarded Children (PARC)* v. *Commonwealth of Pennsylvania* (1971). In this class action suit, the PARC and parents of certain retarded children brought suit against the state of Pennsylvania, seeking a ruling against statutes excluding retarded children from educational programs and training in public schools, and claiming the statutes were unconstitutional and should not be enforced. Four expert witnesses testified that all mentally retarded persons are capable of benefiting from a program of education and training. As the result of a consent agreement, it was determined that the state could not apply any law that would postpone, terminate, or deny mentally retarded children access to a free, publicly supported education. In the final analysis, children could not be denied a public education or be excluded from school on the grounds that they were "unable to profit" from school attendance. (Table 1.1 provides a summary of major court cases.) Singletary, Collings, and Dennis (1977) conclude that litigation in exceptional child education may be summarized as follows:

1. Exceptional child litigation has been developmental in concept. In *Pennsylvania Association for Retarded Children* v. *Commonwealth of Pennsylvania*, it was established that the Commonwealth has an obligation to place each mentally retarded child in a free, public program of education and training appropriate to the child's capacity. Appropriateness of education was expanded to educational adequacy in *Mills* v. *Board of Education of the District of Columbia* (1972). In addition, the Mills case addressed the issue of the child's needs.

2. Exceptional child litigation has a resounding success rate with rulings in favor of the children with special needs.

3. Exceptional child litigation has not attempted to establish that there is a Constitutional right to an education or "fundamental interest" as was planned in *Serrano* v. *Priest.* Once a state elects to provide an education for some, however, the state must provide an education for all.

4. A large number of child advocacy groups support exceptional child litigation.

5. Exceptional child litigation is often led by young attorneys who are aware of the social and legal responsiveness to rights for special children, a situation somewhat similar to the establishment of civil rights in the sixties.

6. Passage of mandatory state statutes establishing the possibility for program development for special youngsters has enhanced exceptional child litigation.

7. Exceptional child litigation is increasing in incidence.

8. Exceptional child litigation has evolved to cover a variety of legal ramifications in establishing rights for exceptional children. Because it has been a step-by-step evolution, a state's total financing scheme is not disrupted.

9. Exceptional child litigation has used legal concepts and consultants from many disciplines.

10. The basic concern of each landmark case discussed is that if we provide an education for some, we must provide it for all, and in providing an education, we must ensure the child's rights to screening, testing, labeling, placement, and development of a comprehensive educational plan for his education. (pp. 490–493)

TABLE 1.1 *Summary of court cases*

Year	Court Cases
1954	*Brown* v. *Topeka Board of Education* (Kansas) Established the right of all children to an equal opportunity to an education.
1968	*Hobson* v. *Hansen* (Washington, D.C.) Declared the track system, which used standardized tests as a basis for special education placement, unconstitutional because it discriminated against black and poor children.
1970	*Diana* v. *State Board of Education* (California) Declared that children cannot be placed in special education on the basis of culturally biased tests or tests given in other than the child's native language.
1972	*Mills* v. *Board of Education of the District of Columbia* Established the right of every child to an equal opportunity for education; declared that lack of funds was not an acceptable excuse for lack of educational opportunity.

(TABLE 1.1, continued)

Year	Court Cases
1972	*Pennsylvania Association for Retarded Citizens* v. *the Commonwealth of Pennsylvania* Class action suit to establish the right to free public education for all retarded children
1972	*Wyatt* v. *Stickney* (Alabama) Declared that individuals in state institutions have the right to appropriate treatment within those institutions.
1979	*Central York District* v. *Commonwealth of Pennsylvania Department of Education* Ruled that school districts must provide services for gifted and talented children whether or not advance guarantee of reimbursement from the state has been received.
1979	*Larry P.* v. *Riles* (California) (first brought to court in 1972) Ruled that IQ tests cannot be used as the sole basis for placing children in special classes.
1979	*Armstrong* v. *Kline* (Pennsylvania) Established right of some severely handicapped children to an extension of the 180-day public school year.
1982	*Rowley* v. *Hendrick Hudson School District* (New York) First case based on PL 94–142 to reach the U.S. Supreme Court. While denying the plaintiff's specific request to have a sign language interpreter in their child's mainstream class, the decision upheld each handicapped child's right to a personalized program of instruction and necessary supportive services, no matter what their cost. The *Rowley* decision affirmed the role of parents in educational decisions as well as made school systems accountable for proving that a handicapped child's education is beneficial (Shrybman, 1982).
1985	In a class action suit filed against the Georgia Department of Education and the Savannah-Chatham County Board of Education, the U.S. Supreme Court upheld a ruling that local school systems may be forced to provide mentally or emotionally handicapped children with year-round schooling ("Year-round schooling," 1985).

Mandell and Fiscus (1981) believe that litigation is likely to be a force demanding the rights of children in the future. It seems certain that litigation will continue to play a major role in developing federal and state policies for the education and welfare of the handicapped. The results of several earlier cases clearly indicate that the courts will intervene when equal educational opportunities are denied to the handicapped. In the case of the

Pennsylvania Association for Retarded Citizens v. *Commonwealth of Pennsylvania,* for example, the three-judge federal panel emphatically stated:

> We have absolutely no hesitation about approving the Agreements as fair and reasonable to the plaintiffs. Approval means that plaintiff retarded children who heretofore had been excluded from a public program of education and training will no longer be so excluded after September 1, 1972. Today, with the following Order, this group of citizens will have new hope in their quest for a life of dignity and self-sufficiency. (Lippman & Goldberg, 1973, pp. 133–134)

Shrybman (1982) offers the following observation:

> The 1980s appear to be ushering in an era in which the trend of the federal government returning to the states and localities more control over their special education policy will increase. The U.S. Department of Education has adopted the general objective of reducing the burdens and costs of existing and future PL 94–142 regulations. The department will continue to review the regulations in an on-going process to:
>
> ☐ Avoid unnecessary regulation
> ☐ Reduce compliance requirements
> ☐ Increase agency accountability for regulatory actions
> ☐ Ensure the societal benefits of the regulations outweigh the cost to society
> ☐ Eliminate burdensome, unnecessary, and unproductive paperwork
> ☐ Minimize the cost of rulemaking to the federal government
> ☐ Ensure that the department is collecting only the information it needs
> ☐ Specifically, reduce burdens for small entities (p. 41).

Legislation

In discussing litigation and legislation, Cartwright, Cartwright, and Ward (1981) stress that although logically the provision of education and other services to the handicapped has been humanistic, the compelling reason has been legislation and court decrees requiring such services. In short, we now have free public education for handicapped children because it is the law. Legislation is the second major force (litigation being the first) in the dramatic development and expansion of special education services. Legislation may be defined simply and straightforwardly as the passage and enactment of laws by the United States Congress or state legislature.

Ysseldyke and Algozzine (1984) noted that although there is a relatively long history of legislation for providing services to handicapped persons, prior to 1950 such legislation was directed primarily toward providing institutional care or rehabilitative services. Federal legislation increased for exceptional persons during the late 1950s and early 1960s. Table 1.2 summarizes the major legislative developments from 1958 to 1978.

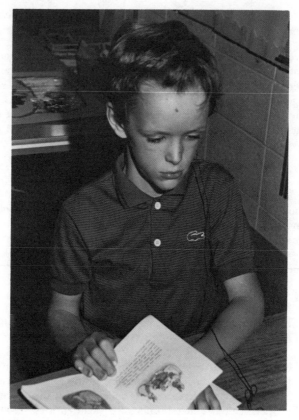

Free public education for handicapped children is the law.

TABLE 1.2   *Legislative developments from 1958 to 1978*

Year	Legislation
1958	PL 85–926 National Defense Education Act Provided funds for teaching professionals to train teachers of mentally retarded children.
1961	PL 87–276 Special Education Act Provided funds for teaching professionals to train teachers of deaf children.
1963	PL 88–164 Mental Retardation Facility and Community Center Construction Act Extended support given in PL 85–926 to training teachers of other handicapped children as well as teachers of mentally retarded children.
1965	PL 89–10 The Elementary and Secondary Education Act Provided money to states and local districts to develop programs for

(TABLE 1.2, continued)

Year	Legislation
	economically disadvantaged and handicapped children.
1966	PL 89–313 Amendment to Title 1 of The Elementary and Secondary Education Act
	Provided funding for state-supported programs in institutions and other settings for handicapped children.
1966	PL 89–750 Amendments to the Elementary and Secondary Education Act
	Created the Bureau of Education for the Handicapped.
1969	PL 91–320 The Learning Disabilities Act
	Defined learning disabilities; provided funds for state-level programs for learning-disabled children.
1970	PL 91–230 Amendments to the Elementary and Secondary Education Act
	Recognized handicapped and exceptional children as a single population with special needs.
1973	PL 93–112, Section 504 Rehabilitation Act (actually adopted in 1977)
	Declared that handicapped people cannot be excluded from any program or activity receiving federal funds on the basis of the handicap alone.
1974	PL 93–380 Education Amendments
	Extended previous legislation. For the first time provided money to state and local districts for programs for gifted and talented students. Also protected rights of handicapped children and parents in placement decisions.
1975	PL 94–103 Developmental Disabilities Assistance and Bill of Rights Act
	Affirmed rights of mentally retarded citizens and cited areas where services must be provided for the retarded and developmentally disabled.
1975	PL 94–142 Education for All Handicapped Children Act
	Mandated free, appropriate public education for all handicapped children regardless of handicap severity; protected rights of handicapped children and parents in educational decision making; required that an individualized education program (IEP) be developed for each handicapped child and that handicapped students receive educational services in the least restrictive environment.
1978	PL 95–561 Gifted and Talented Children's Education Act
	Provided financial incentives for states and local education agencies to identify and educate gifted and talented students, to provide in-service training, and to conduct research.

The passage of the Education for All Handicapped Children Act of 1975 (frequently referred to as Public Law 94–142 or PL 94–142) made public education of the handicapped a reality and is thus often considered the most important legislation in the special education movement. Approved by margins of 375 to 44 in the U.S. House of Representatives and 83 to 10 in the U.S. Senate (and signed by President Gerald Ford on November 29, 1975), PL 94–142 has become law, and thus the quiet revolution to achieve basic educational rights for all children with handicaps nears its goal (Abeson & Zettel, 1977).

In its opening passages, PL 94–142 states:

> There are more than eight million handicapped children in the United States, and these children have special educational needs that are not being fully met. More than half of them do not receive appropriate educational services. One million [are in fact] excluded entirely from the public school system.

PL 94–142 also notes that many other handicapped children, because their handicaps have not been detected, are not succeeding in school.

PL 94–142 was significant for several reasons: first, it expanded the educational rights established in PL 93–380 and increased federal regulatory control of special education; second, it promised substantial federal investment in special education; third, it established the right to education among other issues as a national priority in special education; and finally, PL 94–142 is permanent legislation without an expiration date, a rarity in federal legislation that is indicative of Congress' commitment (Lilly, 1979).

The provisions of PL 94–142 are too lengthy to cover in full detail; however, this legislation does contain certain key elements that should be noted:

☐ A mandatory provision states "in order to receive funds under the Act every school system in the action must make provision for a free, appropriate public education for every child between the ages of 3 and 21 (unless state law does not provide free public education to children 3 to 5 or 18 to 21 years of age) regardless of how, or how seriously, he may be handicapped." 94–142 also provides each handicapped child the right to be educated in the *least restrictive environment* (LRE).

☐ Each handicapped child shall be entitled to a written individualized education program (IEP) developed by a local education agency representative, the teacher, the parents or guardian of the child, and whenever appropriate, the child concerned.

☐ In school placement procedures or in any decisions concerning a handicapped child's educational needs and placement, the child's parents or guardian must be consulted.

☐ The right to due process was established, which protects the individual from erroneous classification, inappropriate labeling, and unequal education with the nonhandicapped.

☐ PL 94–142 protects against discriminatory testing in diagnosis. Tests and other evaluation material used in placing handicapped children will be prepared and administered in the child's native tongue without racial or cultural discrimination.

☐ State and local educational agencies shall take steps to ensure that handicapped children have the variety of programs and services available to non-handicapped children, including industrial arts, home economics, and vocational education.

☐ The results of evaluation and placement must be kept confidential; however, the parents or guardian may have access to records regarding their child.

As Shrybman (1982) has noted, "the entire thrust of the law [PL 94–142] is based on the right of all children, with no exceptions, to an education. Its intent is to give all children, including the most severely handicapped, the learning opportunities they need to achieve their potential and become as self-sufficient as possible" (p. 14).

Mainstreaming

Terms such as *mainstreaming, normalization,* and the *least restrictive environment* are very much in vogue today and part of the educational jargon when speaking about placement of handicapped children. Precise definitions of mainstreaming vary. According to Hutt and Gibby (1976),

> they have in common the philosophy that the retarded child should be moved back into the regular classroom as rapidly as possible, or if that is not feasible, he should have some time each day when he can interact with, and learn with, normal children in regular classroom settings. (p. 391)

Magoon and Garrison (1976) offer the following views on mainstreaming:

> The current trend in American education is toward mainstreaming exceptional children rather than isolating them in special education classes. Mainstreaming refers to placing exceptional children in the regular classroom. Of course, the placement must consider the scope of the child's psychophysical capabilities. Hence, a crippled youngster might be assigned to a regular classroom for affective and cognitive activities and to an alternative physical education class.
>
> The relative merits of mainstreaming have been debated for many years, and the dialogue continues unabated. Historically, special education—like all education—swings from one philosophy to another. First, the movement may be toward isolating special children from the general student body. Then the pendulum swings back toward integration. Two forces—the popularity of the humanist movement and the meteoric rise in the cost of education—are behind today's swing toward mainstreaming. In addition, supporters of mainstream-

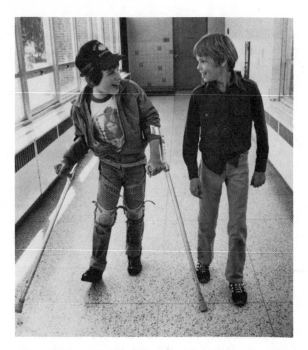

A crippled youngster may be mainstreamed in a regular classroom for affective and cognitive activities and assigned to an alternative physical education class.

ing point out that (1) exceptional children should be educated in the same environment in which they will have to live (i.e., the school should teach them to cope with outside society); (2) exceptional children (with the possible exception of the gifted) need to have "normal" models to emulate; and (3) (as noted earlier) labeling and isolating children is often inappropriate. Opponents of mainstreaming argue that: (1) the regular classroom teacher is already overburdened with socioeducational problems; (2) the regular teacher has not been trained to identify or provide for exceptional students; and (3) the economic attractiveness of mainstreaming has led school administrators (and some of the general public) to "conveniently overlook" the best interests of exceptional children. The opponents argue that mainstreaming is not humanistic, in spite of supporters' claims to the contrary. When viewed from an educational perspective, mainstreaming is not necessarily in the best interests of the individual special child, who may not always receive the optimum education to allow him to maximize his potential for development.

In the future we may very well move toward a compromise, a middle-of-the-road position. Arguments such as these feed the fires of debate and assure that the educational provisions for exceptional children will never become static. (pp. 116–117)

Dybwad (1980) speaks of the heated controversy and misconceptions attached to the catchwords *mainstreaming, normalization,* and the *least restrictive environment.* He points out that these terms sometimes seem to represent an intrusion by a coalition of meddlesome civil rights lawyers and discontented parents on well-established philosophy and practices in the field of special education. According to Dybwad, this argument is an over-simplification, if not a distortion, that ignores significant historical development. To clarify much of the confusion and misunderstanding, Kneedler (1984) offers the following definitions:

> *Normalization*
> Making the handicapped child's life, including his or her education, as much like that of the nonhandicapped as possible.
>
> *Mainstreaming*
> Placing handicapped and nonhandicapped children together for education.
>
> *Least restrictive environment*
> Placing the handicapped child in as normal an environment as is consistent with an appropriate education.

Mandell and Fiscus (1981) point out that the least restrictive environment does not mean that all exceptional children will be educated in regular classrooms; it does not mean that all pupils with handicaps will be placed in self-contained special classes or even in special education programs. What it *does* mean is that when determining the most appropriate setting for a handicapped child, educators must select the least restrictive program alternative relative to the normal school processes. It is assumed that a variety of special programs and types of placements must be available if handicapped children cannot succeeed in regular classes. Leinhardt and Pallay (1982) conducted a comprehensive review of available literature about the least restrictive environment and found that the variables most important for a successful student can occur in most settings, and that for moral and ethical reasons the least restrictive environment is preferred. Educators should, therefore, focus less on debates of setting and more on identifying and implementing sound educational processes.

Early Identification and Intervention

Hayden and McGinnes (1977) stress early identification and intervention in educating the handicapped: "Until we are able to point to a well-established system of public education for the handicapped child from the moment when his handicap is identified, we cannot rest content" (pp. 153–154).

They advocate early intervention for the following reasons:

1. Early experience does have an influence that affects all areas of functioning.
2. Research has shown that there are critical periods for the development of certain skills, most of which occur during the first three years of life.

3. Failure to provide a stimulating early environment leads not only to a continuation of the development status quo, but to actual atrophy of sensory abilities and to developmental regression.
4. All systems of an organism are interrelated in a dynamic way—failure to remediate one handicap may multiply its effect in other developmental areas.
5. With a delay in remediating an intellectual or cognitive handicap, there is a decrease in cumulative achievement even within a single area of functioning.
6. Early intervention has been shown to help; it can work to reduce the effects of a handicapping condition more surely and rapidly than later intervention.
7. The cost-benefit rationale of early intervention is usually more economical than later intervention.
8. Parents need support during early weeks and months, models of good parenting behavior with a handicapped child, and specific instructions for working with the child before patterns of parenting become established.

Bryan and Bryan (1979) have noted some problems that accompany efforts to detect and help children who may experience future academic difficulties. First, it is not clear how such predictions can be made. Which tools, what procedures, which rate of false negative and false positive diagnosis should be employed in detection? Second, labeling the child as high-risk may produce a self-fulfilling prophesy. Once a child is diagnosed as being high-risk, will negative reactions from others increase the likelihood of the child's academic failure? Regardless of these problems in early detection and intervention, those witnessing the development and initiation of early childhood special education services and programs are optimistic. Heward and Orlansky (1984) point out that virtually every special educator today recognizes the importance of early intervention for both handicapped and high-risk children, and most agree that the earlier the intervention begins, the better.

Mandell and Fiscus (1981) have outlined four stages of early identification: population/program definition, screening, diagnosis, and intervention (see Table 1.3). Each stage depends on the preceeding one, although a child may enter the process at the diagnosis level when referred directly by parents or agencies.

Labeling/Classification of Exceptional Children

In his book *The Futures of Children: Categories, Labels, and their Consequences,* Hobbs (1975) refers to classification as serious because it can profoundly affect what happens to a child. Classification can open doors to services and experiences the child needs for growing competence. On the other hand, inappropriate classification can blight the life of a child—it can reduce opportunity, diminish competence and self-esteem, cause alienation

TABLE 1.3   *The early identification process*

Steps	Activities	Outcome
1. Population/ Program Definition	a. Determine geographic region to be served b. Determine age group to be screened c. Describe problems to be identified d. Define pass/refer criteria e. Determine appropriate outreach method	Clear purpose for initiating screening program is identified
2. Screening	Administer appropriate tests, parent questionnaires, interviews	Children having potential problems are referred for diagnosis
3. Diagnosis	Provide in-depth examination by professionals of suspected problem area	Confirmation or denial of problem—children with diagnosed problem receive intervention
4. Intervention	Implement appropriate treatment and/or educational plan based upon diagnostic information	Amelioration, remediation of identified learning and behavior deficit

from others, and prevent realization of the child's potential. Few topics in special education have received more attention than the effects of labels. Meyen (1982) suggests that most special eductors agree that labeling exceptional children not only conveys negative information about the labeled child, but also tends to have a negative influence on the child's life.

Kirk and Gallagher (1983) explore the major differences of opinion about classifying exceptional children in subgroups. They find that those who oppose categorizing usually feel that (1) classification leads to misclassification and mislabeling, particularly in low-income families; (2) categories do not lead to educationally relevant programs; and (3) categories and labels are detrimental to the self-concept of the labeled children. Those who favor classification state that (1) the purpose of classification is to bring the special child into contact with trained personnel who will provide a special educational program; (2) categorizing exceptional children focuses the attention of lawmakers on their problems and aids in obtaining legislation to support special programs; (3) categories allow us to pursue the causes of the handicapping conditions; and (4) categories, when used properly, aid in communication.

While acknowledging that classification is a necessary activity in all disciplines, Heward and Orlansky (1983) present a compelling argument against the traditional classification systems now in practice. Their strongest objection is that current systems are not educationally relevant. Knowing that a child is classified as "mentally retarded" indicates neither what specific skills the child needs to learn nor how the skills may best be taught. In light of the relevancy issue, Heward and Orlansky suggest that alternative classification systems be devised based on educationally relevant variables, leading to strategies tailored to a child's individual needs. In a similar vein, Reynolds (1984) suggests that special education classification should be oriented toward dimensions, such as academic achievement and educational potential, rather than categories. Several years earlier, Reynolds and Balow (1972) stressed the importance of variables using an analogue with the weather: If temperature, humidity, and atmospheric pressure (the variables) can be measured reliably, why not use the variables directly to characterize the weather on a particular day rather than simply describing the weather as "hot" and "muggy." As the question of the effects of labeling children lingers on, it appears that the creation of new labels is not the solution. Instead, we should continue seeking alternative treatment systems rather than focusing on simple and often misleading descriptions of handicapping conditions.

CHAPTER SUMMARY

It is important that professionals who interact with parents of exceptional children develop and practice appropriate helping skills. Using the suggested five-step process on page 2 to improve these crucial communication skills will increase the likelihood that our contacts with parents of exceptional children will be more productive and beneficial.

The term *special education* is used to denote the services, special equipment, and materials usually extended to children whose needs cannot be met in the regular classroom. Special education, therefore, is for the exceptional child. By definition, this child deviates from the norm in performance or ability as a result of sensory handicaps, mental deviations, communication disorders, learning disabilities, or health impairments.

Several issues were discussed to supply the reader with some essential information in gaining an overall perspective of the field of special education. A working knowledge and understanding of *litigation* is important because the courts have ruled in a number of cases (many of them class actions) in favor of handicapped children. In doing so, the right of the handicapped to a free and appropriate public education has been reaffirmed.

Appropriate *legislation* at the federal/state levels has also ensured the handicapped of their right to an appropriate education. PL 94–142 currently stands out as the best example of such legislation. *Mainstreaming, least restrictive environment,* and *normalization* were included and discussed not only because the meanings are often confused, but because of the profound effect they had upon special education. *Early detection and intervention* is a prevailing belief among professionals that early identification coupled with proper prenatal care and a nurturing environment play a profound role in shaping the handicapped child's intellectual, social, emotional, and physical development. *Labeling,* or the classification of exceptional children, continues to spark controversy and discussion primarily because a label tends to say very little about the child and provides scant information for planning appropriate educational programs and services.

REFERENCES

Abeson, A., & Zettel, J. (1977). The end of the quiet revolution: The Education for All Handicapped Children Act of 1975. *Exceptional Children, 44,* 114–128.

Bryan, J. H., & Bryan, T. H. (1979). *Exceptional Children.* Sherman Oaks, CA: Alfred.

Cartwright, G. P., Cartwright, C. A., & Ward, M. E. (1981). *Educating special learners.* Belmont, CA: Wadsworth.

Cowles, A. (1985, February 20). Year-round schooling plan upheld: Handicapped students win high court victory. *The Atlanta Constitution,* pp. 1A, 7A.

Dybwad, G. (1980). Avoiding misconceptions of mainstreaming, the least restrictive environment and normalization. *Exceptional Children, 47,* 85–88.

Hayden, A. H., & McGinness, G. D. (1977). *Educational programming for the severely and profoundly handicapped.* Reston, VA: The Council for Exceptional Children.

Heward, W. L., & Orlansky, M. D. (1984). *Exceptional children.* Columbus, OH: Charles E. Merrill.

Hobbs, N. (1975). *The futures of children.* San Francisco: Jossey-Bass.

Hutt, M. L., & Gibby, R. G. (1976). *The mentally retarded child: Development, education and treatment.* Boston: Allyn & Bacon.

Johnson, D. W. (1981). *Reaching out: Interpersonal effectiveness and self-actualization* (2nd ed.). Englewood Cliffs, NJ: Prentice-Hall.

Kirk, S. A., & Gallagher, J. J. (1983). *Educating exceptional children.* Boston: Houghton Mifflin.

Kneedler, R. D. (1984). *Special education for today.* Englewood Cliffs, NJ: Prentice-Hall.

Leinhardt, G., & Pallay, A. (1982). Restrictive educational settings: Exile or haven? *Review of Educational Research, 52,* 557–558.

Lilly, M. S. (1979). *Children with exceptional needs.* New York: Holt, Rinehart, & Winston.

Lippman, L., & Goldberg, I. I. (1973). *Right to education.* New York: Teachers College Press.

Magoon, R. A., & Garrison, K. C. (1976). *Educational psychology: An integrated view.* Columbus, OH: Charles E. Merrill.

Mandell, C. J., & Fiscus, E. (1981). *Understanding exceptional people.* St. Paul: West.

Meyen, E. L. (1982). *Exceptional children and youth: An introduction* (2nd ed.). Denver: Love.

Reynolds, M. C. (1984). Classification of students with handicaps. In E. W. Gordon (Ed.), *Review of Research in Education* (pp 63–92). Washington, DC: American Educational Research Association.

Reynolds, M. C., & Balow, B. (1972). Categories and variables in special education. *Exceptional Children, 38,* 357–366.

Schmid, R. E., & Nagata, L. M. (1983). *Contemporary issues in special education.* New York: McGraw-Hill.

Shrybman, J. A. (1982). *Due process in special education.* Rockville, MD: Aspen Systems.

Singletary, E. E., Collings, G. D., & Dennis, H. F. (1977). *Law briefs on litigation and the rights of exceptional children, youth, and adults.* Washington, DC: University Press of America.

Weintraub, F., & Aberson, A. (1974). New education for the handicapped: The quiet revolution. *Phi Delta Kappan, 55,* 526–529.

Ysseldyke, J. E., & Algozzine, B. (1984). *Introduction to special education.* Boston: Houghton Mifflin.

SELECTED REFERENCES FOR FURTHER READING AND STUDY

Anastasiow, N. J. (1981). Early childhood education for the handicapped in the 1980s: Recommendations. *Exceptional Children, 47,* 276–282.

Garrett, J. E., & Brazil, N. (1979). Categories used for identification and education of exceptional children. *Exceptional Children, 45,* 291–292.

Gottlieb, J. (1982). Mainstreaming. *Education and Training of the Mentally Retarded, 17,* 79–82.

Halpern, R. (1982). Impact of PL 94–142 on the handicapped child and family: Institutional responses. *Exceptional Children, 49,* 270–273.

Jones, R. L. (1972). Labels and stigma in special education. *Exceptional Children, 38,* 553–564.

Knoff, H. M. (1983). Effect of diagnostic information on special education placement decisions. *Exceptional Children, 49,* 440–444.

Lichtenstein, R. (1982). New instrument, old problem for early identification. *Exceptional Children, 49,* 70–72.

Mercer, C. D., Algozzine, B., & Trifiletti, J. J. (1979). Early identification: Issues and considerations. *Exceptional Children, 46,* 52–54.

Nadler, B., Merron, M., & Friedel, W. K. (1981). Public Law 94–142: One response to the personnel development mandate. *Exceptional Children, 47,* 463–464.

Raiser, L., & Van Nagel, C. (1980). The loophole in PL 94–142. *Exceptional Children, 46,* 516–520.

Reschly, D. J., & Lamprecht, M. J. (1979). Expectancy effects of labels: Fact or artifact? *Exceptional Children, 46,* 55–58.

Zigler, E., Balla, D., & Hodapp, R. (1984). On the definition and classification of mental retardation. *American Journal of Mental Deficiency, 89* (3), 215–230.

PART ONE

*I*n this section you will explore the art (the "how") and the science (the "what") of counseling. Other purposes of this section are (a) to explain the term *counseling* by offering several definitions, (b) to propose a definition of counseling parents of exceptional children, (c) to identify and discuss the counseling process and four approaches, and (d) to analyze issues that impact on the helping relationship. Throughout this section I want to encourage you to arrive at your own conclusions about the skills needed by effective helpers. Concern, caring, compassion, even good intentions are not sufficient for helping most parents of exceptional children. After studying this section, I hope you will realize that effective counselors must have an array of skills and attitudes that extend beyond a willingness and genuine desire to help others.

2 Overview of Counseling

After mastering the material in this chapter, you should be able to

1. Compare and contrast definitions of counseling.

2. Understand the essential differences between *counseling* and *giving advice*.

3. Discuss counseling philosophically, considering both the client's and counselor's search for values.

4. Discuss the kinds of people that should counsel parents of exceptional children as well as the methods they should use.

5. Define the process and differentiate among the distinguishing characteristics of counseling parents of exceptional children.

If you are to make a difference in your helping relationships with others, it means helping others to change their lives in such a way as to make the consequence of their living more satisfying.
—Harold Hackney and Sherilyn Nye

The meaning of life is something that each person must define for himself, and the way a person gives meaning to life will profoundly affect the way in which he lives it.
—Verda Heisler

*T*his chapter begins with a fundamental question: What is counseling? Since this book is about the counseling process and those who practice it, some definitions of counseling are in order. From a historical perspective, counseling was equated with giving advice, and this idea is still prevalent, causing conflict and confusion when educational and noneducational counselors view their function as more than parceling out advice. Further confusion arises when those in search of help are offered assistance by many types of persons who call themselves counselors such as geriatric counselors, financial counselors, mental health counselors, employment counselors, vocational counselors, etc.

WHAT IS COUNSELING?

Counseling has become a catch-all term meaning a variety of practices including encouragement, the giving of advice and information, testing and test interpretation, and even the highly sophisticated and technical practice of psychoanalysis. Some representative definitions of counseling reflect many of the subtle differences that have evolved over the years as well as illustrate that the definition of counseling is not universally agreed upon. According to various authorities, counseling may be defined as

☐ a structured, permissive relationship allowing the client to gain self-understanding that leads to taking positive steps toward the new orientation (Rogers, 1942).

☐ a process that takes place in a one-to-one relationship between a troubled individual and a professional whose training and experience may be used to help others reach personal solutions (Smith, 1955).

☐ that interaction which (a) occurs between two individuals called a counselor and client, (b) takes place in a professional setting, and (c) is initiated and maintained to facilitate changes in the client's behavior (Pepinsky & Pepinsky, 1954).

☐ helping an individual become aware of personal reactions to the behavioral influences of the environment, and helping the individual establish some meaning for this behavior. Counseling also helps the client to develop and clarify a set of goals and values for further behavior (Blocker, 1966).

☐ a process by which a troubled person (the client) is helped to feel and behave in a more personally satisfying manner through interaction with an uninvolved person (the counselor). The counselor provides information and reactions that stimulate the client to develop behaviors for dealing more effectively with oneself and the environment (Lewis, 1970).

☐ attempting to change one's view of oneself, others, or the physical milieu. As a result, one is helped to achieve identity as a person and take steps toward feelings of worth, significance, and responsibility (Bernard & Fullmer, 1977).

☐ generating alternatives, aiding the client in loosening and breaking old patterns, facilitating the decision-making process, and finding viable solutions to problems (Ivey & Simek-Downing, 1980).

☐ empowering the client to cope, to participate in activities that lead to growth, and to make decisions. Counseling helps the counselee to gain control over immediate problems and future possibilities (Patterson & Eisenberg, 1983).

By contrast, Patterson (1967) says counseling is not

1. giving information, though information may be a part of the process.
2. pointing out what the client should do in any given situation.
3. influencing attitudes, beliefs, or behavior by means of persuading, leading, or convincing.
4. influencing behavior by admonishing, warning, threatening, or compelling.
5. interviewing. (Interviewing is involved, but it is not synonymous.)

The nature of counseling is often philosophical. Advocating a developmental approach, Mathewson (1962) contends that the counselor has the responsibility to help the counselee discover values to live by, and then to choose and act accordingly. Curran (1960) also sees the counseling process as a search for values. The counselor's goal, according to Curran, should be to assist the client in searching, then to allow the client to make goal choices. On a personal level, this means seeking the answers to three fundamental questions: Who am I? Where am I going? Why am I going there? Coleman (1969) says that these questions deal with one's self-concept, one's life plans, and one's value patterns—in essence with the self-knowledge involved in self-direction. In contrast to stressing the client's values, Corey, Corey, and Callanan (1984) discuss the counselor's values and possible conflicts that may arise during counseling sessions. It is, of course, possible that a conflict of values can impair a helping relationship.

The burden must be on counselors to honestly assess whether their values are likely to interfere with the objectivity they need to be useful to their clients. To make such an assessment, counselors must be clear about their feelings concerning value-laden issues, they must be honest about their limitations, and they must be honest with potential clients when they think value conflicts will interfere with the therapeutic relationship. (p. 81)

In bringing together these definitions, counseling may be viewed as human interaction that establishes a unique relationship. According to Munson (1971), the counselor can provide an opportunity for others to examine their feelings, attitudes, values, and beliefs and the manner in which they express them in day-to-day behavior. The helper can provide acceptance, understanding, and trust. The counselor doesn't do these things in a counseling cubicle; instead, the counselor tries to be a genuine person and strives to relate to others in "human" ways.

Carl Rogers (1961) has clearly described the helping relationship by suggesting a series of probing questions for the counselor:

Can I *be* in some way which will be perceived by the other person as trustworthy, as dependable, or consistent in some deep sense?

Can I be expressive enough as a person that what I am will be communicated unambiguously?

Can I let myself experience positive attitudes toward this other person—attitudes of warmth, caring, liking, interest, respect?

Can I be strong enough as a person to be separate from the other?

Am I secure enough within myself to permit him his separateness?

Can I let myself enter fully into the world of his feelings and personal meaning and see those as he does?

Can I receive him as he is? Can I communicate this attitude?

Can I act with sufficient sensitivity in the relationship that my behavior will not be perceived as a threat?

Can I free him from the threat of external evaluation?

Can I meet this other person who is in the process of becoming, or will I be bound by his past and by my past? (pp. 50–55)

The term *counseling* is difficult to define with exactness and precision—it can and does vary from one person to another. For example, what does the word mean to you? What is significant, however, is that counseling consists of a relationship between a helper and a client (or parent) where necessary skills or attitudes are used to resolve their unique problems or concerns.

A Helping Activity

Counseling is considered one of the helping professions along with social work, psychiatry and psychology (both clinical and school). Since this book is intended for the varied personnel who work with parents of exceptional children, we need to define who the helpers are. In his article "Who Can Be a Helper?" Brammer (1977) noted that two opposing views surround counseling. One view emphasizes helping as a specialized enterprise based

A counselor must be gentle, thoughtful, and considerate, but still firm and knowledgeable.

on a firm foundation in behavioral and medical science. The other view sees helping as a broad human function using helping skills possessed by most of the population.

This text favors the second view, which Brammer also advocates, that in the context of a helping relationship, effective counseling of parents of exceptional children can be conducted by minimally trained people. A particular word of caution is necessary, however. Demos and Grant (1973) define counseling as a one-to-one, face-to-face relationship between an individual who is seeking help and another who is professionally trained to give this help. To meet the criterion of "professional," the person should have a graduate degree or its equivalent and be in an occupation that helps people become better human beings. The final criterion of a professional is that the practitioner must adhere to a code of ethics. Demos and Grant conclude that an individual does not have to be called a "counselor" to be qualified to counsel, but the person must be a professional limiting his counseling to the scope of professional competency. Recognition of competency is important because in assisting parents of exceptional children, the helper must always be aware of personal strengths and limitations, never attempting to do more than means, capability, and level of expertise allow. Norton (1976) adds that the counselor must be gentle, thoughtful, and considerate, but still firm and knowledgeable about how to assist parents. Sufficient knowledge and experience are fixed and unequivocal criteria. Throughout the remainder of this text, then, all references to counseling and helping will affirm the idea of a person with specialized knowledge of the parent's concern helping within his or her realm of competency.

Because they are closely related, *counseling* and *helping* are used synonomously throughout this text. If a professional listens to parents, making constructive suggestions or offering reassurance, this constitutes a helping relationship. For example, Bassin and Kreeb (1978) give some characteristics of parents with newborn or recently diagnosed retarded children:

1. Parents are looking for answers.
2. They are generally uninformed about mental retardation.
3. Many are receiving ill-timed or poor advice from many people.
4. They are unaware of community programs and services that may be available to them.
5. They may be feeling guilt, depression, or anxiety.
6. Parents often feel isolated and alone—as if they were the only family with a retarded child.
7. They want to talk.
8. They need someone to listen.

When we analyze this list of parental needs and concerns, it seems that a knowledgeable helper could provide the urgently needed support and assistance to these parents. The helper or counselor could serve as a sounding board for parents who want to talk; this would make the parents able to interact more easily, effectively, productively, and lovingly with their retarded child. Demos and Grant (1973) say essentially the same thing when they observe that helping is the core, the foundation, and the essence of counseling.

A Proposed Definition

As we've discovered, *helping* is a difficult word to define because of its different meanings for different people. A definition of counseling parents of exceptional children is appropriate, however, to establish the working boundaries and focal points of counseling. Being aware of these facets of helping is important before even beginning a helping relationship. Here is a proposed definition:

> Counseling is a helping relationship between a knowledgeable professional and the parents of an exceptional child who are working toward a better understanding of their unique concerns, problems, or feelings. Counseling is a learn-

ing process that focuses on the personal growth of the parents, who learn to acquire, develop, and utilize the necessary skills and attitudes for resolving their problem or concern. Parents are helped in becoming fully functioning individuals who assist their child and value a well-adjusted family.

This definition contains several distinguishing characteristics that are either stated or implied: (a) counseling is a helping relationship with a professional who possesses certain skills and competencies, (b) the counselor attempts to aid the parents in identifying and understanding their problem, (c) learning, or a change in behavior, is necessary to bring about a satisfactory solution, (d) acquiring, developing, and utilizing appropriate coping skills can lead to greater self-confidence, (e) the arrival of a handicapped child has an impact on the whole family, (f) while the thrust of helping is working with parents, this does not minimize the needs of the exceptional child's siblings or family—any meaningful way of helping parents should also help the entire family, (g) as a term, *fully-functioning* is similar in meaning to what Abraham Maslow (1970) referred to as *self-actualization*, or the manifestation of one's potential. This humanistic outlook implies that parents can exercise their own potential for learning—they are responsible for using their own resources for development and continued growth.

Our primary goal is to help parents of exceptional children make the best use of their ability and potential. Self-actualization is closely related to any helping function, for it is a dynamic process of becoming, of adapting, of growing, and of changing.

CHAPTER SUMMARY

Historically, the lack of a precise definition of the role and function of a counselor has caused confusion. Many persons profess to be counselors, and parents of exceptional children are likely to receive counseling services from a diverse group of people with varying educational backgrounds, helping skills, and competencies. The viewpoints of this chapter of what counseling is and is not should assist the reader in identifying the essence of the helping relationship. All helpers must be aware of their strengths and weaknesses and refrain from rendering services beyond their ability or level of competency. The proposed definition of counseling parents of exceptional children can help to identify and focus attention on the counseling aspects so vital to working effectively with these parents.

ACTIVITIES, EXERCISES, AND IDEAS FOR REFLECTION AND DISCUSSION

1. Defend or refute the author's proposed definition of counseling parents of exceptional children. What additions or changes would you make? Why?
2. What are some other reasons that make counseling difficult to define?

3. Devise your own definition of counseling. Defend it in terms of purpose, clarity, and expected outcomes.
4. Argue the following statement: A counselor (by definition) serves a unique function and therefore should have formal (professional) training prior to counseling parents of exceptional children.
5. Look back at the series of questions on page 29 that Rogers proposed for the counselor's personal evaluation. On a continuum from 0 to 10, honestly evaluate your feelings as you read each question.

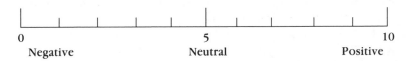

0	5	10
Negative	Neutral	Positive

For example, if intense interest in other people usually leads you to do too much for them, and you feel you are not a strong enough person to be separate from another, you might give yourself a 2 on this characteristic.

After you have finished this rating procedure for all ten questions, go back and carefully analyze your responses. If your responses were mostly positive (6 through 10), you possess similar characteristics to those persons who work effectively in the helping relationship according to Rogers.

If some or most of your responses were negative (0 through 4), carefully analyze each question for possible explanations. You might consider such factors as experience, training, the complexity of the helping relationship, or factors relating to your own personality (attitudes, beliefs, values, openness, and acceptance). The counselor alone must decide how to handle the counseling relationship. In this regard, it would be tragic for the counselor to remain ignorant of his or her own value system and personality.

6. Do you agree or disagree that effective counseling can occur even if the helper lacks formal or professional training in counseling or a related field? Do you agree with the definition that helping is teaching people how to help themselves?
7. Is it realistic to believe that a helper can assist clients and parents to become self-actualizing individuals (individuals who reach or achieve their capabilities and potential to the fullest)?
8. Discuss what is meant by "maintaining a firm and abiding faith in the worth and dignity of the individual." As a supplementary activity, read some of the works of Earl C. Kelley, Carl R. Rogers, Abraham H. Maslow, and Arthur W. Combs. How do they define the helping relationship? How does respect for the individual enhance the relationship?

REFERENCES

Bassin, J., & Kreeb, D. D. (1978). *Reaching out to parents of newly diagnosed retarded children.* St. Louis: St. Louis Association for Retarded Citizens.

Bernard, H. W., & Fullmer, D. W. (1977). *Principles of guidance.* New York: Thomas Y. Crowell.

Blocker, D. H. (1966). *Developmental counseling.* New York: Roland.

Brammer, L. M. (1977). Who can be a helper? *Personnel and Guidance Journal,* *55,* 303–308.

Coleman, J. C. (1969). *Psychology and effective behavior.* Glenview, IL: Scott, Foresman.

Corey, G., Corey, M. S., & Callanan, P. (1984). *Issues and ethics in the helping professions* (2nd ed.). Belmont, CA: Brooks/Cole.

Curran, C. A. (1960). Some ethical and scientific values in the counseling psycho-therapeutic process. *Personnel and Guidance Journal, 34,* 15–20.

Demos, G. D., & Grant, B. (1973). *An introduction to counseling: A handbook.* Los Angeles: Western Psychological Services.

Ivey, A. E., & Simek-Downing, L. (1980). *Counseling and psychotheraphy: Skills, theories, and practice.* Englewood Cliffs, NJ: Prentice-Hall.

Lewis, E. C. (1970). *The psychology of counseling.* New York: Holt, Rinehart, & Winston.

Maslow, A. H. (1970). *Motivation and personality* (rev. ed.). New York: Harper & Row.

Mathewson, R. R. (1962). *Guidance policy and practice.* New York: Harper & Row.

Munson, H. L. (1971). *Foundations of developmental guidance.* Boston: Allyn & Bacon.

Norton, F. H. (1976). Counseling parents of the mentally retarded child. *The School Counselor, 23,* 200–205.

Patterson, C. H. (1967). *The counselor in the school.* New York: McGraw-Hill.

Patterson, L. E., & Eisenberg, S. (1983). *The counseling process* (3rd ed.). Boston: Houghton Mifflin.

Pepinsky, H., & Pepinsky, P. (1954). *Counseling theory and practice.* New York: Roland.

Rogers, C. R. (1942). *Counseling and psychotherapy.* Boston: Houghton Mifflin.

Rogers, C. R. (1961). *On becoming a person.* Boston: Houghton Mifflin.

Smith, G. E. (1955). *Counseling in the secondary school.* New York: MacMillan.

SELECTED REFERENCES FOR FURTHER READING AND STUDY

Benson, J. & Ross, L. (1972). Teaching parents to teach their children. *Teaching Exceptional Children, 5,* 30–36.

Clements, J. E., & Alexander, R. N. (1975). Parent training: Bringing it all back home. *Focus on Exceptional Children, 7,* 1–10.

Cowen, E. L. (1982). Help is where you find it. *American Psychologist, 37,* 385–395.

Davis, J. W. (1981). Counselor licensure: Overskill? *Personnel and Guidance Journal, 60*(2), 83–85.

Gehring, D. D. (1982). The counselor's duty to warn. *Personnel and Guidance Journal, 61*(4), 208–210.

Grabowski, S. M. (1976). Educational counseling of adults. *Adult Leadership, 24,* 225–227.

Hosie, T. W. (1979). Preparing counselors to meet the needs of the handicapped. *The Personnel and Guidance Journal, 58,* 271–275.

Kelly, F. D. (1976). The counselor's role in parent education. *The School Counselor, 23,* 332–338.

McDowell, R. L. (1976). Parent counseling: The state of the art. *Journal of Learning Disabilities, 9,* 614–619.

O'Connell, C. Y. (1975). The challenge of parent education. *Exceptional Children, 41,* 554–556.

Parker, C. A. (1974). The new scope of counseling. *Personnel and Guidance Journal, 52,* 348–350.

Pueschel, S. M., & Murphy, A. (1976). Assessment of counseling practices at the birth of a child with Down's Syndrome. *American Journal of Mental Deficiency, 81,* 325–330.

Seligman, M., & Seligman, P. A. (1980). The professional's dilemma: Learning to work with parents. *The Exceptional Parent, 10,* 511–513.

Smith, D. (1982). Trends in counseling and psychotherapy. *American Psychologist, 37*(7), 802–809.

Tarkelson, C. (1976). Making contact: A parent-child communication skill program. *Elementary School Guidance and Counseling, 11,* 89–96.

Watkins, C. E. (1983). Burnout in counseling practice: Some potential professional and personal hazards of becoming a counselor. *Personnel and Guidance Journal, 61*(5), 304–308.

3 Characteristics and Skills of Effective Helpers

After mastering the content in this chapter, you should be able to

1. Define and discuss the following terms and concepts:

   acceptance   genuineness
   trust   attentiveness
   empathy   ethical behavior
   rapport   human behavior

2. Understand and appreciate how specific attitudes and skills of the helper influence the relationship between parent and helper.

3. Increase your awareness of how you communicate with others in the context of a helping relationship.

*Active listening is appropriate whenever emotion is evident in
the parent. If you anticipate a strong response to a topic you
are going to raise, allow time in the agenda for parents to react
and for active listening to their response.*

Sharon Roberts-Baxter

*Respect or positive regard, in turn, has its origin in the respect
which the individual has for himself. He cannot respect the feelings and experiences of others if he cannot respect his own feelings and experiences.*

Robert R. Carkhuff and Bernard G. Berenson

---

*T*his chapter focuses on some of the significant traits, characteristics, and attitudes usually associated with effective counselors and
helpers. The direction and outcome of any helping relationship is heavily
influenced by the skills, characteristics, and traits of the helper, and research
equates effective counseling with the type of relationship provided by the
helper. One school of thought contends that the counselor's own personality
is the most significant resource a helper brings to a relationship and that
the most significant variable is the helper's self-understanding.

Shertzer and Stone (1980) believe that the attitudes, the methods of
approaching the individual, and the actions of the counselor all influence
the counseling relationship to a marked degree. The counselor is the key
to the initiation and development of the relationship. Counselor traits and
characteristics are vitally important because the consequences are often
far-reaching.

Research tells us that there is no single ideal personality that a counselor
must possess. In the context of the helping relationship as defined in Chapter
Two, many kinds of people, each with individual personalities, can and do
become effective helpers. Many authors have attempted to list counselor
traits that are essential or desirable for effective counseling. For example,
Tyler (1969) believes that intellectual competence and emotional stability
are necessary for counseling. She adds that attitudes of acceptance and understanding are also necessary characteristics.

Parents of exceptional children are faced with many complex and diverse problems associated with their child's handicap. The following discussion of counselor traits will therefore be broad, yet inclusive enough to
offer specific guidelines and suggestions to helpers for becoming more skill-
ful in their interpersonal relationships with parents of exceptional children.

In addition, this chapter can help you to consider on a more personal
level the type of personality a helper should possess to produce the most

effective counseling relationship. If the helper possesses or develops these traits, he or she will be more effective in assisting parents of exceptional children.

This chapter presents a brief discussion of the essential counselor skills and attitudes (sometimes called facilitative dimensions) that contribute to the success or failure of the helping relationship. That these skills are essential is emphasized by Boyd (1978) who says that the crucial element in a counselor's effectiveness is not adopting a particular theory or using a given technique, but offering a therapeutic relationship based on empathy, respect, concreteness, and genuineness.

INTEREST IN PEOPLE

One basic characteristic of being an effective helper is liking people. The counselor must have respect for and faith in those seeking help. It is essential that counselors have the courage to ask themselves if they genuinely like people without being afraid of what feelings may be discovered. Since counseling is one of the helping professions, the counselor must be willing to help by spirit and action as well as words. Coleman (1969) emphasizes that caring for something outside of oneself is one of the most gratifying and self-fulfilling human experiences. The helper must have a deep and sincere capacity to care for others and to help them grow and find meaning and satisfaction in their lives.

ACCEPTANCE AND TRUST

Acceptance requires respect for the client as a person of worth. This is best illustrated by Roger's (1961) statement:

> By acceptance I mean a warm regard for him as a person of unconditional self-worth—of value no matter what his conditions, his behavior, or his feelings. It means a respect and liking for him as a separate person, a willingness for him to possess his own feelings in his own way. It means an acceptance of a regard for his attitudes of the moment, no matter how negative or positive, no matter how much they may contradict other attitudes he has held in the past. (p. 34)

Counselor acceptance may be demonstrated by words, gestures, and postures that convey the message "I accept you." This often means the helper will have to develop and practice the ability to be nonjudgmental. Total acceptance of another person is unconditional; the focus is on self-worth. Acceptance, although important throughout the counseling session, is especially important during the initial phase because it reflects a desire to help but not to control.

Shertzer and Stone (1980) describe acceptance as a positive, tolerant attitude on the part of the counselor that enables the counselee to change.

They suggest that to be accepting of the counselee, the counselor must have self-acceptance and understanding.

Trust is akin to acceptance but more abstract. Trust is manifested by confidence in another person. Munson (1971) points out the importance of trust in the counseling relationship by suggesting that

> A counselor must be trusting—that is, he must trust others. If he is unable to trust others in his own living, it is difficult to transfer this lack of trust outside the counseling relationship to one of trust in it. This feeling of trust, then, is something that the counselor must experience himself in order that the other person can feel free and able to reciprocate and respond in the process of communication. (p. 133)

According to Brammer (1979), a crucial relationship dimension is "trust-distrust." Helpees are generally willing to accept help from people they trust. For trust to develop, helpees must have confidence in their helpers' validity. The helpee experiences the relationship as a shared problem-solving activity to achieve growth. Distrust, then, often causes the helpee to reject offers of help. Brenner (1982) comments that to the degree that trust is absent, clients are apt to be suspicious, withholding, evasive, and unwilling to discuss the private thoughts and feelings that led them to you.

It is important for helpers to make effective use of a communication process that will enhance and encourage free and open communication. You and I, then, must work toward developing a relationship built on trust. Jones, Lepley, and Baker (1984) contend that trust is the basis of effective communication, allowing a person to freely express inner feelings and thoughts.

EMPATHY/UNDERSTANDING

Everyone desires to be understood. The counselor must, therefore, understand the parents with whom they work if the relationship is to be beneficial. Benjamin (1974) notes that we must call on our common humanness to understand how the other person thinks, feels, and sees the world. This means ridding ourselves of our internal frame of reference and adopting the other person's. The point is not to agree or disagree, but to understand what it is like to be the other person.

A special kind of understanding widely recognized in counseling literature is empathy, or the ability to put oneself in the other person's shoes to comprehend his needs and feelings. As the lawyer Atticus Finch said to his children in Harper Lee's *To Kill a Mockingbird*, "You never really understand a person until you consider things from his point of view—until you climb into his skin and walk around in it." Brammer (1979) and others believe that empathy is the principal route to understanding helpees. The recognition and awareness of attitudes, thoughts, feelings, and perceptions between counselor and client are an integral part of an empathic understanding. Understanding and empathy are very similar in meaning. Both mean that the counselor "feels with" the counselee. When we empathize with another person, we are conveying a simple yet meaningful message that "I understand," not "I feel sorry for you." Feeling sorry (sympathy) implies that we may feel superior and more fortunate in some way. The parents of a handicapped child usually need understanding and empathy instead of sympathy or pity.

Ivey and Simek-Downing (1980) suggest important skills necessary in achieving primary empathy. These consist of basic attending behavior, minimal encouragers, paraphrases, reflections of feelings, and summarizations. Ivey and Simek-Downing also point out another beneficial aspect of empathy: If you truly hear the client, you will be more likely to choose appropriate counseling interventions, offer appropriate degrees of warmth and respect, be sufficiently concrete and immediate, and be genuine.

When counseling parents, we must have (or develop) an ability to understand their thoughts and feelings. For example, a parent may strenuously object to what the counselor feels is a logical course of action. If the counselor perceives this as stubborn or foolish behavior, the counselor has failed to be sensitive towards the parent's feelings and will likely be unable to genuinely assist the parent.

RAPPORT

Shertzer and Stone (1980) describe rapport as an essential condition to a comfortable, unconditional relationship between counselor and counselee. It is a bond of interest, responsiveness, and sensitive emotional involvement. Rapport is established and maintained through the counselor's genuine interest in and acceptance of the client—it must be natural, not forced or contrived. Weiner (1975) illustrates the danger of artificiality by the following:

> Patients are also quick to identify when a therapist is behaving in ways that are not natural for him. A customarily somber therapist who decides his patient needs an additional show of warmth and forces himself to smile is being ungenuine. A forced smile, which most patients will recognize immediately, bears eloquent testimony to therapist insincerity, not genuine warmth. Warmth is meaningful only when it is expressed by a person who is being real. Similarly, a therapist who attempts to improve communication with his patient by talking in the patient's vernacular, when he cannot do so comfortably, will appear ungenuine. Anyone not trained in the performing arts who makes a conscious effort to use profanity, slang, dialect, pedantic words, or technical terms that are not ordinarily a part of his speech will stumble and strain in ways that communicate phoniness and pretense. (p. 27)

The establishment of rapport is vital to the success of any helping relationship, especially during the initial counseling session when both counselor and client may be uncertain about each other's roles and expectations. Establishing and maintaining a relationship marked by cooperation, harmony, trust, confidence, and understanding is not easily attained. Rapport goes beyond a friendly greeting and a superficial attempt to make parents feel comfortable and at ease. As Shertzer and Stone note, rapport is an intangible entity characterized by pleasantness, confidence, cooperation, sincerity and interest—all qualities difficult to measure, impossible to turn on in a mechanical way, and difficult to initiate by recipe.

GENUINENESS/CONGRUENCE

In regard to the qualities and attitudes that facilitate learning, Carl Rogers (1969) has stated that

> Perhaps the most basic of these essential attitudes is realness or genuineness. When the facilitator is a real person, being what he is, entering into a relationship with the learner without a front or facade, he is much more likely to be effective. (p. 106)

Genuineness is simply being real in your relationships with parents. You should, therefore, always strive to be yourself—an authentic person truly interested in the welfare of the other person. Honesty and genuineness cannot be turned on and off; it must be a unique part of one's total personality. Benjamin (1974) has pointed out that the helper should cast aside any mask, facade, or other "professional equipment" that creates barriers between the

The counselor's emotional security and stability are closely related to genuineness and humanness.

interviewee and the counselor. The helper should conduct the helping interview in an open manner so that the interviewee may draw closer not only to the counselor, but other people as well. A genuine person is congruent; there is no discrepancy between outer actions and inner feelings, nor is the person cold and aloof one day and warm and friendly the next. The genuine person says only what is meant and does only what is comfortable and natural. Many parents will recognize discrepancies between what the helper is saying and thinking and may immediately label the helper as false.

The counselor's emotional security and stability are closely related to genuineness and humanness. If the helper feels secure there is less danger of falseness. The helper is an authentic person, able and willing to allow parents to share their thoughts and feelings in an open, trustful, and nondefensive manner.

RESPECT/CARING/UNCONDITIONAL POSITIVE REGARD

Boyd (1978) says that respect includes acceptance, interest, concern, warmth, liking, and unconditional caring, allowing parents the freedom to be themselves with the counselor. Respect is an acceptance of parents as people, regardless of attitudes or behaviors that may be unacceptable to the helper. Respect also involves a belief that parents are generally capable of working through their own difficulties, making the right or best decisions for themselves. Boyd maintains that respect and understanding are in a direct relationship—as respect increases, understanding increases. Carl Rogers explains respect as an *unconditional positive regard* for another person regardless of his or her behaviors.

ATTENTIVENESS/LISTENING

Attentiveness is basic and fundamental to all helping skills, involving an awareness of a client's verbal and nonverbal communications. If attentiveness is to go beyond a superficial level, the helper must listen. Benjamin (1974) emphasizes that genuine listening requires work—little about it comes naturally. Listening is closely related to acceptance and understanding because listening conveys to the client that the counselor is interested in and sensitive to the client's concerns. From a historical perspective, Nichols and Stevens (1957) pointed out that the need to listen was recognized about 4,400 years ago when Prahhotep, one of the pharoahs, instructed the viziers and officers about listening: "An official who must listen to the pleas of clients should listen patiently and without rancor, because a petitioner wants attention to what he says even more than the accomplishing of that for which he came." To this day, the importance and need for active and purposeful listening remains a basic and essential skill, particularly when working with parents of handicapped children. To be more confident in responding to parents' and childrens' needs, Powell (1981) states, "First, professionals must develop listening skills." A helper must listen patiently instead of probing to provide parents with an opportunity to discuss problems or concerns from their point of view. Listening with comprehension and being aware of the speaker's real feelings is a very active process (as opposed to passive) that must be practiced and learned.

Brammer (1979) has noted the usefulness of attentiveness, especially when beginning an interview. Brammer established the following guidelines for attending behavior:

1. Establish contact by looking at the helpees when they talk.
2. Maintain a natural, relaxed posture that indicates your interest.
3. Use natural gestures that communicate your intended messages.
4. Use verbal statements that relate to what the helpee has said, refraining from interruptions, questions, or new topics.

Ten Guides for Effective Listening* are presented as follows:

1. Stop talking!
   You cannot listen if you are talking. Polonius (Hamlet): "Give every man thine ear, but few thy voice."
2. Put the talker at ease.
   Help a person feel free to talk. This is often called a permissive environment.
3. Show a talker that you want to listen.
   Look and act interested. Do not read your mail while someone talks. Listen to understand rather than to oppose.
4. Remove distractions.
   Don't doodle, tap, or shuffle papers. Will it be quieter if you shut the door?
5. Empathize with talkers.
   Try to help yourself see the other person's point of view.
6. Be patient.
   Allow plenty of time. Do not interrupt a talker. Don't start for the door or walk away.
7. Hold your temper.
   An angry person takes the wrong meaning from words.
8. Go easy on argument and criticism.
   This puts people on the defensive, and they may "clam up" or become angry. Do not argue: Even if you win, you lose.
9. Ask questions.
   This encourages a talker and shows that you are listening. It helps to develop points further.
10. Stop talking!
    This is first and last because all other guides depend on it. You cannot do an effective listening job while you are talking.

---

*"Ten Guides for Effective Listening" from *Human Behavior at Work* by Keith Davis. Copyright 1977. Used with permission of McGraw-Hill Book Company.

☐ Nature gave people ears but only one tongue, which is a gentle hint that they should listen more than they talk.

☐ Listening requires two ears, one for meaning and one for feeling.

☐ Decision makers who do not listen have less information for making sound decisions.

Carl Rogers (1980) comments that

We think we listen, but very rarely do we listen with real understanding, true empathy. Yet listening, of this very special kind, is one of the most potent forces for change that I know. (p. 116)

ETHICAL BEHAVIOR

The observance and practice of professional ethics is one of the most important responsibilities of helpers. Because the helper is concerned with helping parents and is often given confidential or personal information, the helper must demonstrate a professional and ethical attitude in his work. Several years ago, Schwebel (1955) suggested that unethical behavior may occur for various reasons: The counselor behaves out of ignorance, the counselor does not have sufficient training, or the counselor acts out of self-interest. More recently, Heller (1983) commented that "Ethics serve as the conscience for the field [of special education], assuring that practice is consistent with what is known to be 'good' or 'right'." Parents, therefore, have the right to expect helpers to act in accordance with high standards of professional and ethical behavior during every phase of their relationship.

In order to determine whether or not a behavior is unethical, each profession needs to formulate general guidelines to assist in evaluating daily activities, such as a professional code of ethics. To be meaningful, a code of ethics should reflect not only the agreed-upon values of the profession represented but also values generally accepted by the society the profession serves. Before a group can state an ethical code, it must first agree upon values and responsibilities. After a series of such attempts at defining basic values, the American Personnel and Guidance Association (APGA) adopted a code of ethics and published it in October, 1961. The APGA revised its ethical standards in 1974. Some of the major points made in the 1974 revision are as follows:

1. Ethical behavior among professional associates, members, and nonmembers is expected at all times.
2. The member's primary obligation is to respect the integrity and promote the welfare of the counselee(s) whether the counselee(s) is (are) assisted individually or in a group relationship.
3. The counseling relationship and information resulting therefrom must be kept confidential, consistent with the obligations of the member as a professional person.

4. Counselees shall be informed of the conditions under which they may receive counseling assistance at or before the time when the counseling relationship is entered. This is particularly so when conditions exist of which the counselee would be unaware. In individual and group situations, particularly those oriented to self-understanding or growth, the member-leader is obligated to make clear the purposes, goals, techniques, rules of procedure, and limitations that may affect the continuance of the relationship.

5. If the member is unable to be of professional assistance to the counselee, the member avoids initiating the counseling relationship or the member terminates it. In either event, the member is obligated to refer the counselee to an appropriate specialist. (It is incumbent upon the member to be knowledgeable about referral resources so that a satisfactory referral can be initiated.) In the event the counselee declines the suggested referral, the member is not obligated to continue the relationship.

While a code of ethics has no legal force, it offers general guidelines that help an organization to evaluate a member. However, an ethics code will not always allow a person to resolve every dilemma that may be encountered. Many ethical problems lie in a gray area. Adhering to the APGA ethical standards, and practicing professional, mature decision making will enhance any helper's ability to observe and practice high ethical standards. You may find it informative and worthwhile to read and analyze the *Code of Ethics and Standards for Professional Practice* adopted by the Council for Exceptional Children (CEC) Delegate Assembly in April of 1983. Please refer to Appendix C at the end of this text to locate this important set of beliefs that guide the practitioner in making professional judgments concerning what constitutes competent practice.

One major area of ethical practice is the counselor's obligation to maintain confidentiality. Once a trust is violated by a counselor who talks freely about his clients, it is difficult, if not impossible, to regain their confidence. There will be general situations in which maintaining confidentiality will be difficult, especially for the inexperienced counselor. Schneiders (1963) believes that the counselor's obligation to maintain confidentiality varies with both the nature of the information imparted and the effect that revelation would have on the client. A good guideline to follow when in doubt about such matters is to always ask for the client's or parents' permission. Information given by the client within a counseling relationship belongs to the client unless he or she releases it for other use.

UNDERSTANDING OF HUMAN BEHAVIOR

Demos and Grant (1973) point out that what the counselor needs to know about any individual results from understanding the behavior of individuals; in other words, the counselor requires a basic and thorough knowledge of human behavior. Atkin (1972) has noted that counselors must work to represent our understanding of the human dynamics of learning and see that these insights are incorporated into the learning environment. In a provocative article by Berdie (1972), he proposes that counseling as we know it will be replaced by another discipline called *applied behavioral science.* The applied behavioral scientist would understand social influence theory, reinforcement theory, cognitive development theories, field theory, psychoanalytic theory, trait and factor theory, role theory, and decision theory.

More recently, Dixon (1979) stated that the therapist needs a comprehensive understanding of human behavior from which to begin. Allowing for the individuality and uniqueness of each individual, Dixon suggests some basic assumptions about human behavior:

1. All human behavior has a cause, and the cause always involves many complex interpersonal interactions between the individual, other people, and the environment.
2. Human behavior is purposeful. People try to satisfy needs, to adapt to the social environment, and to defend themselves against any stimulus that threatens their emotional equilibrium.
3. All human beings experience the same feelings and behaviors. The basic differences between people are not differences of kind but differences of degree.
4. The individual and his or her social environment are a united interactional field.
5. Stress and conflict are an inevitable part of life. To live happily and productively, human beings must learn patterns of behavior that let them restore and maintain a sense of equilibrium.
6. The way a person functions psychosocially is the accumulative result of his or her life experiences and socialization processes.
7. Effective social functioning is related to the nature of biological endowment, the social environment, and specific phases of the life cycle.
8. An individual's social functioning can range from highly effective to ineffective.
9. Social dysfunction can be ameliorated by therapeutic intervention after assessing and evaluating contributing factors in the individual and the environment.

We now know more about the nature of human behavior than ever before. Effective counselors can and should use this knowledge in order to help clients and parents avoid making costly and needless mistakes that may result in a loss of their potential to become self-sufficient individuals striving toward self-fulfillment. Are we willing to expend the time, effort, and energy needed to broaden our understanding about the dynamics of human behavior? In this endeavor, helpers cannot afford anything less than exerting their best effort to expand their knowledge and understanding about the dynamics of human behavior.

CHAPTER SUMMARY

This chapter has stressed the importance of the helper's attitudes, skills, and traits in any helping relationship. The attitudes and approach of the counselor can have a profound influence on the success or failure of one person aiding or assisting another. It takes skill, tact, and a working knowledge of helping skills for a professional to communicate effectively with different kinds of parents who have different needs.

There is a wealth of professional literature reminding us of characteristics that distinguish effective counselors from ineffective ones. This chapter has discussed nine specific traits or attitudes deemed especially crucial in increasing the effectiveness of the helping relationship. It is hoped that, above all else, this discussion of counselor attitudes and skills will help you to recognize your own strengths and weaknesses, and to strive constantly to improve any deficiencies.

Finally, the helper skills discussed in this chapter are simply a representative and arbitrary selection; they are not intended to cover the entire array of possible helper characteristics. For example, a review of the literature might include other traits and attitudes such as commitment, concreteness, cooperation, encouragement, flexibility, immediacy, objectivity, reassurance, reflection of feelings, and sensitivity. While it is beyond the scope of this book to provide coverage of all the possible helping skills, it is important to identify and discuss selected skills and traits that typically are characteristic of effective helpers.

ACTIVITIES, EXERCISES, AND IDEAS FOR REFLECTION AND DISCUSSION

1. Think of other significant counselor characteristics, such as sensitivity or flexibility, which should have been included as significant counselor traits. Defend your choices.
2. Describe, in your own words, the ideal counselor or helper.
3. Recall when a person once assisted you in the context of a helping relationship. What unique characteristics did this person possess? Did a change in your behavior (resolution of problem) result from this helper's skills, knowledge, and abilities? How? Why?
4. Nine specific counselor characteristics were discussed in this chapter. Rank these according to which traits you feel are most important in the helping relationship. Then write a statement beside each to defend and support your choice.
5. Many believe that proficiency in understanding another person is a skill or ability that is not acquired easily. To what extent do you agree with this statement? How would you go about increasing your understanding of another person?
6. In the spaces provided, list some verbal responses that would convey empathic understanding to a client or parent who lacks self-esteem and self-confidence to the extent that he or she is hesitant or afraid to make major personal deci-

sions affecting the family's or personal daily functioning. (Would you say, "You know, that's my impression of you also"?)

a. _____

b. _____

c. _____

d. _____

e. _____

7. Skill in active listening is not acquired by accident or a magic formula. Think of systematic ways or methods that your listening skills can be improved.

8. There is considerable evidence that self-acceptance and acceptance of others are closely related—individuals who are self-accepting are usually more accepting of others. What are the implications of this statement? What are some characteristics of self-accepting individuals?

9. Can rapport be taught to you by others or does it primarily come about by having the opportunity to experience this relationship in helping others? Explain.

10. Interview a guidance counselor (or another member of the helping professions) to learn more about a counselor's role and responsibilities. What specific characteristics or attitudes are most important to this person? Why?

REFERENCES

American Personnel and Guidance Association. (1974). *Ethical Standards.* Washington, DC: The Association.

Atkin, J. (1972). Counseling in an age of crisis. *Personnel and Guidance Journal, 50,* 723.

Benjamin, A. (1974). *The helping interview.* Boston: Houghton Mifflin.

Berdie, R. F. (1972). The 1980 counselor: Applied behavioral scientist. *The Personnel and Guidance Journal, 50,* 451–456.

Boyd, J. (1978). *Counselor supervision.* Muncie, IN: Accelerated Development.

Brammer, L. M. (1979). *The helping relationship: Process and skills.* Englewood Cliffs, NJ: Prentice-Hall.

Brenner, D. (1982). *The effective psychotherapist: Conclusions from practice and research.* New York: Pergamon Press.

Coleman, J. C. (1969). *Psychology and effective behavior.* Glenview, IL: Scott, Foresman.

Davis, K. (1977). *Human behavior at work: Organizational behavior.* New York: McGraw-Hill.

Demos, G. D., & Grant, B. (1973). *An introduction to counseling: A handbook.* Los Angeles: Western Psychological Services.

Dixon, S. L. (1979). *Working with people in crisis: Theory and practice.* St. Louis: C. V. Mosby.

Heller, H. W. (1983). Special education professional standards: Need, value, and use. *Exceptional Children, 50*(3), 199–203.

Ivey, A. E., & Simek-Downing, L. (1980). *Counseling and psychotherapy: Skills, theories, and practice.* Englewood Cliffs, NJ: Prentice-Hall.

Jones, D.A., Lepley, M.K., & Baker, B.A. (1984). *Health assessment across the life span.* New York: McGraw-Hill.

Munson, H. L. (1971). *Foundations of developmental guidance.* Boston: Allyn & Bacon.

Nichols, R. G., & Stevens, L. A. (1957). *Are you listening?* New York: McGraw-Hill.

Powell, M. L. (1981). *Assessment and management of developmental changes and problems in children.* St. Louis: C. V. Mosby.

Rogers, C. R. (1969). *Freedom to learn.* Columbus, OH: Charles E. Merrill.

Rogers, C. R. (1961). *On becoming a person.* Boston: Houghton Mifflin.

Rogers, C. R. (1980). *A way of being.* Boston: Houghton Mifflin.

Schneiders, A. A. (1963). The limits of confidentiality. *Personnel and Guidance Journal, 42,* 252.

Schwebel, M. (1955). Why unethical practice? *Journal of Counseling Psychology, 2,* 122–128.

Shertzer, B., & Stone, S. C. (1980). *Fundamentals of counseling.* Boston: Houghton Mifflin.

Tyler, L. (1969). *The work of the counselor.* New York: Appleton-Century-Crofts.

Weiner, I. B. (1975). *Principles of psychotherapy.* New York: John Wiley.

SELECTED REFERENCES FOR FURTHER READING AND STUDY

Brown, J. H., & Brown, C. S. (1975). Environmental management: A step toward counselor effectiveness. *The School Counselor, 23,* 108–113.

Dyer, W. W., & Vriend, J. A. (1977). A goal setting checklist for counseling. *Personnel and Guidance Journal, 55,* 469–471.

Gehring, D. D. (1982). The counselor's duty to warn. *Personnel and Guidance Journal, 61*(4), 208–210.

Ivey, A. E., & Matthews, W. J. (1984). A meta-model for structuring the clinical interview. *Journal of Counseling and Development, 63*(4), 237–243.

Margolin, G. (1982). Ethical and legal considerations in marital and family therapy. *American Psychologist, 37*(7), 788–801.

Maurer, R. E., & Tindall, J. H. (1983). Effect of postural consequence on clients' perception of counselor empathy. *Journal of Counseling Psychology, 30,* 339–345.

Talbutt, L. C. (1981). Ethical standards: Assets and limitations. *Personnel and Guidance Journal, 60*(2), 110–112.

Vriend, J., & Dyer, W. W. (1976). Counseling the reluctant client. *The School Counselor, 23,* 165–174.

Weinrach, S. G. (1975). How effective am I? Five easy steps to self-evaluation. *The School Counselor, 22,* 202–205.

Wrenn, C. G. (1983). The fighting, risk-taking counselor. *Personnel and Guidance Journal, 61*(6), 323–326.

Zonca, P. H. (1977). Openness: A formula for communication. *The Clearing House, 50,* 201–203.

4 Overview of the Counseling Process

After mastering the content in this chapter, you should be able to

1. Define and discuss the following terms and concepts:
    counseling process
    initial counseling encounter
    structure in the relationship
    phases of counseling

2. List and explain the characteristics of persons who seek counseling.

3. List and discuss the realities of a new relationship.

4. Recognize and discuss the importance of the initial counseling encounter.

5. Explain the importance of structure—What? Why? When? How?

6. Compare and contrast the phases of counseling according to the models of Stewart, Brammer, and Ivey and Simek-Downing.

Because of their special goals, helping encounters are also characterized by special kinds of processes which may not be found in the daily experiences of the persons who are seeking aid. For these reasons, people entering the helping relationship must be helped to understand its nature and ways of functioning.

—Combs, Avila, and Purkey

The term process *helps to communicate much about the essence of counseling. A process is an identifiable sequence of events taking place over time. Usually there is the implication of progressive stages in the process.*

—Lewis E. Patterson and Sheldon Eisenberg

*B*efore studying this chapter, you should remember that the following discussion refers to the broad and general aspects of the *counseling process*. Later chapters will, in a more detailed way, amplify and focus on this process as an approach to working with parents of exceptional children. You are, therefore, encouraged to examine this content thoughtfully and carefully to develop the knowledge and insight necessary to become a more productive and effective helper.

The counseling process actually begins with the first contact between helper and helpee and follows an orderly progression beginning with the establishment of a relationship and usually ending with the termination of that relationship. Between these two steps, the helper assists the client in developing an understanding of his or her problems. This chapter will provide you with insight into this process that is often referred to as the stages or phases of counseling.

WHY PEOPLE SEEK HELP

Prior to a detailed analysis of the counseling process, it would be beneficial to understand why people seek counseling. According to Lewis (1970), people seek counseling for many reasons, but three common characteristics can be noted:

1. The person is experiencing some sort of personal dissatisfaction and is unable to reduce this dissatisfaction sufficiently. The person perceives a need to change the dissatisfactory behavior without knowing how to go about it.
2. The person approaches counseling with a substantial amount of anxiety and uncertainty about not only some aspect of his or her life which is inadequate, but about stepping into a strange and foreboding land—the counselor's office.

3. The person who seeks counseling expects that the counselor will be able to help, but has no clear ideas about what will occur.

While the first two points made by Lewis might be frightening (especially to the beginning counselor), you should note that an optimistic tone pervades the initial encounter. Both counselor and client normally enter the relationship with the expectation that its outcome will result in an agreed-upon behavior change.

Brammer (1979) stresses the importance of the helper's awareness of the realities of a new relationship. He cites the following realities as especially significant:

1. It is not easy to receive help.
2. It is difficult to commit one's self to change.
3. It is difficult to submit to the influence of a helper; help is a threat to esteem, integrity, and independence.
4. It is not easy to trust a stranger and to be open with him.
5. It is not easy to see one's problem clearly at first.
6. It is difficult to share problems easily because they sometimes seem too large, too overwhelming, or too unique.

Parents of exceptional children seek help for many reasons. As an example, Ehlers, Krishef, and Prothero (1977) state:

> Usually, parents want and need help. They may not understand why their child is retarded, and they may feel that in some way they are to blame for something they did or did not do. They may react to their feelings by rejecting the child or being overprotective or overdemanding. These parents need help in solving the problems with which they are confronted. They need to know what type of home atmosphere and training the child will require to fully develop his limited capabilities. (p. 189)

The main point is that most parents want and need help, whether it is information about their child's handicapping condition or the opportunity to talk with a helper about the difficulties and uncertainties which may lie ahead. Many parents urgently need help in solving practical day-to-day problems. Rendering assistance is not limited to a professional helper—help may result from interaction and personal sharing with other parents who have experienced and worked through similar problems. By our previous definition, these other parents who listen and offer support then become helpers.

THE INITIAL COUNSELING ENCOUNTER

Most human interactions have a goal or purpose, and this is especially true of the counseling relationship. The initial interview between counselor and client is significant since it affords the first opportunity for two people to begin a relationship within a counseling context. Munson (1971) has suggested some assumptions that can be made about the initial interview: The counselee wants or needs help, nothing specific needs to be accomplished beyond the structure required by the counselor, and the initial session is merely a beginning stage in a relationship between two individuals. Patterson and Eisenberg (1983) have noted:

> Counseling has a beginning, a middle, and an end. At the outset the client and counselor discuss the concerns of the client. The counselor attempts to learn as nearly as possible what the client is experiencing and what has brought him or her to counseling. (p. 7)

Tyler (1969) suggests these objectives for the counselor: (1) get a sound counseling relationship started, (2) open up the psychological realm of feelings and attitudes within the person, and (3) clarify the structure of the helping process. Bucheimer and Balogh (1961) divide the initial interview into three phases: the statement of a problem, exploration, and closing and planning for the future. They believe that this represents a purposeful and goal-directed approach to counseling.

With this outlined purpose of the initial interview, you should remember that beginning interviewers, through lack of experience, usually commit many types of common errors. Emerick (1969) has compiled a practical list of common errors that the beginning counselor should avoid during the interview or counseling session:

1. Avoid questions that may be answered "Yes" or "No." Try to frame the question to elicit more complete responses.
2. Avoid asking questions that inhibit freedom of response. Do not say, "You didn't have any difficulty with the child's toilet training, did you?"
3. Avoid talking too much. It is much better to rephrase what the respondent has said or make some comment like "I see," "Tell me more," or "Anything else?"
4. Avoid concentrating on the child's physical symptoms and their causes to the exclusion of the parent's feelings and attitudes.
5. Avoid providing information too soon. There will be plenty of time to clear up misconceptions later in the interview.
6. Ask questions straightforwardly, maintaining eye contact.
7. Avoid negative or moralistic responses—verbal or nonverbal—to the parent's statements. The flow of information will stop rapidly and the relationship will be severely impaired if the parent senses that you find his or her behavior distasteful.
8. Avoid abrupt transitions in bringing the parent back to a point. The ability to make smooth transitions characterizes the experienced interviewer.
9. Avoid allowing only superficial or surface answers. Seek deeper, more significant responses from parents.
10. Avoid letting the parent reveal too much in one interview. Sometimes a beginning interviewer makes the mistake of trying to get everything in one session.
11. Avoid trusting your memory. Put the clinical situation, procedures, observations, and recommendations in writing as soon as possible.

STRUCTURING THE HELPING RELATIONSHIP

Structure is evident in the helping relationship, especially one that extends over a period of time. In this regard, Shertzer and Stone (1980) write:

> Structure varies, depending upon the type of helping relationship, but its essential features—patterns of stimuli and response—are always present. Structure enables the relationship to eventuate in growth and productivity. In reality, responsibility for the structure is reciprocal. Both the helper and person to be helped have needs—to achieve, to be recognized, to be adequate—that determine structure and set in motion responses which the helping person must be prepared to meet to build a helping relationship. (p. 9)

Structure defines the nature, limits, and goals of the prospective helping relationship. According to Brammer (1979), structure outlines the roles, responsibilities, and possible commitments of both helper and helpee. At the outset, many helpers will feel compelled to outline procedures to follow during the counseling relationship. Keep in mind, however, that hard and fast rules are difficult to develop because one counselor's theoretical frame of reference may differ markedly from another's. While one counselor would prefer to present the counseling approach (the roles and functions of both parties), another counselor may wish to simply proceed with the task of counseling and leave structure (assuming it is necessary) to develop during the course of the relationship.

If formal structuring is necessary, you should realize that the circumstances favor the counselee's acceptance of the counselor's approach. The client may be anxious and uncertain; the counselor is confident and calm and has the status of an authority figure. The counseling relationship will be enhanced and directed as the client develops faith in the counselor and the approach they will take. This faith involves the client's commitment for it implies going beyond mere acceptance of the counselor's approach. The approach set forth by the counselor will not always be easy for the client to accept, however. Much depends on the client's preconceived ideas of the counseling sessions and the role of each person in the counseling process. Should disagreement occur, allow a period of time for accommodation and further deliberations.

One of the most vital initial transactions involves the counselor and client agreeing on a procedure that will be followed during future meetings. Talk must be translated into a course of action to attain a counseling goal. The parent's concern is often vaguely and poorly verbalized; thus the first step in resolving the problem is to define it. This is often referred to as *statement of the problem.*

PHASES OF COUNSELING

Helping is often marked by a definite internal structure previously referred to as *phases.* While any listing of phases will vary, counseling may be thought

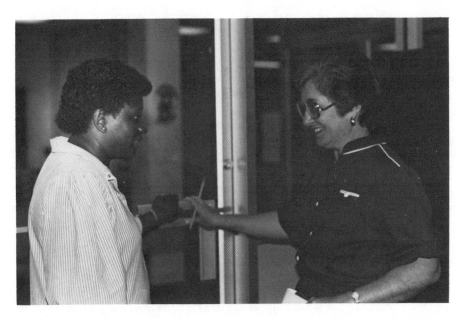

The counselor must convey to the client that she considers her a valuable person.

of as six steps or phases that are not always fixed. Benjamin (1974) has stated that sometimes phases fuse into each other until it is difficult to tell them apart. If stages are absent, this may indicate that there were none, or that stage one was never reached, for example. On the other hand, movement from one stage to another may be so swift that it is difficult to determine where one stage ends and the next one begins.

Nevertheless, a working knowledge of phases is essential to counseling and should be a fundamental part of any helper's counseling skills. The first counseling model is the Stewart model in which counseling consists of the following six sequential phases:

Initiation or Establishment of Purpose   In this first phase, the helper and helpee establish the subject of their meeting. During this step, the helpee should indicate his or her purpose for seeking help. This is important both from a motivational and a directional viewpoint because this identifies a goal toward which both client and counselor may work. It is also during this phase that the counselor becomes an active listener and attempts to convey to the client that he or she is valued as a person.

Defining the Counseling Process   The counselor and counselee should agree on how to achieve a mutually acceptable goal. During this phase the client needs assistance in developing some ideas about the nature and function of counseling. Counselor and client, then, attempt to reach a mutual agreement about the purpose and direction of their relationship. Rapport is established so that a comfortable communication of thoughts and feelings may be exchanged between counselor and client.

Understanding of Client's Needs   The next step is to clarify the nature of the client's difficulty and to seek insight into the dynamics of the client's behavior. The counselor is concerned with the client's perception of personal difficulties and the feelings surrounding them. The counselor and client, working together, attempt to examine as many facets of the difficulty as possible so that an appropriate plan of action can be formulated.

Understanding alone is not sufficient. The counselor must verbally express understanding to the client. It is during this phase that empathy, or the ability to perceive the client's thoughts and feelings and to communicate this understanding, assumes special significance. Learning to develop empathy with the client takes both time and practice. It is learning to hear the client and to convey that you heard. For example, if the client becomes tearful, the counselor should attempt to understand the feeling underlying the tears and thereby help the client acknowledge and accept those feelings.

Exploring the Possible Alternatives   Helpers have the responsibility to point out the many possible solutions and alternatives to a situation; in other words, they should make progress toward the client's goal. It is not the counselor's duty to decide what decisions to make or what course of action to choose for the counselee. Decisions are and rightfully should be the counselee's own, but understanding why and how they were made is important. The counselee should also learn to estimate the consequences of any actions in terms of personal effort, sacrifice, time, money, risk, and other significant variables that may affect progress toward the ultimate goal.

Planning a Course of Action   As the client becomes more aware of thoughts and feelings with the assistance of the counselor, the client begins to move steadily toward the counseling goal. Executing a plan of action is normally much easier if the client has personally made the selection. If a parent has decided on the course of action, we may expect a personal commitment and a concentrated effort to carry it out. The counselor must remember that the human personality varies considerably and should, therefore, not be disappointed if the desired ends (the counseling goals) are not fully attained as a result of counseling.

This phase, often called the *progress* phase of counseling, continues until the client and counselor agree that the counseling can and should be concluded. Agreement to terminate the sessions indicates either that the goal has been reached or that the client feels capable of continuing alone without further assistance. Prior to termination, encourage the client to review his or her counseling experiences, especially regarding probable future development. The rationale here is to encourage the client to recognize and take advantage of insights gained, and to apply self-understanding toward future

With the assistance of the counselor, the client begins to move toward the counseling goal.

endeavors. Counseling should lead to a general improvement not only in the client's ability to cope, but also with his or her ability to meet the situational demands of daily functioning.

Terminating the Session   The final step in the counseling session is usually referred to as *termination*. This may be considered from two points of view: First, from a temporary one in which the client continues contact with the counselor later, and second, a permanent termination if the client feels that the goal has been reached. In any event, the effects of the counseling session will hopefully continue beyond termination.

The session is best terminated on a positive note, allowing the client to face new difficulties without a counselor. In terminating counseling either temporarily or finally, it is important that the parents depart with a feeling that something constructive has been accomplished. This positive attitude will normally prevail if an adequate job is done by the counselor; however, this feeling will be enhanced if the counselor is systematic and exercises tact and diplomacy in closing the counseling relationship.

Ideally, the decision to terminate counseling should be a mutual one, although either party should feel free to discuss the possibility at any time during the counseling encounter. A good rule that Stewart (1978) provides is that the client should assume the major responsibility for this decision as with all his decisions.

Finally, Ward (1984) has noted that "the termination of counseling is a process that seems to have been inadequately addressed in the literature, in training programs, and therefore most probably in counseling practice" (p. 21). Ward also suggests that appropriate termination not only is a significant stage in the counseling process but also serves three primary functions:

1. assessing client readiness for the end of counseling and consolidating learning;
2. both resolving remaining affective issues and bringing about appropriate closure of the significant and often intense relationship between the client and the counselor; and
3. maximizing transfer of learning and increasing the client's self-reliance and confidence in his or her ability to maintain change after counseling has ended. (p. 22)

Using a slightly different order and emphasis, Brammer (1979) has identified eight basic stages of the helping process.

Phase 1: Building Relationships

1. Entry: Preparing the helpee and opening the relationship
2. Clarification: Stating the problem or concern and the reasons for seeking help
3. Structure: Formulating the contract and the structure
4. Relationship: Building the helping relationship

Phase 2: Facilitating Positive Action

5. Exploration: Exploring problems, formulating goals, planning strategies, gathering facts, expressing deeper feelings, learning new skills
6. Consolidation: Exploring alternatives, working through feelings, practicing new skills
7. Planning: Developing a plan of action using strategies to resolve conflicts, reducing painful feelings, and consolidating and generalizing new skills or behaviors to continue self-directed activities
8. Termination: Evaluating outcomes and terminating the relationship (p. 52).

This general model of the helping process is designed to incorporate problem-solving, skill-development, life-planning, and awareness models. This sequence of events is typical of helpers' and helpees' experiences of moving from the first contact through the final outcome. Brammer notes two other significant factors related to stages in the helping process.

☐ This general sequence is not dependent on helping style or helping theory; it is an unfolding of a natural process of problem solving.

☐ The stages are typical of the process, but they do not always exist in this exact sequence, nor are all stages always present, since helpees typically determine the sequence and length of stages. (p. 51)

In order to stress the importance of structure in the counseling process, a third and final approach for structuring the interview and aiding the decision-making process is presented. Ivey and Simek-Downing (1980) suggest three stages in decision making and problem solving that they believe provide the basis of most approaches to counseling. These consist of the problem definition phase, the work phase, and the decision for action phase. You are urged to study these phases and their component subparts in Figure 4.1.

The conclusions drawn by Ivey and Simek-Downing are worthy of our consideration.

Decision making undergirds the counseling process. All counseling and therapy are oriented toward effective decision making. Critical to intentional counseling is the counselor's ability to assist the client to develop a large number of ways in which a problem or concern can be defined. (p. 48)

CHAPTER SUMMARY

To work effectively with others, helpers should have a thorough and complete understanding of the counseling process. You should be familiar with not only why people seek help but also the realities of entering into a new relationship. The initial encounter with a client is vitally important because it conveys confidence in the client's ability to profit from the helping relationship. Structure as a part of the process focuses attention upon the commitments, obligations, and responsibilities of both parties as they begin the relationship. It is here that counseling phases take on added importance; three specific approaches to phases were presented to help you. What is important is that you the helper be aware of how the sequence of the helping stages relates to the client's ability to improve his or her problem-solving and decision-making skills. The skills, attitudes, knowledge, and behavior of the helper determine to a large degree the effectiveness of the client's successful passage through the stages.

ACTIVITIES, EXERCISES, AND IDEAS
FOR REFLECTION AND DISCUSSION

1. Recall a time that you felt a need for counseling. Apply Lewis's three characteristics of people who seek counseling to your personal situation. Did you actually seek counseling? Why or why not? What was the outcome?

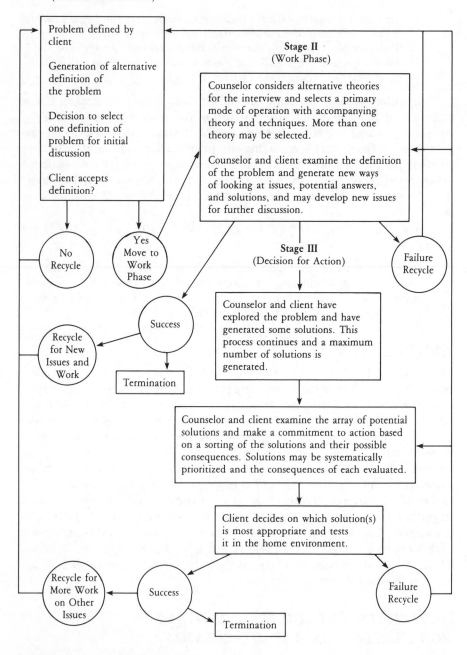

Stage I
(Problem Identification)

Problem defined by client

Generation of alternative definition of the problem

Decision to select one definition of problem for initial discussion

Client accepts definition?

Stage II
(Work Phase)

Counselor considers alternative theories for the interview and selects a primary mode of operation with accompanying theory and techniques. More than one theory may be selected.

Counselor and client examine the definition of the problem and generate new ways of looking at issues, potential answers, and solutions, and may develop new issues for further discussion.

No Recycle

Yes Move to Work Phase

Stage III
(Decision for Action)

Failure Recycle

Success

Recycle for New Issues and Work

Termination

Counselor and client have explored the problem and have generated some solutions. This process continues and a maximum number of solutions is generated.

Counselor and client examine the array of potential solutions and make a commitment to action based on a sorting of the solutions and their possible consequences. Solutions may be systematically prioritized and the consequences of each evaluated.

Client decides on which solution(s) is most appropriate and tests it in the home environment.

Recycle for More Work on Other Issues

Success

Failure Recycle

Termination

FIGURE 4.1 *The three stages in decision making*

SOURCE: Allen E. Ivey, Lynn Simek-Downing, *COUNSELING AND PSYCHOTHERAPY: Skills, Theories and Practice,* © 1980, p. 37. Reprinted by permission of Prentice-Hall, Inc., Englewood Cliffs, N.J.

2. Do you think that a person having a personal, social, or emotional problem is usually unwilling to approach a professional person for counseling? What factors might account for one's hesitancy in initiating a counseling relationship?
3. To what extent should the counselor expect to fully understand the client's needs? How much client understanding and awareness is necessary to proceed with the counseling relationship? To what degree might one expect this to develop during the relationship?
4. Devise and structure a role-playing situation that conveys empathy. Analyze the types of verbal communication and nonverbal actions that establish empathy.
5. Devise and structure a role-playing situation where counseling is to be terminated or termination is to be discussed. (Taping or recording the session will allow for detailed analysis.) How can you improve your ability to terminate a counseling relationship?
6. Is it correct to assume that most parents of exceptional children will cooperate readily if they sense you want to help their children? Should this be the dominant theme in your initial meeting with the parents? How might you convey your willingness to help in a genuine and positive manner?

REFERENCES

Benjamin, L. M. (1974). *The helping interview.* Boston: Houghton Mifflin.

Brammer, L. M. (1979). *The helping relationship: Process and skills* (2nd ed.). Englewood Cliffs, NJ: Prentice-Hall.

Bucheimer, A., & Balogh, S. C. (1961). *The counseling relationship.* Chicago: Science Research Associates.

Ehlers, W. H., Krishef, C. H., & Prothero, J. C. (1977). *An introduction to mental retardation: A programmed text.* Columbus, OH: Charles E. Merrill.

Emerick, L. (1969). *The parent interview.* Danville, IL: Interstate Printers and Publishers.

Ivey, A. E., & Simek-Downing, L. (1980). *Counseling and psychotherapy: Skills, theories, and practice.* Englewood Cliffs, NJ: Prentice-Hall.

Lewis, E. C. (1970). *The psychology of counseling.* New York: Holt, Rinehart, & Winston.

Munson, H. L. (1971). *Foundations of developmental guidance.* Boston: Allyn & Bacon.

Patterson, L. E., and Eisenberg, S. (1983). *The counseling process* (3rd ed.). Boston: Houghton Mifflin.

Shertzer, B., & Stone, S. C. (1980). *Fundamentals of counseling* (3rd ed.). Boston: Houghton Mifflin.

Stewart, J. C. (1978). *Counseling parents of exceptional children.* Columbus, OH: Charles E. Merrill.

Tyler, L. E. (1969). *The work of the counselor.* New York: Appleton-Century-Crofts.

Ward, D. E. (1984). Termination of individual counseling: Concepts and strategies. *Journal of Counseling and Development, 63,* 21–25.

SELECTED REFERENCES FOR FURTHER READING AND STUDY

Day, R. W., & Sparacio, R. T. (1980). Structuring the counseling process. *Personnel and Guidance Journal, 59,* 246–249.

Ellis, A. (1982). Major systems. *Personnel and Guidance Journal, 61,* 6–7.

Goldfried, M. R. (1980). Toward a delineation of therapeutic change principles. *American Psychologist, 35,* 991–999.

Goodyear, R. K. (1981). Termination as a loss experience for the counselor. *Personnel and Guidance Journal; 59,* 347–350.

Huber, C. H. (1983). A social-ecological approach to the counseling process. *AMHCA Journal, 5,* 4–11.

Ivey, A. E., & Matthews, W. J. (1984). A meta-model for structuring the clinical interview. *Journal of Counseling and Development, 63*(4), 237–243.

Jackard, C. R. (1974). The American male rejects counseling. *Adult Leadership, 23,* 9–10.

Krumboltz, J. D. (1980). A second look at the revolution in counseling. *Personnel and Guidance Journal, 58,* 463–466.

Marinoff, S. L. (1973). When words are not enough—VIDEOTAPE. *Teaching Exceptional Children, 5,* 66–73.

Rosenblatt, H. S. (1975). How I counsel. *Personnel and Guidance Journal, 54,* 44–45.

Scher, M. (1981). Men in hiding: A challenge for the counselor. *Personnel and Guidance Journal, 60*(4), 199–202.

Smith, D. (1982). Trends in counseling and psychotherapy. *American Psychologist, 37,* 802–809.

5

Basic Counseling Strategies

After mastering the material in this chapter, you should be able to

1. Identify, explain, and discuss the *nondirective* counseling approach.

2. Identify, explain, and discuss the *directive* counseling approach.

3. Identify, explain, and discuss the *eclectic* counseling approach.

4. Identify, explain, and discuss the *action/behavioral* counseling approach.

5. Discuss significant factors that determine the counseling approach a helper might use in working with others.

Counseling and psychotherapy have a long tradition of arguing which therapy is best, rather than determining which therapy is best for which individuals under what conditions.
—Allen E. Ivey and Lynn Simek-Downing

A particular technique is effective to the degree to which it is acceptable to and compatible with the personality of the individual being counseled. The counselor must, therefore, be well informed on theory and be imaginative in the application of concepts gained from theory.
—Lester N. Downing

---

*D*owning (1975) comments that the counselor must be well-informed on the major counseling theories; it is from this knowledge of appropriate techniques and procedures that the counselor is able to accommodate the client. This chapter presents four basic counseling theories that will aid individuals in the helping professions. Each of these theories translates into a counseling approach that a helper may use within a counseling relationship. By understanding these strategies, the helper will be better able to intervene at the appropriate time and help parents of exceptional children. Demos and Grant (1973) comment that mastering the specifics, or techniques, of counseling will make an effective helper. The important thing in helping parents is that the helper selects the best strategy for the situation.

The following approaches may appear rather simple, and this is deceptive. The selection and effective application of these strategies require a person with sufficient skills, training, and experience. The helper must recognize personal limitations when attempting to use a wide range of techniques; limit your involvement to parents you can assist by the competencies you hold. The beginner must study and especially practice (preferably in role-playing situations) before mastering the competencies necessary for effective helping. Because counseling is concerned with developing and utilizing personal competencies to help individuals (parents) recognize and utilize their own potential, skilled helpers can select the technique most appropriate for helping parents with their particular problems or concerns.

THE THREE TRADITIONAL APPROACHES

According to Stewart (1974), counseling, for many years, was heavily influenced by three traditional approaches: (1) the directive or counselor-centered approach, (2) the nondirective, client-centered, or Rogerian approach, and (3) the eclectic approach. Other approaches are now popular among various practitioners in our society, such as Existential (May), Gestalt (Perls), Psychoanalytic (Freud), Logo (Frankl), Rational Emotive Therapy (Ellis), and Transactional Analysis (Berne).

This chapter provides an in-depth discussion of the three traditional approaches of counseling, with the addition of action or behavioral counseling. The effective counselor must be knowledgeable about the basic concepts and principles underlying each approach.

The Directive Approach

The directive approach is often referred to as clinical, trait factor, or counselor-centered counseling. E. G. Williamson (1950) has been acclaimed as the founder of the counselor-centered method. His book entitled *Counseling Adolescents* provides additional information on the directive approach. According to Williamson, the basic goal of counseling is to help the client develop excellence in all aspects of human life.

Williamson (1959) proposes that an individual's freedom "to become" includes self-destructive and antisocial forms of individuality as well as positive development. He adds that people have potential for either good or evil; the purpose of counseling is to assist in actualizing the good potential in people, particularly with a client who lacks the environmental experiences necessary to foster the good drives and impulses. The counselor's background and training should lead to an understanding of the patient's concerns as well as provide the counselor with the means to help the patient adjust to an unpleasant situation. Because the helper is involved in analyzing, diagnosing, presenting information, and clarifying issues, the helper is active in the learning process of the client. The clinical counselor must not be too therapeutically ambitious; accept the fact that you will be of limited use to parents with problems that are primarily long-term emotional reactions—these are best solved by therapeutic help.

Williamson divided the work of the clinical counselor into six steps that represent a rational approach to life's problems. Shertzer and Stone (1980) note these steps.

> *Analysis*—involves collecting data from a wide variety of sources to obtain an understanding of the client.
> *Synthesis*—refers to the summarizing and organizing of data to determine the client's strengths and liabilities.
> *Diagnosis*—the counselor's conclusions about the problem's causes and characteristics.
> *Prognosis*—refers to the counselor's prediction of the counselee's future development or the implications of diagnosis.
> *Counseling*—means the steps taken by counselor and counselee to bring about adjustment and readjustment.
> *Follow-up*—includes whatever the counselor does to assist the counselee with new or recurring problems as well as the evaluation of counseling effectiveness. (p. 173)

The helper is involved in analyzing, diagnosing, presenting information, and clarifying issues when using the directive approach.

A frequent criticism of the Williamson approach is that it over-emphasizes counselor control often resulting in the counselee's becoming too dependent on the counselor for direction and proper courses of action. This viewpoint interprets Williamson too rigidly. In helping parents adjust to difficult experiences, the counselor does not dictate. The counselor does, however, offer experiences and understanding related to the parents' difficulty. The helper does not hesitate to use special skills in giving advice about decisions or courses of action. One major disadvantage of the counselor-centered approach is that poor counselor judgment may lead to adverse consequences.

According to McGowan and Porter (1967), a major advantage of the counselor-centered approach is that since it usually requires only a limited number of interviews, it is a more realistic approach for schools and agencies with a time limit. The judgment and experience of the counselor allow the client to test ideas using the counselor as a "sounding board." Since this is the type of counseling help most people expect when they enter a counseling relationship, the process can usually proceed with a minimum amount of structuring.

The basic assumption underlying the counselor-centered approach is that people must make many and varied decisions—decisions that often call for knowledge and experience that the client is capable of acquiring, but has not had the opportunity to do so. As a result, the client needs to use the knowledge, experience, and technical information that a trained, skilled counselor can provide. Using the counselor's experience, the parent can learn to make and test decisions that will lead to optimal growth and happiness.

Much of a helper's work with parents of exceptional children will call for a directive approach. To be effective in this type of counseling, the counselor should be well-trained in counseling techniques, have adequate diagnostic skills, and possess mature judgment. The helper, as an active participant in the counseling process, will frequently use specific counseling techniques such as (a) asking factual questions that will develop the problem further, (b) supplying the parents with information about themselves and their environment, (c) giving suggestions and advice concerning decisions, and (d) proposing alternative courses of action. Generally, counseling sessions with parents of exceptional children will center on explaining the problem or concern to the parents and then considering the possible results of applying the offered solution.

Coleman (1969) notes that a directive approach appears to be most useful and practical when the client's chief need is for information or reassurance, or when a lack of time dictates an immediate decision that the client is too immature or emotionally upset to make. Davis (1977) points out that directive counseling mostly takes an advisory role, but it also reassures, communicates, gives emotional release, and to a lesser extent, clarifies thinking. Most people enjoy giving advice, counselors included, and it is usually easy to suggest to another person what they should or should not do. Is advice-giving effective? The helper must really understand the parent's problem and possess the technical knowledge of human behavior to make a right decision. Even if the decision is right, the parents may not follow it, or the advice may be rejected or misunderstood. Benjamin (1974) offers an excellent illustration of what a helper might say in order to tactfully refrain from giving advice:

> Now arises the question of whether I, the interviewer, feel I have the right on moral, professional, or simply human grounds to give advice. If I conclude that I do not, I should say so openly and clearly.
>
> "It's hard for you to decide, but I feel I have no moral right to do it for you. These are your children, and the decision as to whether to leave them with your wife's parents or to stay with them is one, I'm afraid, you'll have to make on your own.
>
> This lies beyond my professional competence. All I can do is to recommend a qualified physician who may be able to give you sound advice. But even here, different doctors have different approaches; and my guess is that, ultimately, you will have to make up your own mind.
>
> What should I do in your place? Honestly I can't say. I've tried to understand how things seem to you, but I cannot say whether they would look like this to me if I were you. As you will have to live with your decision, I don't want to influence it unduly. I have a feeling, however, that we have not yet considered all the aspects of the home in. . . ." (p. 131)

Helpers, then, should always be cautious about giving advice. Unless providing educational or vocational information, it is usually best to encourage parents to work out a solution for themselves. Brammer (1979) points out that another limitation of giving advice is that it reinforces dependency on experts, shifting responsibility for solutions to the helper. The helper who takes the "If I were you . . . " approach is often projecting personal needs, problems, or values into the advice rather than keeping the helpee's needs foremost. Brammer concludes with a basic rule to follow: Do not give advice unless it is a tentative suggestion based on solid expertise. Advice may also be in the form of a possible alternative that has been successfully tried by other parents of exceptional children. In any event, the helper should be extremely cautious about giving advice because as Brammer notes, "the helpee may take the helper's advice and later find that it was invalid. The helper then is blamed when things don't turn out right in the helpee's life" (p. 97).

The Nondirective or Client-Centered Approach

Nondirective counseling is often referred to as self-theory, client-centered, or Rogerian counseling. This counseling approach may be used by a variety of qualified professional counselors; however, all helpers may use Rogerian techniques as they encounter and counsel parents of exceptional children. The acknowledged authority of this school of counseling is Carl R. Rogers, whose theories about helping were destined to profoundly change the counseling profession. Rogers's approach is essentially based on the humanistic belief that people's problems are primarily emotional, and that most clients already possess the objective information they need to make a decision about a problem.

Patterson and Eisenberg (1983) note:

> Client-centered counseling is based on a theory of personality referred to as self theory. One's view of self within the context of his or her environment determines one's behavior and personal satisfaction. If provided with a nurturing environment, people grow in confidence toward self-actualization—becoming all they can be. If they do not receive the love and support of significant others, they will likely come to see themselves as lacking in worth and others as untrustworthy. (p. 194)

Rogers has a deep and abiding faith in the goodness of people and in their potential for positive growth given the proper conditions, such as a supportive environment. He argues that people have the basic capacity to set a goal and make correct choices if they are able to see problems objectively in a nonthreatening situation. This is why Rogers originally referred to this type of counseling as *nondirective*—the counselor or therapist does not lead the client but stresses the client's ability to determine the important issues and the potential to solve his or her own problems.

A significant aspect of Rogerian counseling is establishing a warm, permissive, and accepting climate that permits the client to express feelings and gain meaningful insight into the problem. The counselor provides an atmosphere in which the parent feels free to discuss concerns with some one who is genuinely willing to listen. Once the counselor has established a relationship characterized by feelings of understanding, acceptance, lack of evaluation, and lack of threat, parents can lower their self-defenses and begin to gain insight into their feelings. This insight allows them the freedom to examine, incorporate, and express previous experiences. Through conditions of acceptance and understanding, the counselor assists the parents in self-discovery and in reaching a better understanding of their problem or concern.

To enhance the counseling relationship, the client-centered counselor must learn to share the individual's internal frame of reference. Rogers (1951) notes, "The best vantage point for understanding behavior is from the internal frame of reference of the individual himself" (p. 494). The counselor must be able to convey to the client an attitude of genuine liking, a complete absence of value judgments, a total concentration on the client's problems, and finally, an ability to share this perceptual framework without losing self-identity. As Rogers (1951) states:

> It is the counselor's function to assume insofar as he is able, the internal frame of reference of the client, to perceive the world as the client sees it, to lay aside all perceptions from the external frame of reference while doing so, and to communicate something of this empathic understanding to the client. (p. 29)

A crucial element in nondirective counseling, then, is the counselor's participation as a genuine person. Helpful counseling techniques that you might use are listening in-depth, reflecting on attitudes and feelings, and clarifying. Many counselor responses are open-ended or nonstructured leads that prompt the client to express the emotions accompanying a problem. Hackney and Nye (1973) suggest that a good way to help the client identify and express feelings is to model this process; the counselor expresses a feeling that the client may be experiencing. The counselor might say, "I think we've really gotten somewhere today and I feel good about that." The counselor might also model the client's situation by saying, "If she had treated me that way, I think I would have been pretty angry." This strategy helps the client who is unable, for whatever reason, to make appropriate emotional responses.

Davis (1977) points out that Rogerian counseling is a skilled process, unlike what is jokingly called "uh-huh counseling" where the counselor nods his head, smiles at the client, and repeatedly says "uh-huh." The helper must completely concentrate on the client's problem to communicate empathic understanding, allowing the client to gain insight and greater self-understanding. Davis refers to this type of counseling as a fluid, sensitive relationship that requires close attention to detail.

McGowan and Porter (1967) indicate that a major advantage of Rogerian counseling is that clients depend less on the counselor to make their decisions. Instead, responsibility falls on the client to find solutions to problems. The client's past experiences, which cannot be changed, are minimized and attention focuses on present adjustment. Client-centered counseling provides an emotional release as well as a permanent form of self-suggestive growth.

Lewis (1970) notes that the strengths of the client-centered approach are its emphasis on positive development of the individual, and its use of a therapeutic technique that does not involve years of intensive training to master. He warns that Rogerian counseling is not easy or simple, however. The basic concepts are easily understood, but the true client-centered therapist must possess a self-awareness and a capacity for forming relationships not usually encountered. A great deal is required of the therapist as a person rather than as a therapist. The helper's attitudes of respect, empathy, and warmth are often more important than the technique employed.

Perhaps the major disadvantage of client-centered counseling is that it assumes an emotional cause behind every problem; all clients fit the mold of having emotional problems regardless of their own perceptions. Two other disadvantages mark client-centered counseling. First, the counselor is expected to be neutral, neither condemning nor condoning the actions or feelings of the client. Is it possible for any counselor to be valueless in an interpersonal situation? Second, because of the specific techniques necessary in Rogerian counseling, a series of interviews or conferences is usually required. Nondirective counseling is often considered too time consuming and expensive to be realistic.

As a contemporary note, Carl Rogers (1977) now speaks of a person-centered approach. He states:

> A person-centered approach, when utilized to encourage the growth and development of the psychotic, the troubled, or the normal individual, revolutionizes the customary behaviors of members of the helping professions. It illustrates many things: (1) A sensitive person, trying to be of help, becomes more person-centered, no matter what orientation she starts from because she finds that approach more effective. (2) When you are focused on the person, diagnostic labels become largely irrelevant. (3) The traditional medical model in psychotherapy is discovered to be largely in opposition to person-centeredness. (4) It is found that those who can create an effective person-centered relationship do not necessarily come from the professionally trained group. (5) The more this person-centered approach is implemented and put into practice, the more it is found to challenge hierarchical models of "treatment" and hierarchical methods of organization. (6) The very effectiveness of this unified person-centered approach constitutes a threat to professionals, administrators, and others, and steps are taken—consciously and unconsciously—to destroy it. It is too revolutionary. (p. 28)

More recently, Rogers (1980) identified the central hypothesis of the person-centered approach. According to Rogers, "individuals have within themselves vast resources for self-understanding and for altering their self-concepts, basic attitudes, and self-directed behavior; these resources can be tapped if a definable climate of facilitative psychological attitudes can be provided" (p. 115).

The Eclectic Viewpoint

Several years ago, Hitchcock (1964) defined the eclectic approach to counseling as an approach where directive, nondirective, and other techniques are employed to aid the client in adjusting to life's problems. This approach is often referred to as the "middle-of-the-road" approach. As Shertzer and Stone (1980) note, the word *eclectic* means to select, to choose appropriate doctrines or methods from various sources or systems. The eclectic counselor, then, believes that procedures, techniques, and concepts from many sources will best serve the needs of the person seeking help. Shertzer and Stone further note that through the eclectic counselor's knowledge of perception, development, learning, and personality, a wide repertoire of helping approaches is available to the counselor, who then must choose the most appropriate in terms of the particular problem, the situation, and the personality of the client or parent.

Ivey and Simek-Downing (1980) warn helpers about relying on a single model of helping by stating:

> Common to many people in helping is an overzealous commitment to one single most effective way of helping. Commitment and belief are important if one is to be competent and make a difference in the lives of others, but a single-minded commitment to a sole theoretical school can represent a rigidity which makes it impossible to reach and help many people who might respond to another point of view. The task is to become versatile in many theories and approaches and to remain open to new ideas. (p. 7)

Frederick Thorne contributed most to the development of eclecticism. In his book, *Principles of Personality Counseling,* he discussed the scientific application of eclecticism—a technique that calls for a study of all methods of diagnosis and treatment. As Thorne (1961) expresses it:

> To the degree which eclecticism is able to integrate all operational methods and find ways available at time and place, it appears to us that it must represent the last word concerning what we can validly understand and apply in practice. (p. 240)

The eclectic model is based on two assumptions: (1) that people differ in their capacity to cope with life and its problems and therefore need different types of assistance, and (2) that an adequate diagnosis is essential to any science that proposes to identify and appropriately treat problems. According to Thorne (1950), the process of personality counseling involves five stages:

1. Diagnosis of the cause of personality maladjustments
2. Making a plan for modifying the causal factors
3. Securing proper conditions for efficient learning
4. Stimulating the client to develop his own resources and assume responsibility for practicing new modes of adjustment
5. Handling any related problems that may contribute to adjustment. (pp. 88–89)

As with other approaches, eclectic counseling is characterized by warmth, understanding, and acceptance, but adds an emphasis on reassurance and information-giving to promote client learning. A counselor who intends to use eclecticism should have a scientific view of man, broad diagnostic skills, and an openness that allows flexible style and technique.

The advantage of eclecticism over other counseling methods is that Thorne has analyzed and integrated the best aspects of each. This diversity and flexibility of technique theoretically allows the counselor to work with a more diverse clientele.

A common criticism of the eclectic approach, however, is that it is not realistic to expect counselors to be expert in so many methods and styles. Counselors have a tendency to develop their own personal style and often lose effectiveness when trying another technique. It is also unrealistic to expect most counselors to possess the academic and diagnostic training necessary for successful eclectic counseling.

Hackney and Nye (1973) observe that once the counselor and client have identified specific goals, the counselor's expertise is needed. The counselor must establish rapport and a helping relationship as well as possess a repertoire of counseling strategies to help the client achieve the established goals. These strategies become *modus operandi* (plans of action) to achieve specific client outcomes.

COMPARISON AND CONTRAST OF DIRECTIVE/NONDIRECTIVE/ECLECTIC METHODS

Demos and Grant (1973) offer an outline of differentiation between the three traditional counseling approaches.

Directive
1. Relies on data gathered by the counselor
2. Concerns intellect (reacting to intellectual content)
3. Predominantly scientific
4. Primarily concerned with educational and vocational areas
5. Emphasizes problems of the client

Nondirective
1. Relies on data offered by the client
2. Concerns emotions (reacting to emotional content)
3. Predominantly focuses on the art of human relations
4. Primarily concerned with the personal-social area
5. Emphasizes the process of interviewing

Eclectic
1. Relies on data gathered by the counselor or offered by the client
2. Concerns intellect or emotions
3. Involves a scientific approach or the art of human relations
4. Includes educational, vocational, and personal-social areas
5. Emphasizes the problem or process

An unanswered question remains: How does a helper determine the appropriate or best helping strategy? Although there is no absolute answer, knowledge, training, experience, and flexibility appear to be the most critical factors in determining when to adopt directive, nondirective, or eclectic theories of counseling. Skill and proficiency in the method or theory used is also crucial—probably more than the particular method used. Demos and Grant acknowledge that they do not single out any technique as being superior to the others. Each technique has its own merits in a given situation.

Hackney and Nye (1973) maintain that common elements exist in all the counseling approaches, and comment that

> Counseling involves responding to both feelings and thoughts of the client. Or, thinking of this in another way, the counselor deals with both attitudes and behaviors of the client. Existing theoretical approaches differ with respect to emphasis and order of responsiveness to feelings and behavior. Some approaches (client-centered; existential) favor an emphasis on feelings; others (rational-emotive; reality therapy; behavioral) emphasize the importance of behaviors and actions. An eclectic counseling model, however, would acknowledge the importance of being able to identify and respond appropriately to both feeling states and behaviors. (p. 5)

Counselors and psychologists continue to prefer eclecticism above other counseling types. Smith (1982) conducted a survey that indicated a 41% majority of the therapists surveyed identify with an eclectic orientation from a choice of twelve theoretical orientations (Adlerian, Behavioral, Cognitive-behavioral, Eclectic, Existential, Family, Gestalt, Person-centered, Psychoanalytic, Rational-emotive, Reality, and Transactional analysis). Psychoanalytic and Cognitive-behavioral orientations accounted for the next highest preferences with approximately 10% for each.

THE BEHAVIORAL OR ACTION APPROACH

Because none of the traditional counseling techniques was flexible enough to help all clients, supplementary counseling techniques became necessary.

One of the techniques recognized and accepted by practitioners is behavioral or action counseling. Several years ago, Lewis (1970) noted that only recently have counselors responded to the challenge presented in 1962 by Michael and Meyerson in their article, "A Behavioral Approach to Counseling and Guidance." In this provocative article, the authors state that "observable behavior is the only variable of importance in the counseling and guidance process, and it is the only criterion against which the outcome of the process can be evaluated"(p. 395–396). Operant conditioning, proposed by B.F. Skinner, is based on the idea that we tend to repeat behaviors that bring about positive consequences; behaviors that elicit negative responses are not repeated. Operant responses, then, are given to gain some type of positive outcome (Weiten, 1983). Proposing this same idea, Michael and Meyerson (1962) point out that "behavior is controlled by its environmental consequences and an effective procedure for producing behavioral change is the manipulation of the environment so as to create consequences that will produce the desired behavior."

Thoresen (1966) made a five-fold statement that captured the essence of behavioral counseling:

1. Most human behavior is learned and is therefore subject to change.
2. Specific changes of the individual's environment can assist in altering relevant behaviors; counseling procedures seek to bring about relevant changes in student behavior by altering the environment.
3. Social learning principles, such as those of reinforcement and social modeling, can be used to develop counseling procedures.
4. Counseling effectiveness and the outcome of counseling are assessed by changes in specific student behaviors outside the counseling interview.
5. Counseling procedures are not static, fixed, or predetermined, but can be specifically designed to assist the student in solving a particular problem. (pp. 395–396)

Patterson and Eisenberg (1983) also discuss the nature of behavioral counseling. Their viewpoints are worthy of noting:

☐ Behavioral counseling is based on learning theory. The fundamental assumption is that all behavior is learned and can therefore be changed by implementing strategies to produce new learning.
☐ The purpose of behavioral counseling is to change ineffective behavior, and only measurable behavior change is regarded as evidence of successful counseling.
☐ Behavioral counseling places great emphasis on the clear definition of goals. Goals are stated in terms of behavior change so that observation will provide evidence of measurable change.
☐ Counseling strategies are based on the principles of learning. The client is taught to think differently about a behavior or is simply conditioned to behave differently.

The most significant aspect of the behavioral counseling relationship is setting up a structure that enhances specific, positive, observable changes in client behavior. This type of counseling emphasizes identifying the behavioral events that are to be modified as well as determining the present stimuli reinforcing the behaviors. It is important, then, to define, or pinpoint, the client's particular concern. From a learning theory framework, to define a client's difficulty as having a poor self-concept is insufficient. Instead, state the problem in terms of overt behavior (Hansen, Stevic, & Warner, 1972). Any observed behavior is measurable, offering concrete evidence of any change. For example, the nondirective counselor might suggest a counseling goal such as "improving the client's self-concept"; the behavior-oriented counselor would specify the behaviors that would give the client new ways of coping with problems and that would eventually lead to an improved self-concept.

Ullman and Krasner (1965) suggest three initial questions that the behavioral counselor might ask:

1. What behavior is maladaptive; that is, what subject behaviors should be increased or decreased?
2. What environmental contingencies currently support the subject's behavior?
3. What environmental changes, usually reinforcing stimuli, may be manipulated to alter the subject behavior?

Dustin and George (1973) describe action or behavioral counseling as consisting of three essential phases. In Phase 1, the counselor begins contact with the client by listening and communicating empathic understanding to develop a special kind of relationship. Phase 2 is the stage when the counselor and client decide how to meet the client's needs and what techniques will be most effective. In Phase 3, the client follows an action plan. More and more of the conversation between the counselor and client is based on what the client did or would like to do, and what they can do to meet the client's objectives. According to Dustin and George, combining these three phases of relationship, choice, and action provides an effective approach toward behavior change.

One advantage of behavioral counseling is its in-depth approach that stresses observable behavioral changes. Another advantage is the positive reinforcement given to clients to motivate them to continue the change process. The disadvantage is that those who aspire to be effective behavioral counselors have had only a superficial exposure to learning theories and may not be competent in using the behavioral method. If you adopt a behavioral approach, you must be well-versed in learning theory to assist clients to grow in self-understanding.

Helping Parents Understand and Apply Behavioral Principles

Education has often excluded parents from direct involvement with their children's education, providing them only with information and advice instead. Professionals in parent intervention programs are becoming more aware of the productive contributions that parents can make toward their child's development. In fact, parents are now valued as major contributors to parent-child interactions, as well as primary agents for changing these interactions. Parents *can* be taught the principles and skills of behavior management and they are capable of bringing about specific changes in their child's behavior.

Karnes and Zehrback (1972) state that the success of a parental involvement program depends on three factors:

1. The attitude of the professional—there must be a positive attitude about the parents' contribution to the growth of their child.
2. The recognition that there is more than one way to involve parents—parents have individual needs that must be recognized to help them select the best way to involve themselves in the educational program of their child.
3. The belief that each parent is capable of growth—the amount of growth of parents will vary. The extent depends on the degree to which the teacher changes, expands, and increases the breadth and depth of activities in the parent involvement program.

In addition to these factors, parents must realize the importance of committing time and effort, maintaining a positive attitude toward their child, and adhering to a consistent application of newly acquired skills. You as a helper must encourage parents if they begin to feel frustrated, fatigued or disappointed.

O'Dell (1974) states some advantages to using behavior modification approaches for training parents to manage children's behaviors. The advantages include the following:

1. Behavior modification techniques are easy to learn. Persons who are unskilled in sophisticated therapy techniques can learn the principles of behavior modification. A college education or professional training is not a prerequisite for successful management of a child's behavior repertoire.
2. Parents and professionals alike prefer a management model that is not oriented to sick behavior and patterned after the traditional medical model.
3. The majority of children's behavioral responses possess common features that are amendable to change by the systematic application of behavioral principles.
4. The behavioral principles can be carried out in the natural environment where the behavioral problems are being manifested by the child and responded to by the parents. (p. 419–420)

According to Karnes and Zehrback (1972),

The basic thrust of this approach requires the parent to specify exactly which child behaviors are his concern, gather data to record the frequency of such behavior, develop a specific procedure for changing the child's behavior, and then note the degree of change in the child's behavior. (p. 14)

They also note that parents who profit most from this approach seem to be fairly stable, consistent, and seem to need to bring about a positive change in their child's behavior.

What are some principles that parents should be aware of before using behavior modification techniques? They should have an understanding of what a behavior is, how behaviors are learned, and how to influence (change) a behavior.

The basic principle of behavior modification is that behavior is learned; it is taught. If it is learned it can be relearned or unlearned. Much of our behavior is learned through interaction with the surrounding environment. From our childhood, parents, teachers, peers, brothers, sisters, and even strangers have provided cues and rewards for our responses to the environment. The food we eat, the people we like, the clothes we wear, and so forth are learned from our friends and society. We learn not only desirable behavior but undesirable as well, for we act in a manner that we feel will help us get along best in that environment. When observing a child one sees various types of behavior. This behavior may be attributed to aggression, neglect, or lack of motivation, but all one can really see is the behavior—the overt, physical, or psychomotor act. Behavior, in this context, is a series of observable responses.

What Constitutes a Behavior?

Three characteristics define a behavior. First, the behavior must be directly observable and capable of being clearly described so that any person could accurately identify its occurrence. As we established before, an observed behavior is measurable. Second, the behavior should involve movement. Acts such as sitting, resting, daydreaming, and being quiet are really the absence of behavior, and are noticeable only because some other behavior is not occurring. Third, the behavior should be repeatable. If a behavior cannot be repeated, then it cannot be examined. It must occur a sufficient number of times for the counselor to work with it.

The basic law of behavior is the *law of reinforcement*. Behaviors that are rewarded tend to be repeated and behaviors that are not rewarded tend not to be repeated. A behavior, then, is repeated because its consequences have been rewarding or pleasing to the person; otherwise, that behavior would not reoccur. If we observe a behavior occurring repeatedly, there must be some reward or desired outcome that supports it. This is astounding when one considers that inappropriate or undesirable behaviors are also being rewarded. In fact, the reward must be so important that the behavior continues in spite of any unpleasant results.

How to Influence Behavior

There are four basic ways that a parent can influence, change, and manage a child's behavior:

1. Increase—The parent may increase or strengthen a good behavior that doesn't happen often enough. One method for learning new behavior is observation and imitation. A child may copy or imitate a behavior if someone else performs it and is rewarded. This type of imitative behavior is called modeling. Children learn to speak, ride bicycles, identify with their sex, and so forth by imitating the actions of others.
2. Decrease—A parent may decrease or weaken a bad or displeasing behavior that happens too frequently. If a child exhibits undesirable behaviors, the objective is to not reinforce them.
3. Shape—If a behavior has never been performed by a child it is impossible to reward the behavior. To teach a behavior, parents must reward ones that approximate the desired behavior. As the general response is performed more frequently, parents should reward only those a step closer to the desired specific behavior.
4. Maintain—To maintain a child's existing behavior that is pleasing, parents should continue to reward the child for the behavior.

To benefit from our discussion of the major counseling theories, it would be helpful to identify some principles that apply to all counseling theories. Downing (1975) believes that instead of moving directly to a counseling technique to help the individual, the counselor should first consider some sound principles that dictate to a degree the appropriateness of a technique. According to Downing, some principles appropriate to all counseling approaches, or to an integrated approach, might include the following:

(a) Always view each problem revealed from the viewpoint of the client. Attempt to perceive the total situation from the perspective of the individual.
(b) Create a nonjudgmental atmosphere in which the person is encouraged to express himself with candor and freedom. Minimize any possibility of his thinking that the counselor will judge or punish behavior.
(c) View each individual as a whole, or as a totality of personality traits and characteristics. Realize that the isolation and treatment of a single symptom is likely to be unproductive in terms of total growth. Wholeness is essential here.
(d) Avoid the temptation to focus upon a particular behavior, personality trait, or problem as if the resolution of a particular difficulty were the answer to the person's needs. Anticipate the existence of underlying conditions with a relationship to the main problems, and assume a condition of interrelationships among personality traits and among the causes of difficulties.

(e) Always direct efforts toward helping the individual identify and fulfill his needs. Assume that progress toward need fulfillment will also result in the resolution of many of an individual's problems.

(f) Proceed as if the best solutions to a person's problems are to be found within himself. It is the internal strength of the individual upon which he can rely most confidently for answers to his problems.

(g) Demonstrate a belief in the individual from which he may gain added confidence and through which appropriate actions may be triggered. Help him to see a justification for the confidence shown in him by believing in him and by reinforcing his efforts.

(h) Continually emphasize an attitude of high regard for him as a worthy human being. Help him to see his importance as a unique, deserving human being.

(i) Demonstrate enthusiasm and optimism in the relationship, and help him to see the humor as well as the seriousness of his situation. A hopeful, cheerful, optimistic attitude should be a prerequisite to a concerted attack upon existing problems.

(j) Focus all efforts upon strengthening and building up the individual. It is upon the increasing strength and capacities of the individual that he will be able to depend for actions and judgments.

(k) Structure each counseling session in such a fashion as to identify possibilities for developing and improving needed skills. Greater competence adds to self-confidence and attracts the kind of attention that continues to bolster self-esteem.

(l) Continually emphasize the notions that counseling is a shared and a sharing relationship and that all decisions are mutually achieved. Help him to feel that the tone and the quality of the relationship are a source of encouragement upon which he may draw indefinitely.*

There are other principles, but these are representative of common goals to establish in all types of counseling. The precise nature or number of principles is not important; however, it is important to observe principles for the improvement of counseling.

A final question remains that needs attention. What factors affect the counselor's chosen approach or strategy? There are many factors that influence the counselor's approach and course of action. Some of the major considerations and variables are

☐ the counselor's philosophy of counseling,
☐ the counselor's concept of his or her role,
☐ the knowledge, competencies, and experience of the counselor
☐ the particular concern of the parent (Parents present different kinds of problems and need different kinds of help.),
☐ the parent's ability to assume a responsible role in the counseling process, and
☐ the helper's realization that there are no simple solutions to complex problems.

---

*SOURCE: Lester N. Downing, *Counseling theories and techniques summarized and critiqued.* Chicago, IL: Nelson-Hall, 1975, pp. 182–183. Reprinted with permission.

Although considering these factors may be helpful, the technique or techniques to use when counseling the parent of an exceptional child remains relatively open. Remember that people behave and act differently at every moment of their lives depending on their need for personal realization.

When helping people solve their problems, Johnson (1981) suggests observing two basic rules.

> The first rule in helping other people solve their problems and understand distressing situations is to remember that all insights, understandings, decisions, and solutions occur within the other people, not within you. No matter how convinced you are that you know what the other people should do, your goal is helping must be to assist them in reaching their own decisions and forming their own insights.
>
> The second rule in helping others solve their problems is to differentiate between an internal frame of reference (how the other person sees and feels about the situation) and an external frame of reference (how you see and feel about the other person's situation). You are able to give help to the extent that you understand and respond to the sender's frame of reference rather than imposing your frame of reference on the problem situation. (p. 159)

CHAPTER SUMMARY

Although specific counseling strategies and techniques for working with parents of exceptional children will be discussed in Chapters Eight, Nine, and Ten, any person who seeks to help others should understand the basic and fundamental counseling strategies. This understanding will help you capture the essence of helping, and may help you make choices of technique and strategy. This chapter should guide your own individual assessment and development of helping theories. Working effectively with others involves adopting specific actions, and since virtually all helping involves the counselor's efforts to teach counselees to solve their own problems, the helper needs to be familiar with basic helping strategies.

ACTIVITIES, EXERCISES, AND IDEAS FOR REFLECTION AND DISCUSSION

1. Cite individual variables that might influence the approach you would take in a counseling situation.
2. Which of the four approaches discussed in this chapter might be most difficult for a person without formal training in counseling? Why?
3. What type of counseling approach would appear to work best for individuals who need information, understanding, emotional support, and acceptance to make a correct decision?
4. Choose two people to represent a client and counselor. Define a problem, and role-play a counseling session employing a particular counseling approach. See if the class can identify which approach was used by analyzing the exchange between client and counselor.

5. Complete this statement: A counselor's approach to counseling is governed in part by his _____ . Compare your response with another person.
6. Of the counseling approaches discussed, which one seems to be the most systematic? Why?
7. Of the counseling approaches discussed, which one seems to be the most valid on a scientific basis? Why?
8. Do you agree with Carl Rogers's belief that people's problems are primarily emotional and that most clients already possess the objective information needed to make a decision about a problem? Substitute the words *parents of exceptional children* for *clients*. Has your opinion changed?
9. Which of the approaches discussed would probably work best with individuals who, by nature, are timid and reserved and quite fearful of seeking help or becoming actively involved in a counseling relationship? Why?
10. Is this statement valid? It is impossible for a counselor to provide the correct form of counseling service (treatment) without first identifying what it is that the client needs (diagnosis).
11. Should the beginning teacher/counselor experiment with the different types of counseling approaches or use only the one that has become most comfortable? What are some advantages and disadvantages of experimentation with counseling approaches?
12. Do you agree or disagree that giving advice is a purposeful counseling activity?
13. Once counseling decisions are made, what factors influence their implementation?
14. List specific ways in which goals, decisions, and behavioral operations may be evaluated.
15. Do you agree or disagree that the counselor of parents of exceptional children is dealing with problems of human behavior and, therefore, is essentially working with the fundamentals of psychology? What implications does this have?

REFERENCES

Benjamin, A. (1974). *The helping interview*. Boston: Houghton Mifflin.

Brammer, L. M. (1979). *The helping relationship: Process and skills* (2nd ed.). Englewood Cliffs, NJ: Prentice-Hall.

Coleman, J. C. (1969). *Psychology and effective behavior*. Glenview, IL: Scott, Foresman.

Davis, K. (1977). *Human behavior at work: Organizational behavior*. New York: McGraw-Hill.

Demos, G. D., & Grant, B. (1973). *An introduction to counseling: A handbook*. Los Angeles: Western Psychological Services.

Downing, L. N. (1975). *Counseling theories and techniques: Summarized and critiqued*. Chicago: Nelson-Hall.

Dustin, R., & George, R. (1973). *Action counseling for behavior change*. New York: Intext Educational Publishers.

Hackney, H., & Nye, S. (1973). *Counseling strategies and objectives*. Englewood Cliffs, NJ: Prentice-Hall.

Hanson, J. C., Stevic, R. R., & Warner, R. W. (1972). *Counseling: Theory and process.* Boston: Allyn & Bacon.

Hitchcock, W. L. (1964). *The counseling service.* Atlanta, GA: Georgia Department of Education.

Ivey, A. E., & Simek-Downing, L. (1980). *Counseling and psychotherapy: Skills, theories, and practice.* Englewood Cliffs, NJ: Prentice-Hall.

Johnson, D. W. (1981). *Reaching out: Interpersonal effectiveness and self-actualization* (2nd ed.). Englewood Cliffs, NJ: Prentice-Hall.

Karnes, M. B., & Zehrbach, R. R. (1972). Flexibility in getting parents involved in the school. *Teaching Exceptional Children, 5,* 6–19.

Lewis, E. C. (1970). *The psychology of counseling.* New York: Holt, Rinehart, & Winston.

McGowan, J. F., & Porter, T. L. (1967). *An introduction to the vocational rehabilitation process.* Washington, DC: U.S. Department of Health, Education, and Welfare.

Michael, J., & Meyerson, L. (1962). A behavioral approach to counseling and guidance. *Harvard Educational Review, 32,* 395–396.

O'Dell, S. (1974). Training parents in behavior modification: A review. *Psychological Bulletin, 81,* 418–433.

Patterson, L. E., & Eisenberg, S. (1983). *The counseling process* (3rd ed.). Boston: Houghton Mifflin.

Rogers, C. R. (1977). *Carl Rogers on personal power.* New York: Delacorte.

Rogers, C. R. (1951). *Client-centered therapy.* Boston: Houghton Mifflin.

Rogers, C. R. (1980) *A way of being.* Boston: Houghton Mifflin.

Shertzer, B., & Stone, S. C. (1980). *Fundamentals of counseling* (3rd ed.). Boston: Houghton Mifflin.

Smith, D. (1982). Trends in counseling and psychotherapy. *American Psychologist, 37* (7), 802–809.

Stewart, J. C. (1974). *Counseling parents of exceptional children: Principles, problems and procedures.* New York: MSS Information Corporation.

Thoresen, C. E. (1966). Behavioral counseling: An introduction. *The School Counselor, 14,* 13–21.

Thorne, F. C. (1961). Clinical judgment. *Journal of Clinical Psychology, 22.*

Thorne, F. C. (1950). Principles of personality counseling. *Journal of Clinical Psychology,* 88–89.

Ullman, L. P., & Krasner, L. (1965). *Case studies in behavior modification.* New York: Holt, Rinehart, & Winston.

Weiten, W. (1983). *Psychology applied to modern life: Adjustment in the 80s.* Monterey, CA: Brooks/Cole.

Williamson, E. G. (1959). Some issues underlying counseling theory and practice. In W. E. Dugan (Ed.), *Counseling points of view.* Minneapolis: University of Minnesota Press.

Williamson, E. G. (1950). *Counseling adolescents.* New York: McGraw-Hill.

Williamson, E. G. (1980). In B. Shertzer and S. C. Stone, *Fundamentals of counseling* (3rd ed.). New York: Houghton Mifflin.

SELECTED REFERENCES FOR FURTHER READING AND STUDY

Ball, T. S., Coyne, A., Javis, R. M., & Pease, S. (1984). Parents of retarded children as teaching assistants to other parents. *Education and Training of the Mentally Retarded, 19,* 64–69.

Brown, D., & Brown, S. (1975). Parental consultation: A behavioral approach. *Elementary School Guidance and Counseling, 10,* 95–102.

Ewing, D. B. (1977). Twenty approaches to individual change. *Personnel and Guidance Journal, 55,* 331–338.

Ginnot, H. G. (1965). *Between parent and child.* New York: Avon.

Glasser, W. (1965). *Reality therapy.* New York: Harper & Row.

Gordon, T. (1970). *Parent effectiveness training.* New York: Peter H. Wyden.

Harris, T. A. (1969). *I'm o.k.—You're o.k., A practical guide to transactional analysis.* New York: Harper & Row.

MacNamara, R. (1977). The complete behavior modifier: Confessions of an over-zealous operant conditioner. *Mental Retardation, 15,* 34–37.

Parloff, M. B. (1976, February 21). Shopping for the right therapy. *Saturday Review,* 14–20.

Roos, P. (1974). Human rights and behavior modification. *Mental Retardation, 12,* 3–6.

6 Specific Topics and Issues in the Helping Relationship

After mastering the content in this chapter, you should be able to

1. Discuss the importance of the physical setting to the counseling relationship.

2. Discuss the purpose, causes, and handling of long periods of silence during counseling.

3. Briefly describe the purpose, nature, and significance of nonverbal communication.

4. Summarize the basic principles of group counseling.

5. Define and describe the referral process.

6. Identify and briefly discuss ten basic principles of referral.

7. Explain why systematic evaluation of the counselor's services is an important phase in the helping relationship.

8. Identify two or more methods of evaluating the helper's services.

Group counseling can be conducted for remedial purposes, for developmental purposes, or be preventive in nature, hoping to prevent problems from growing to the point where the individual needs special help to cope with them.
—Bruce Shertzer and Shelley C. Stone

Evaluation is a critical part of the entire therapeutic process and thus should not simply be left out until after intervention strategies have been applied. In its most effective form, evaluation and thus data gathering for evaluation purposes is ongoing.
—Leroy G. Baruth and Charles H. Huber

*C*hapter Six completes Part One by identifying and discussing some of the topics and problems that inevitably occur during the counseling process. An in-depth understanding of these topics will enable the helper to assume a more professional role in effectively assisting parents of exceptional children.

THE PHYSICAL SETTING

The client's first impressions of counseling are based on more than simply the actions of the helper. The helpee's attitude may also be influenced by the counseling setting. The physical setting and its atmosphere may have an important bearing on the success of a counseling relationship. Benjamin (1974) points out that the helper's goal is to provide an atmosphere conducive to communication. Although each person must decide what type of setting this is, Benjamin suggests a room or area that is not overwhelming, noisy, or distracting. Interruptions, distractions, and interferences should always be avoided if possible. Instead, the room or area should be comfortable and attractive, conveying a warm, friendly, nonthreatening atmosphere.

According to Shertzer and Stone (1980),

The most important prerequisite of the physical setting is privacy and if the confidence of the counselee is to be secured, the feeling of security engendered by privacy cannot be overemphasized. Individuals desire and have a right to both auditory and visual privacy from peers, teachers, and others when they enter into a helping relationship. (p. 336)

No office, room, or other area can encourage effective communication if conversations can be easily overheard.

The arrangement of chairs or seating is often a significant factor in a particular counseling technique. The presence or absence of a desk between the helper and parents conveys meaning to a client. For example, a nondirective counselor would normally avoid the authoritative position of being behind a desk and having the client seated directly facing him.

Lewis (1970) suggests that the beginning counselor try various arrangements of furniture to find the most comfortable one that seems to communicate best the kind of counseling relationship to be established.

SILENCE IN COUNSELING

Shertzer and Stone (1980) state:

> Silence is difficult to master as a technique for most counselors who have been teachers because they often believe that client silence is synonymous with counselor failure and become uncomfortable when it occurs. Because silence in social situations tends to be looked upon as rejection, defiance, or disapproval, this meaning, from a different context, is quite often transferred to the counseling relationship. When pauses occur, the counselor may be overcome with the desire to break the silence rather than tolerate it. (p. 280)

You should understand that a great deal of communication may occur without verbal exchanges—no rule exists that says silence should always be replaced with spoken words.

A successful counseling relationship requires both listening and talking. Perhaps the most common error beginning counselors make is that they tend to talk too much. Silence is sometimes difficult to tolerate—a 30-second period of silence seems to last for much longer, and the helper often reacts by talking. With experience and practice, most helpers will learn to differentiate between types of silences and respond to them accordingly.

Periods of silence can be useful and can actually enhance the helping relationship. Benjamin (1974) illustrates this by saying,

> There is, for example, the silence the interviewee may require to sort out his thoughts and feelings. Respect for this silence is more beneficial than many words from the interviewer. When ready, the interviewee will continue, usually quite soon—in a minute or so. This minute will seem quite long to us at first, but with experience we shall learn to measure time internally. Should the silence endure, we may want to interject a brief remark to help him go on; one can get lost in silence and appreciate the indication of a possible way out. For example, we might say: "There must be lots going on within; I wonder if you are ready to share some of it with me" or "I can see by the expression on your face that there's much going on behind the scenes; I'm ready to participate if you're ready to have me." Silence of this sort can be most helpful if the interviewer does not feel threatened by it or uncomfortable with it but can handle it with ease as part of an ongoing process. (p. 24)

There are several logical reasons for silence. Shertzer and Stone (1980) give the following:

1. the person being counseled may be the "naturally quiet" type and have difficulty expressing thoughts and feelings,

2. silence may occur because either the counselor or the client has reached the conclusion of a thought and does not know what to say next,
3. silence may indicate that the client is experiencing emotions that are difficult to express, yet would like to do so,
4. a pause may mean that the client seeks the counselor's assurance, support, or encouragement,
5. silence may be the result of a highly emotional expression by the client,
6. the helpee may be silent to resist what may appear as the counselor's probing,
7. the client may be reflecting on what has just been said, and
8. silence may indicate a desire not to reveal too much or to expose feelings.

When should a helper interrupt a pause or silence? According to Hackney and Nye (1973), there is no general rule to help you determine when to remain silent and when to interrupt. Although some counselors remain silent when the client initiated the pause, the counselor must be sensitive in each particular situation. You should recognize that silence does not necessarily indicate a halt in the counseling process. Periods of silence will inevitably occur and usually indicate that the client is thinking about feelings and emotions that have just surfaced. Remember that silence may be a productive element in the helping relationship if the client uses it as a means to stimulate personal awareness and sort out thoughts and feelings.

NONVERBAL COMMUNICATION: MEANING BEYOND WORDS

Dr. Fredrick Perls, a leading Gestalt psychologist, says, "Verbal communication is a lie. The real communication is beyond words." Similarly, the French writer Victor Hugo said, "When a woman is speaking to you, listen to what she says with her eyes." Hugo was talking about what is now commonly known as nonverbal communication. Body language, an important part of nonverbal communication, has recently received a great deal of both clinical and popular attention. Davis (1977) reports that studies provide evidence of body language as an important supplement to verbal communication in most parts of the world. This form of communication can be eloquent in its capacity to confirm one's spoken words; it is equally true that people often communicate contradictory feelings in their words and body language. Speech is only a part of people's effort to communicate.

Nichols and Stevens (1957), note that

The pitch and timbre of a person's voice; the way he pauses between words; the rhythm with which the words flow from his mouth; oddities in pronunciation; the speed at which words are spoken—all of these things have something to say, over and above that which is being communicated by words alone. (pp. 59–61)

Nichols and Stevens illustrate this with the word *oh*—a word that says little when seen in printed form. When spoken, however, *oh* can acquire many meanings. Using different voice inflections, *oh* can mean: "You surprised me," "I made a mistake," "You're a pain in the neck," "You make me so happy," "I'm bored," "I'm fascinated," "I understand," or "I don't understand."

As you can see from this example, nonverbal messages can reinforce, modify, and sometimes even contradict the words that a person speaks. In certain instances, the nonverbal part of a client's communication is far more important than the verbal part. For example, if you can detect the facial changes that reflect emotion, you should be in a better position to lead the interview in the appropriate direction.

Hackney and Nye (1973) suggest that nonverbal communication may help the counselor interpret client silence. By watching the client, the counselor will be able to gather some clues. Is the client relaxed? Are the client's eyes fixed on something without focusing? A fixed stare usually means the person is thinking about something, perhaps examining a new idea. Is the client tense or nervous, looking from one object to another and avoiding eye contact? This may mean avoidance of some topic or idea. The interaction between counselor and client will often depend on the nonverbal communication between the two.

Johnson (1981) believes that to communicate effectively with other individuals, it may be more important to master nonverbal communication than fluency with words. He cites a study showing that in a normal two-person conversation, 65 percent of the meaning comes from nonverbal messages. To be an effective helper, then, you should have a working knowledge of nonverbal communication to be aware of the messages your client sends to you, as well as those you send to your client, such as understanding and support, or the lack of them (Hansen, Stevic, & Warner, 1972). Nonverbal communication can no longer be ignored as a major force in shaping our understanding of another person.

GROUP COUNSELING

Group counseling has developed in only the past 30 to 40 years. It was slow to gain acceptance, but group counseling has expanded rapidly during the last decade in both school and nonschool settings. This rapid growth has led to concerns about its effectiveness. Mahler (1971), for example, stated:

> It appears that our favorite child, group counseling, has attained the adolescent stage of development, with all the anxiety and confusion accompanying it. One major concern is the too frequent naive view that the mere placing of individuals in a group will be good for them. (p. 601)

In spite of such criticism, group counseling has become increasingly popular. Shertzer and Stone (1981) comment that although in the past group counseling may have been subordinate to individual counseling, it is currently viewed as a complement to individual counseling. Even though group

Group counseling is an important and effective alternative to individual counseling.

counseling should only be practiced by those professionally trained to do so, you should be aware of this important and effective alternative to individual counseling. In group counseling, one counselor assists the group to set goals and make decisions.

Group counseling may be defined as a social experience usually concerned with developmental problems and situational concerns of members. Cohn, Combs, Gihian, and Sniffen (1963) offer the following definition:

> Group Counseling, as we see it, is a dynamic, interpersonal process through which individuals with a normal range of adjustment work within a peer group and with a professionally trained counselor, exploring problems and feelings in an attempt to modify their attitudes so that they are better able to deal with developmental problems. (p. 355)

According to Lewis (1970), the best objective of group counseling is its positive use of the group situation to help individual members reach their counseling goals. If conducted properly, group counseling should provide the individual members with an opportunity to give help to others and accept help from the group as well as from the counselor. Group counseling is most effective in demonstrating that others have encountered similar difficulties and problems. The group format also helps the nonverbal client or the person who cannot adequately cope with threatening situations. Ohlsen (1983) offers this contemporary view of the group counseling process:

During group counseling, clients learn to help fellow clients as well as to accept their assistance, feedback, support, encouragement, and reinforcement of desired new behaviors. Within this therapeutic atmosphere they discover what really worries and upsets them, learn to discuss their pain openly, define the new behaviors that they must learn (goals) and make the association between implementing their desired new behavior and their relief of pain. They discover that they are not mere victims—that there are many things that they can do to manage their lives more effectively. (p. 39)

In a group situation, the counselor's role is basically the same as in individual counseling: to provide an atmosphere where individuals can engage in self-disclosure and feedback by expressing their attitudes and feelings. Group members must feel they are being understood. The counselor and other group members, then, must learn to listen perceptively and with understanding. This perceptive listening will help the counselor derive the topic from the expressed concerns of the group.

Beckley's (1967) guidelines for group counseling are still valid today.

1. Group counseling should be conducted by an experienced counselor with a good understanding of group dynamics.
2. Participants should be selected from individual counseling cases. The nature and advantages of group counseling should be explained to them, so that they know what is expected from them.
3. Participation should be voluntary.
4. Homogeneity, with respect to age, educational background, economic status, and similarity of problem is desirable.
5. Sessions should be approximately one hour in length.
6. There should be no more than 12 counselees in the group.
7. Group counseling sessions followed by at least one individual counseling session with each participant seem to be most beneficial and produce more lasting results. (p. 2–4)

Lifton (1972) maintains that through sharing perceptions, groups provide

- [ ] a reduction of anxiety,
- [ ] a setting for reality testing,
- [ ] the establishment of consensual validity,
- [ ] the dissemination of information,
- [ ] the development of skills, and
- [ ] emotional support to face threat. (pp. 45–46)

With these characteristics in mind, Lifton comments that groups typically form with at least one of the following objectives:

- [ ] information dispensing
- [ ] skill development
- [ ] decision making
- [ ] self-understanding

☐ reality testing
☐ task orientation
☐ power base to effect change

Vander Kolk (1985) contends that people form groups because they usually have something in common and wish to discuss ways of dealing with a personal, social, medical, or vocational aspect of their lives. Vander Kolk specifically refers to counseling groups that normally have more structure, have specifically defined goals, and have more explicit expectations of group members. He states:

> Another structured group is that which offers information from group leaders, speakers, and fellow group members to parents of handicapped children. A related though less structured group for parents of handicapped children provides support, and is most helpful when children are severely handicapped. Parents learn that they are not alone in their struggles, receive genuine understanding from one another in their struggles, and acquire useful ideas with their responsibilities. (pp. 10–11)

The optimum size of a group is still a matter of discussion. Most authorities suggest six or seven members, with an outside range of five to ten. The group should be small enough so that members can communicate freely, and large enough to stimulate interaction, self-expression, and cooperative sharing. A group that is too small also may create the possibility that a particularly vocal member dominates the other members.

Although group counseling has disadvantages (such as the demand it places on the skills and competencies of the counselor), it can be effective for working with parents, especially if the counselor's time is too limited for individual sessions. Group members are encouraged to develop an accepting, permissive atmosphere of rapport and trust, allowing the release of participant attitudes, thoughts, and feelings. Some group members may find life more meaningful as they share their experiences with others.

THE REFERRAL PROCESS

Referral is the act of transferring a client to another person or agency for specialized assistance. An ethical helper will never undertake an activity beyond his or her competency level. The American Personnel and Guidance Association (1974) is unequivocal in this standard.

> The member shall decline to initiate or shall terminate a counseling relationship when he cannot be of professional assistance to the counselee or client either because of lack of competency or personal limitation. In such instances, the member shall refer his counselee or client to an appropriate specialist. (p. 202)

Learning when and how to make referrals and for what purpose is almost as important as learning to counsel. If referral appears to be a proper course of action, discuss this with the client. You must be familiar with the nature and scope of referral services and agencies before suggesting referral, however. Discover what kind of special service is required, and if the service is available. It is important that the client understands the referral agency, its limitations, and its strengths. When discussing referral with the client, the helper should be tactful, yet straightforward and to the point. Although the client may become apprehensive, the counselor's offer to arrange for more expert help should assure the client of the counselor's acceptance and willingness to help. The trained helper usually makes the initial contact with the referred person or agency, but it is the client who ultimately decides what further action to take.

When helping parents of exceptional children, the referral procedure is no different. Should a problem or concern go beyond a helper's expertise, two courses of action are normally available: (1) terminate the relationship (tactfully explaining why) or, (2) refer parents to another person or agency that can more successfully handle the problem. Referral is usually preferable because it indicates the helper's interest and provides alternatives to the parents.

Brammer (1979) identified ten principles that helpers should consider when making referrals.

1. Know community resources for different kinds of services.
2. Explore the helpee's readiness for referral. Has he expressed interest in specialized help?
3. Be direct and honest about your observations of his behavior which led to your suggested referral. Be honest also about your own limitations.
4. It is usually desirable to discuss the possibility of referral with the referral agency before the problem becomes urgent.
5. Determine what other persons have had contact with this helpee and confer with them before suggesting further steps.
6. If the helpee is a minor, it is wise to inform parents of your recommendations and obtain their consent and cooperation.
7. Be fair in explaining the services of a referral agency by citing the possibilities and limitations of that agency. Do not imply that miracles can be performed there.
8. Let the helpee make his own appointments for the new service, although supportive services like offering transportation would be facilitative.
9. Do not release information to any referral source without written permission from the helpee in the form of a signed release.
10. If you have been having the primary helping relationship with him, it is only ethical to maintain that relationship until the referral is complete and a new relationship is begun. (pp. 123–124)

EVALUATION OF THE HELPER'S SERVICES

The process of evaluation is examining and judging the helper's performance in effectively attaining desired outcomes or goals. Without evaluation, the helper's effectiveness is at best impressionistic and subjective; at worst, it is prejudicial and unjust (Boyd, 1978). Hackney and Nye (1973) also stress the importance of evaluation by saying:

> You and your clients are more likely to succeed if you set down goals that are relevant to the client's concerns, develop strategies that are determined by those goals, and finally, assess your progress continually as you work together toward those goals. (p. 157)

One systematic way to judge the helper's effectiveness is to examine and analyze the level of functioning in the helping relationship. Carkhuff and Berenson (1967) suggest five-point scales to assess the functioning of interpersonal processes and to operationally define empathic understanding, positive regard, genuineness, and concreteness. Using empathic understanding as an example, it may be helpful to examine Carkhuff and Berenson's scales. At level 1, the lowest level of interpersonal functioning, the helper is not attending to the client's expressions. At level 2, the counselor is somewhat responding to the expressed feelings of the helpee. At level 3, the helper is providing the minimum of empathic understanding. When the 4th level is reached, empathic understanding is present, allowing the client to express feelings at a deeper level. Level 5 characterizes a level of understanding that adds significantly to the client's ability to accurately express feelings. As Brammer (1979) notes, when level 5 has been reached, the quality of helper response is consistently high. All helper characteristics can be similarly scaled or ranked—as you become more involved with the growth of others, it is important to rank yourself or ask colleagues who observe your efforts to evaluate your effectiveness.

Other types of rating scales may be used to measure helping effectiveness. Dimick and Krause (1975) suggest approximately twenty basic skill areas of a helper that can be assessed (see Figure 6.1).

In the absence of external evaluation by another qualified person, the responsibility for analyzing and assessing your proficiency in helping skills will rest on your self-evaluation techniques. Rating scales such as those proposed can help the evaluation process if only by reminding us of desirable counselor behaviors and skills.

Citing the need for a research approach to evaluation, Ohlsen (1983) states,

> Looking beyond the individual client, the counselor must determine how efficacious each treatment is for whom under what circumstances by asking herself: "Who were helped most by the techniques used? Who failed to profit from them? Who was hurt by what techniques and/or events? What informa-

FIGURE 6.1   *The Practicum Counselor's Skill in Counseling*

AREAS	Outstanding	Does well	Adequate	Unsatisfactory	Not observed
Ability to provide a theoretical rationale for use of own counseling procedures	4	3	2	1	0
Awareness of ethical standards and confidentiality	4	3	2	1	0
Awareness of own personal and professional limitations	4	3	2	1	0
Ability to apply knowledge, research, and theory from other disciplines to the counselee's situation	4	3	2	1	0
Awareness of the youth culture and its implications in areas of sex, drugs, and moral concerns	4	3	2	1	0
Responds at the counselee's level — If not, circle whether below or above	4	3	2	1	0
Assumes leadership — If not, circle whether too much or too little	4	3	2	1	0
Perceptive in handling the counselee's cues	4	3	2	1	0
Acceptance of the counselee	4	3	2	1	0
Conveys a pleasant mood or relaxed atmosphere in the interview — If not, circle whether too much or not enough	4	3	2	1	0
Seems sincere in working with the counselee — If not, circle whether too much or too little	4	3	2	1	0
Understands the situation the counselee is trying to present	4	3	2	1	0
Gains the confidence of the counselee	4	3	2	1	0
Is a good listener	4	3	2	1	0
Facilitative in specifying the problem in concrete terms	4	3	2	1	0
Emphatically able to bring client to the effective level of awareness	4	3	2	1	0
Real and genuine in the relationship	4	3	2	1	0
Able to facilitate the counselee's resolution of concerns	4	3	2	1	0
Effectiveness of this counselor as evaluated by clients	4	3	2	1	0
Ability as a counselor, overall evaluation	4	3	2	1	0

Comments:

tion may have enabled me to predict prior to counseling and/or in its early stages who would have been hurt or helped by each of the various techniques used? In what ways did my behavior and, in groups, particular clients' behaviors, contribute to or interfere with each client's growth? (p. 358)

Notice that practitioners must ask a more precise question than "Was this counseling technique effective?" Instead, they must ask, "For whom was this particular technique effective, and for what type of clients under what circumstances?" You must decide if the quality of your relationship with clients influenced their growth. Ohlsen adds that the focal point of helping and measuring our counseling effectiveness is how well we help clients define clear, precise behavioral goals that enable them to grow. Clients may then learn to take responsibility for discovering solutions and growth strategies, increasing their commitment to practicing these new behaviors.

CHAPTER SUMMARY

To become an effective helper, you must not only understand basic counseling strategies but also other significant issues in the helping relationship. These other issues are frequently referred to as *core elements* that ease the counseling process. For example, the arrangement of the physical setting may have a significant influence on the success or failure of the relationship. Your counselees need to feel physically comfortable and psychologically secure to profit from the helping relationship. You, the helper, will also feel better about the relationship when the counseling is conducted in an optimal environment. Other counselor skills such as the proper handling of silence and the referral process also contribute to the ultimate success of the counseling relationship. Helpers should always strive to improve their effectiveness in helping and working with clients by evaluation. Because counseling is a purposeful activity, your effectiveness in helping clients reach goals and objectives is a meaningful evaluation measurement.

The quality of the helping relationship will enable parents to recognize that they have the capacities to restructure their lives and solve their own problems.

ACTIVITIES, EXERCISES, AND IDEAS FOR REFLECTION AND DISCUSSION

1. Compare and contrast individual counseling with group counseling.
2. Is it possible that a person could be a skilled, effective individual counselor and fail to work effectively with groups? If so, what are some reasons that might account for this?
3. Is it unethical to discuss a client with another professional person? What guidelines might you suggest for conduct in this area?

4. How should the counselor handle requests for information from, for example, a parent or teacher?

5. To test one's tolerance for silence, select three people for this exercise. One person is the talker, one the listener, and the third person the timekeeper. The talker may talk about anything he wishes. The listener must wait 30 seconds between each response. The timer will signal when 30 seconds have expired. As this becomes tolerable, gradually increase the silent time to 40 seconds, 50 seconds, etc. When the listener can tolerate silence for about two or three minutes without discomfort, exchange roles and repeat the exercise.

6. Arrange to role-play or videotape a hypothetical counseling session. Keep a log of specific instances of nonverbal communication such as raised eyebrows, facial expressions, postures, gestures, mannerisms such as a glance or look, intensity or volume of the voice, raising or lowering of voice pitch and increased or decreased voice tempo. At the end of the session, compare the nonverbal behaviors with the verbal messages for consistency.

7. What steps would you take to survey the referral agencies in your community? Compile a list of agencies in your community/city that offer services to parents of exceptional children. Include important data such as the purpose of the agency, the eligibility criteria, and the nature of service. Are there local civic clubs that render services to the exceptional child?

8. Helpers should know the term *privileged communication* to behave professionally and ethically. What is privileged communication?

9. Why do you think it is important to evaluate the helper's services? Suppose that parents tell you they are satisfied (perhaps highly pleased) with the quality of your help. Should you request written feedback, allowing you to pinpoint your specific strengths and weaknesses?

REFERENCES

American Personnel and Guidance Association. (1974 revision). *Ethical standards.*

Beckley, R. W. (1967). Group counseling provides new insights. From *Counseling,* U.S. Department of Labor, Bureau of Employment Security, U.S. Employment Service, 2–4.

Benjamin, A. (1974). *The helping interview.* Boston: Houghton Mifflin.

Boyd J. (1978). *Counselor supervision.* Muncie, IN: Accelerated Development.

Brammer, L. M. (1979). *The helping relationship: Process and skills* (2nd ed.). Englewood Cliffs, NJ: Prentice-Hall.

Carkhuff, R. C., & Berenson, B. G. (1967). *Beyond counseling and therapy.* New York: Holt, Rinehart, & Winston.

Cohn, B., Combs, C. F., Gihian, E. J., & Sniffen, A. M. (1963). Group guidance: An orientation. *Personnel and Guidance Journal, 42,* 355–356.

Davis, K. (1977). *Human behavior at work: Organizational behavior.* New York: McGraw-Hill.

Dimick, K. M., & Krause, F. H. (1975). *Practicum manual for counseling and psychotherapy* (3rd ed.). Muncie, IN: Accelerated Development.

Hackney, H., & Nye, S. (1973). *Counseling strategies and objectives.* Englewood Cliffs, NJ: Prentice-Hall.

Hansen, J. C., Stevic, R. R., & Warner, R. W. (1972). *Counseling: Theory and process.* Boston: Allyn & Bacon.

Johnson, D. W. (1981). *Reaching out: Interpersonal effectiveness and self-actualization* (2nd ed.). Englewood Cliffs, NJ: Prentice-Hall.

Lewis, E. C. (1970). *The psychology of counseling.* New York: Holt, Rinehart, & Winston.

Lifton, W. M. (1972). *Groups: Facilitating individual growth and societal change.* New York: John Wiley.

Mahler, C. A. (1971). Group counseling. *Personnel and Guidance Journal, 49,* 601.

Nichols, R. G., & Stevens, L. A. (1957). *Are you listening?* New York: McGraw-Hill.

Ohlsen, M. M. (1983). *Introduction to Counseling.* Itasca, IL: Peacock.

Shertzer, B., & Stone, S. C. (1980). *Fundamentals of Counseling.* New York: Houghton Mifflin.

Shertzer, B., & Stone, S. C. (1981). *Fundamentals of guidance* (3rd ed.). New York: Houghton Mifflin.

Vander Kolk, C. J. (1985). *Introduction to group counseling and psychotherapy.* Columbus, OH: Charles E. Merrill.

SELECTED REFERENCES FOR FURTHER READING AND STUDY

Cain, L. F. (1976). Parent groups: Their role in a better life for the handicapped. *Exceptional Children, 42,* 432–437.

Davis, K. L. (1980). Is confidentiality in group counseling realistic? *Personnel and Guidance Journal, 59*(4), 197–201.

Denkowski, R. H., & Denkowski, G. C. (1982). Client-counselor confidentiality: An update of rationale, legal status, and implications. *Personnel and Guidance Journal, 60*(6), 371–375.

Gill, S. J., & Barry, R. A. (1982). Group-focused counseling: Classifying the essential skills. *Personnel and Guidance Journal, 60*(5), 302–305.

Hammond, J. M. (1981). Loss of the family unit: Counseling groups to help kids. *Personnel and Guidance Journal, 59*(6), 392–394.

Hiebert, R. E. (1984). Counselor effectiveness: An instructional approach. *Personnel and Guidance Journal, 62*(10), 597–601.

Huber, C. H. (1979). Parents of the handicapped child: Facilitating acceptance through group counseling. *Personnel and Guidance Journal, 57,* 267–269.

Kimball, K. K., & McCabe, M. E. (1981). Should we have children? A decision-making group for couples. *Personnel and Guidance Journal, 60*(3), 153–156.

Landreth, G. L. (1984). Encountering Carl Rogers: His views on facilitating groups. *Personnel and Guidance Journal, 62*(6), 323–325.

Masson, R. L., & Jacobs, E. (1980). Group leadership: Practical points for beginners. *Personnel and Guidance Journal, 59,* 52–55.

McWhirter, J. J. (1976). A parent education group in learning disabilities. *Journal of Learning Disabilities, 9,* 16–20.

Paritzky, R. S., & Magoon, T. M. (1982). Goal attainment scaling models for assessing group counseling. *Personnel and Guidance Journal, 60*(6), 381–384.

Riggs, R. C. (1979). Evaluation of counselor effectiveness. *Personnel and Guidance Journal, 58,* 54–59.

Rosenthal, R. (1973, September). The Pygmalion effect lives. *Psychology Today,* 56–63.

Schmidt, J. C., & Atlas, J. W. (1976). Teacher-parent communication: A consulting model. *The School Counselor, 23,* 346–352.

Shipp, P. L. (1983). Counseling blacks: A group approach. *Personnel and Guidance Journal, 62*(2), 108–111.

Stiles, W. B., & Snow, J. S. (1984). Counseling session impact as viewed by novice counselors and their clients. *Journal of Counseling Psychology, 31,* 3–12.

Weissman, S., & Montgomery, G. (1980). Techniques for group family enrichment. *Personnel and Guidance Journal, 59*(2), 113–116.

PART TWO

PART TWO

*P*art Two begins with a general overview of the family and some of the major problems, concerns, and issues typically associated with parents and siblings of handicapped children. Chapters Eight and Nine discuss some steps helpers may take in assisting these parents. A multivolume work would be necessary to cover a topic as broad and diverse as helping parents of handicapped children. The primary goal of this section is to raise some basic issues, indicate significant research, and encourage you to pursue additional areas that interest you.

This particular section assumes that you have a reasonable working knowledge of exceptional children and special education. Since Chapter One provided an in-depth discussion of this topic, the emphasis here will not be on the identification and characteristics of handicapped children. Instead, this section is directed toward identifying and understanding parental feelings as well as discussing how helpers can guide parents in resolving their problems by offering support, encouragement, workable suggestions, ideas, and basic information.

Part Two employs a primarily noncategorical approach. This framework is practical and useful because it eliminates the possibility of redundancy, duplication, and overlapping. Although admittedly this approach is imperfect, a discussion of parental reactions to mild/moderate and severe/profound handicapping conditions is best in a book of this size.

Using traditional categories may occasionally be necessary when dealing with such topics as genetic counseling and institutionalization, since both are traditionally associated with mental retardation. You may also expect instances when mild/moderate and severe/profound handicapping conditions may overlap, or may not be precisely clear.

I encourage you to read, study, and direct your energies toward better understanding parents of handicapped children and their counseling needs. Parents of handicapped children vary considerably in their need for counseling, but when they do seek help, they are experiencing problems and need help in finding a possible solution.

Helpers have a unique opportunity to assist troubled parents in attaining productive and rewarding behaviors. Understanding parental feelings, attitudes, and values will enable the helper to effectively intervene in self-defeating and inappropriate behavior patterns. This section is, therefore, directed toward your helping parents to learn and develop appropriate behaviors and coping skills.

7 The Family and the Exceptional Child— Overview and Impact

After mastering the material in this chapter, you should be able to

1. Discuss the concept of the family unit and relate this to the task of being parents of a handicapped child.

2. Briefly describe stress and identify stressful situations that may occur in the family of a handicapped child.

3. Discuss the general effects of a handicapped child on the family.

4. Identify and describe some possible effects of a handicapped child on siblings. What factors might lead to sibling maladjustment?

5. Use strategies that may help siblings cope more effectively with their handicapped brother or sister.

The purpose of the family unit is to create a vessel or environ-
ment for the development of mature, fully-functioning
individuals.

—Laura Sue Dodson

The effect on family units of the addition of a handicapped
member varies widely, despite the gloomy, general descriptions
by physicians and mental health workers of increased stress,
marital disputes, and sibling antagonism.

—Linda Sterupte and Richard O. Bell

---

*T*he impact of an exceptional child on a family is aptly described by Hardman, Drew, and Egan (1984):

> Nowhere is the impact of an exceptional individual so strongly felt as in the
> family. The birth of a disordered infant is likely to alter the family as a social
> unit in a variety of ways. Parents and siblings may react with shock, disappoint-
> ment, anger, depression, guilt, and/or confusion, to mention only a few. Re-
> lationships between family members often change, in either a positive manner
> or a negative manner. The impact of such an event is great, and it is unlikely
> that the family unit will ever be the same. (p. 419)

The purpose of Chapter Seven is to identify and discuss the specific
impact of an exceptional child—especially a handicapped child—on the
social system of the family unit. Particular emphasis is placed on examining
how changes in one family member can consequently affect the entire family
system.

THE HANDICAPPED CHILD'S IMPACT
ON THE FAMILY UNIT

It is important to begin our discussion by defining the term *family unit.*
Dodson and Kurpius (1977) give the following definition:

> The family unit, broadly speaking, is a unit of people who live together and
> share life's basic day-by-day functions. Throughout history, humanity has
> demonstrated need for such a core group, yet also has demonstrated need for
> each individual member to grow. These dual, sometimes contrasting human
> needs create the paradoxes of the family unit, in which exist struggle for
> separateness and togetherness, differences and sameness, protection and
> freedom, support and independence. The purpose of the family unit is to create
> a vessel or an environment for the development of mature, fully functioning
> individuals. The paradox of the family situation is that this end is achieved

only as the individuals in the family are contributing to and participating in the family process. (p. 3)

Schiamberg (1985) offers a similar view:

> The family performs the primary function of socializing the child from birth through at least adolescence. This process of socialization is accomplished through mutual interaction between parent and child. These interactions include the transmission and interpretation of cultural standards of values and behavior. The family can be viewed as a dynamic system that changes over time, as do its members. (p. 249)

These definitions, then, characterize the typical family unit. Now imagine the arrival of a handicapped child into that unit. Although parental reactions to the birth or arrival of a handicapped child into the family are discussed in a later chapter, what is important to understand at this point is that such a traumatic event can create additional stress within the family. Lombana and Lombana (1982) emphasize that although counseling circumstances are diverse, certain types of parents, such as those with handicapped children, appear to experience more stress. Brammer (1979) defines stress as a condition characterized by physiological tension and a persistent conflict of choices that pressure the person to reduce the tension and achieve equilibrium. Holmes and Rahe (1967) studied stress by placing an objective value on certain situations that directly affect a person's physical health. These stressful events, ranging from the death of a spouse to minor violations of the law, were scaled and assigned a value. These rankings are presented in Table 7.1 on page 112.

Noting stress items 11 and 14 should indicate the possible impact of the arrival of a new family member or a change in health of a family member. Stress will increase when that newly arrived family member has a mental, physical, or sensory handicap. Schleifer (1982) poignantly describes how the hopes of parents expecting their healthy firstborn are often shattered:

> Couples have daydreams and images of what this new stage of parenting will bring. Joyful images are modified by the real experiences of parenting. The couple must also make a different kind of commitment to each other and the baby. They will have to resolve how they will work together so that the interests of each can be met. The birth of a child with a serious difficulty complicates this process. First the images of themselves as parents are likely to be changed. This time that would have brought pleasures brings doubts and worries. The ordinary difficulties of helping any child grow arouse frustration and helplessness at some point in all couples. But when parents are having greater difficulty, they find themselves preoccupied with their own efforts and especially their feelings of frustration. (p. 44)

Ehlers, Krishef, and Prothero (1977) note that even parents who have had close contact with retarded children often find themselves in a state of shock when told that their own child is retarded. The counselor's aware-

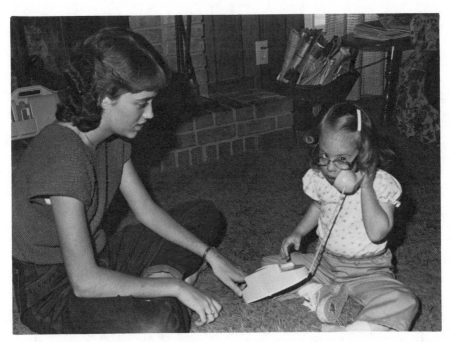

The family performs the primary function of socializing the child.

ness of this shock and finding ways to deal with it separate the counseling of parents with a retarded child from the counseling of most other parents.

Similarly, Robinson and Robinson (1976) offer another perspective on the effects of a handicapped child on the family:

> The path of parenthood is never completely smooth. Patience, understanding, ingenuity, good humor, and strength are demanded in large measure from the parents of any youngster. For the family of a retarded child, however, the situation may be more complicated and more hazardous, and the rewards of parenting more likely to be lost sight of. The child's handicaps; his slow development; the special arrangements needed for his physical care, training, and companionship; the disappointments and the lost dreams—all combine to create pressures which tend to disrupt family equilibrium. Added to these pressures may be financial problems, tensions created by the child's immature self-control, handicaps in communication, and the parent's own lingering doubts about their upbringing practices. Thus, the relationship between a retarded child and his family is potentially more complex and ambivalent than the ordinary one, and more intense and prolonged. (p. 413)

The presence, realization, and impact of a handicapping condition is usually felt by all members of the family because of the emotional, social, educational, and economic demands placed on them. These demands and

TABLE 7.1   Stress rankings

Stress

Rank	Life event	Mean			
1	Death of spouse	100	24	Trouble with in-laws	29
2	Divorce	73	25	Outstanding personal	
3	Marital separation	65		achievement	28
4	Jail term	63	26	Wife begins or stops	
5	Death of a close family			work	26
	member	63	27	Begin or end school	26
6	Personal injury or illness	53	28	Change in living con-	
7	Marriage	50		ditions	25
8	Fired at work	47	29	Revision of personal	
9	Marital reconciliation	45		habits	24
10	Retirement	45	30	Trouble with boss	23
11	Change in health of		31	Change in work hours or	
	family member	44		conditions	20
12	Pregnancy	40	32	Change in residence	20
13	Sex difficulties	39	33	Change in schools	20
14	Gain of new family		34	Change in recreation	19
	member	39	35	Change in church activi-	
15	Business readjustment	39		ties	19
16	Change in financial state	38	36	Change in social activi-	
17	Death of close friend	37		ties	18
18	Change in line of work	36	37	Mortgage or loan less	
19	Change in number of			than $10,000	17
	arguments with spouse	35	38	Change in sleeping	
20	Mortgage over $10,000	31		habits	16
21	Foreclosure of mortgage		39	Change in number of	
	or loan	30		family get-togethers	15
22	Change in responsibil-		40	Change in eating habits	15
	ities at work	29	41	Vacation	13
23	Son or daughter leaving		42	Christmas	12
	home	29	43	Minor violations of the	
				law	11

SOURCE: Chart originally published in "The Social Readjustment Rating Scale" by T. H. Holmes and R. H. Rahe, 1967, *Journal of Psychosomatic Research, 11*, pp. 213–218. Reprinted with permission of Pergamon Press, Inc.

obligations make families of handicapped children particularly vulnerable to stress. Crnic, Friedrich, and Greenberg (1983) state that "the impact of mental retardation is never restricted to retarded individuals; members of the immediate and extended families are affected to varying degrees" (p. 125). Gallagher, Beckman, and Cross (1983) extensively reviewed literature that links a wide variety of factors to parental stress and discovered that stressful factors may come from the handicapped child, the parents, the siblings, the extended family, and even the institutions designed to help the child.

Smith (1984) identified several types of stress commonly associated with parenting a handicapped child. These potential stresses further illustrate the additional and unexpected pressures and responsibilities that parents of handicapped children must deal with. These possible stresses consist of the following:

- ☐ Dream of child shattered
- ☐ Child looks different
- ☐ More attention required
- ☐ Routine caregiving is more difficult
- ☐ Attitudes towards handicapped
- ☐ Exposed to frustrations and humiliations
- ☐ Lowered self-esteem
- ☐ Less time for siblings
- ☐ Spouses have less time together
- ☐ Friends uncomfortable/drift away
- ☐ Avoid situations/social events
- ☐ Fewer rewards for being a parent
- ☐ Separations/disruptions of parent-child relationship
- ☐ Reactions of relatives/family
- ☐ Lack of specific information
- ☐ Increased costs for medical, special equipment, and trips
- ☐ Conflict in opinions
- ☐ Parents' expectations often inappropriate
- ☐ Break in communication/relationship with child
- ☐ Unknown questions regarding future
- ☐ Vulnerable child

ONE PARENT'S PERSONAL ACCOUNT

Reading the following account of a parent's personal experience gives us significant insight into the effect of a handicapped child on the family. Carole Hosey (1973) presents a readable and self-explanatory account that needs no further comment.

> In this account of my son's life in our family circle, I hope to present a strong case for the preservation of every human being and the inclusion of every child in a loving family when possible.
>
> Stephen is 11 years old, profoundly retarded, cerebral palsied, and epileptic. He doesn't walk or talk and he probably never will. He does not understand speech and has few ways to communicate his needs. Stephen also has both visual and auditory perceptual impairment and a variety of seizure dis-

NOTE. From "Yes, Our Child Is Still With Us" by Carole Hosey, 1973, *Children Today, 2,* pp. 14–17, 36.

orders. Although some of the disorders are well-controlled, he has dozens to hundreds of small drop seizures daily.

Stephen is a handsome boy, although he has a wasted, underdeveloped and poorly muscled body. He does not whine, whimper, or cry except when in extreme pain. He has a very sweet expression and a gentle personality.

In this account of his life, I would like to emphasize that I realize that the qualities of each child make him or her—to a greater or lesser degree— easier to take care of in the home. I am not foolish enough to think that every severely handicapped child will be as comparatively easy to take care of as Stephen.

I have longed many times to be able to describe to a doctor how we feel about our handicapped child. I am in my late 40s and my husband is in his early 50s. We have a 20-year-old son and two daughters, aged 16 and 18, living at home, as well as a married daughter. The children were 11, 9, 7, and 5 when Stephen was born. My husband and I married young and adopted our first two children after several childless years. Then I gave birth to our third child, a normal and very intelligent daughter. A short time later, we adopted our fourth child. And then, when I was 37, I gave birth to Stephen after an uncomplicated pregnancy. But the delivery was induced and precipitate, and much later we were told that lack of oxygen was the probable cause of enormous damage to his central nervous system.

Stephen's color was not normal following birth; his lethargy was profound and his sucking ability so poor that his weight fell almost a full pound during his first five days. Nevertheless, Stephen was discharged from the hospital to us as "a normal male infant."

As his first year came to an end, however, I realized that his inability to turn over, sit up, or crawl was not to be explained by his chubby weight or crossed eyes. When he was 14 months old, we asked for comprehensive testing. I stayed in the hospital with Stephi during the week of tests. Each evening the pediatrician would come and tell me the results of the tests and, because I was naive, I was pleased as he reported each negative result. It was only at the end of the week, when he explained, that I started to understand the horror of the situation. The doctor said he had done the tests hoping to find something, anything, that was correctable. But as each of the tests were negative, he realized that we were faced not with a thyroid deficiency or something of that nature but with an undeterminable amount of brain damage and a very crippled little boy. During that week in the hospital I had spent many hours fighting panic—swinging upward when I got the details of a test result, and then down again when I made myself face the facts, as I had begun to face them the day I first called the pediatrician before one of Stephen's well-baby check-ups and told him I thought Stephen was retarded and asked him to talk honestly with me.

I was told there was nothing to be done but wait and see how he developed. I took Stephi home from the hospital to the family. We were in a better position than many young couples who have this experience. First of all, we had raised four normal children, which was a comfort. Secondly, we were both of a mature age, not a young couple untested by problems. But I will always remember my feeling of numb despair. I didn't cry or give much external sign of my inner hysteria but I felt that I would never be able to adjust to this situation.

The shock of the birth of a child like this doesn't come all at once. It's worse in some ways than the death of a child because you gradually realize that this child is never going to live in the fullest sense of the word. It is only after months or years pass that you find out how your family will be affected.

It was difficult for us to absorb the first shock, which is truly physical as well as mental. We were numb, we could scarcely walk about and do our normal day's work, or talk to other people. Still, we had no agonizing decision to make at this point. We loved Stephi, he had been a part of our family for more than a year, and no one would have suggested, even if it had been possible, to allow him to die. He was living and he was healthy then. The shock consisted of knowing that we had a child who would never grow up. He might have a very long life, but he would not experience any of the pleasures of adulthood, such as fatherhood, nor the other lovely pleasures of a normal life.

I feel strongly that no couple, no matter what their age or experience, can make a wise or even a fully conscious decision at a moment like this. I feel that unless a decision is absolutely imperative because of life or death alternatives, it should be postponed. I am firmly convinced that parents' assertion of their instinct to love and cherish their child is essential to a family's mental health. I think that at the moment of first knowledge of their child's damage this instinct may be stunned by the pain they are experiencing. But I know that if someone stands by and encourages them to love the child and, if possible, to take the child home, it is going to help in many ways for the rest of their lives. If this instinct to love and cherish the child asserts itself, then I think that they can make a loving decision about him later on. This may be later in terms of a week, or years, but if they have allowed their natural parental instinct to be developed, they are going to make it *because* they love the child and they will not, instead, have to live with a memory of rejection. It is better to remember in the years to come that you did everything out of love for your child, and not because you lacked courage. If parents have to institutionalize the child, soon or years later, it may be very painful, but they will be comforted by knowing that they loved him.

Because we had to travel with my husband's job in the years following Stephen's birth, we had the opportunity to see more doctors with Stephi than the average family could or would. We found that, as time passed and Stephen's disabilities became more apparent, doctors were *still* explaining to us that he was retarded. Since this would have been obvious to anyone at first glance, we could only conclude that they were really saying, "Why do you still have this retarded child with you?" Or they would be more forthright about it and say, "A child like this is damaging to your other children. You should see about an institutional placement for him. Do you have him on a waiting list? You have your own lives to live."

From the time we were given our first child, our lives had involved our children and they were never to be separated totally from any of them. So now we questioned why our lives and emotions should be separated from the most helpless of all of our children. Doctors did at times express pity and I have heard many other parents of retarded children say rather belligerently that they don't want pity. I don't feel this way. There's nothing wrong with pity as far as I'm concerned; in fact, *I* feel very sorry for myself at times. I think that honest parents of a child like ours do feel that they and certainly their child have had a damn poor shake out of life. It *is* a tragedy! It's heartbreaking. But our children are here. They live. They must not be rejected like broken toys.

I've often wondered why doctors didn't give me credit and support for an intelligent decision to give my child the safe-keeping that I knew I could give him for as long as it was possible for me to give it to him. But so many times I've been made to feel that I love Stephen almost illegally and certainly unintelligently. We were told by one doctor that Stephen was not a productive member of society; therefore, we did not have the right to take family time, money, and energy away from our other four "productive members of society" in favor of Stephi. We had a strong family feeling that each child, as in *all* families, naturally gets the time and money and energy that he or she needs from parents. As far as society goes, I think one of the greatnesses of our country is that the benefits, the fruits of our country, don't go just to the taxpayer, but to all the people. And it is the same in a family. As far as our other children are concerned, we couldn't believe that his presence was going to be detrimental to them. They seemed to be growing normally. They dearly loved Stephen and still do. They don't hesitate to bring their friends home and discuss their little brother. In fact, when one of our daughters was in the fourth grade and her class was discussing mental retardation, she asked me if she could take Stephen in for "Show-and-Tell." The teacher agreed, and I felt that it was beneficial to the children. Handicapped children have been kept in back rooms and in special classes, hidden away, so naturally they are objects of curiosity to be stared at. When they are permitted to enter as much of normal social life as possible, there will be a greater understanding of their problems.

The sorrow of Stephen's condition is a lasting thing, something that flares up at strange times. It hits both of us, my husband and me, many times. Once when I was driving through the mountains of Switzerland, it overpowered me—knowing Stephi would never feel the beauty of approaching evening in the mountains. And at other times, perhaps during a beautiful piece of music that I know that he will never understand. . . .

The day-to-day care of Stephen is not the difficult part. I guess the most difficult thing about these children is facing their future. We can protect him now, but unlike most couples who enter their later years with a fair amount of serenity, looking forward to retirement and the easing of family responsibility as their children leave home, we have one child who will never be independent. We are able to care for him lovingly now, but this isn't enough. He shouldn't be well cared for only during our lifetime, but for all of his. And most families probably find the worst of the nightmare, wondering where their child will live out the end of his life, praying that he won't be neglected, malnourished, or cared for by insensitive people.

I often wondered when Stephen was very young and not having any medical problems how I would have felt if I had had a child who had been diagnosed as gravely damaged at birth and I had had to make a life-or-death decision. Later in Stephen's life, we went through a series of medical crises—several episodes of chain epileptic seizures, months of allergic drug reactions, weeks of forced feedings when he lost his swallowing reflex and wasted almost to death, and, just a year ago, a day and a night of almost fatal hemorrhages after surgery. It was a testing period for me because, as I saw him through those periods, there was no doubt about my feelings. I wanted him to live, just as I would want my normal children to survive.

Stephen is currently enrolled in the Intensive Training Unit for retarded-multihandicapped students at the Montgomery County Association for Retarded Citizens in Silver Spring, Maryland. We found through the years that meeting Stephen's need for training in the basic life skills required the most determined effort on our part. Less damaged children are sometimes accommodated in public school systems, but we had to insist repeatedly that he not be ignored because of the multiplicity of his problems. The quality of his adult life was going to depend on our being able to do something about our conviction that feeding himself was better than being fed, and learning to sit upright in a wheelchair was preferable to lying in a crib for the rest of his life.

In writing all this, I have tried to present the problems of a family with a handicapped child. This is easier to do than to explain the plus side of our life. There is *so much more* of that, but it is harder to put into words. Stephen has given us a great deal of positive happiness. He isn't just tolerated. When he is ill, we pray that he will survive. We had a family celebration at the end of his ninth year, the first year he had not had a stay in a hospital. The family was thrilled when he brought his first bite of food to his mouth by himself, and when he learned to stand up from his wheelchair. I think our children have gained in compassion and maturity. They are more aware than many of their contemporaries of how precious a normal life is, how wonderful an undamaged intellect, and how lucky they are to have whole bodies. Great patience with a slow child can leave you with a sense of warmth and pride. I am sure it is difficult even for a doctor who works with children like Stephen every day to try to imagine himself a parent of a seriously damaged child. I couldn't do it before I had Stephi. I was totally unprepared. But there are no regrets now. I wish very much that Stephen was a normal child. But as long as he is the way he is, I am glad he is ours. I wish that every father and mother who has a handicapped child born to them could be given a chance to love their child. (pp. 14–18, 36)

Heward and Orlansky (1984) indicate that the birth of a handicapped child or the discovery that a child has a disability is unquestionably an intense and traumatic event. Parents can differ widely in their reactions, and the helper or counselor should always be aware of this. Berdine and Blackhurst (1985) list such factors as religion, socioeconomic status, severity of handicap, parental knowledge, and order of birth that can all affect the parental responses of frustration, fear, disappointment, and uncertainty. The reactions and subsequent behavior of parents toward their handicapped child are complex issues—sweeping generalizations are of little or no value. Contrasting views and opinions about parental reactions exist, however.

Kneedler, Hallahan, and Kauffman (1984), for example, feel that despite the problems and the emotional turmoil, the ultimate impact on a family of having an exceptional child is minimal. These families do experience great stress, but they also learn to cope, sometimes better than other families. Kneedler, Hallahan, and Kauffman add that many families become closer and stronger than they might have been otherwise.

Suran and Rizzo (1983) reiterate the idea of the importance of the family unit and its functioning. They state:

> It is also important to maintain a developmental view of family organization and functioning. A family is a dynamic system of relationships in which each member is continually adapting to ongoing changes in other family members. Tensions or problems affecting any member of the family inevitably affects other members. For example, a child's disability will, in some fashion, affect every other family member. In most cases, the family will adapt itself to the child's problem through changes in attitudes and behavior. However, whether these adaptations are positive and satisfying or painful and stifling may well depend on a variety of obvious and subtle factors. We can readily see the impact of social or educational background, parental maturity, or financial security. Less obvious factors influencing the family system are the attitudes and reactions of grandparents and other relatives, neighbors, physicians, teachers, and other professionals. While some of these factors are beyond influence, it is critical that helping agents ensure that their impact is positive and growth promoting. Thoughtful attitudes toward the special conditions of childhood and care in communicating with parents can have crucial results in moving a family in the direction of optimism, growth, and mutual satisfaction. (p. 60)

In order to gain a balanced perspective of the impact an exceptional child will have on the family, it is important to learn the viewpoint of parents of these children. Here, Harra (1975) presents just such a viewpoint:

> Parents, we're pretty terrific! We need to tell each other that periodically. At least once a day would be fine, but we'll settle for every now and then. We can't put our wares on a table like a salesman and we have no professional research papers to present. Unlike politicians, we dare not make grandiose promises about the future. We see the results of our labors in ways that go unnoticed by most others, but are vastly significant to us—we see progress in our children. Sometimes it's a new word learned or pronounced properly, sometimes it's a ball successfully thrown and caught, or it may be the absence of a tantrum. We know that these little things have enormous significance.

We are Pioneers

> In our own way, we're all pioneers. How many of us knew anything at all about disability before we were confronted with the condition in our child? How much have we learned since then? A great deal. Not in professional terms,

NOTE. From "Stop Worrying? Nonsense!" by V. Harra, *The Exceptional Parent*, Jan./Feb. 1975, *5*, 12–15. Copyright 1975 by Psy-Ed Corporation. Reprinted by permission.

perhaps. We don't have the professional's clinical training and broad factual knowledge. But we know our own children exceedingly well. Ours is an exquisite awareness of how a specific child's disability interacts with everything else he is and tries to be.

Some of us were first told of our child's difficulty by a professional. Others of us knew something was wrong and sought help. Whatever the circumstances, we depend on professionals to help our children. Each of us is indebted to more than one such person who has been on the scene at the right time with the right help. This much is clear. What is not so clearly established yet is the extent to which we, the parents, can be of assistance to professional workers in a cooperative effort to help our individual children.

We Orchestrate Our Children's Care

It's slowly being recognized that parents play a unique role in their children's care in several respects. First, we make the final decision about which professional to engage with our child. Second, we have a special kind of information to share with professionals about our children, for only we observe them at home in the routine of their everyday life. Third, when resources are lacking, we are the catalysts, the prime movers, in seeing that resources—educational, medical, recreational or social—are developed. Fourth, I would guess that most of us are engaged in some kind of remedial effort with our children at home, supporting their development and enriching their learning through directed efforts or weaving this "instruction" in informally during the day's activities. We also carry through prescribed medical therapies or physical therapies of one sort or another.

Finally, it is we, the parents, who have the abiding responsibility for our child throughout his dependent life, whether for a few years or well into his adulthood. Often, this ongoing support and effort by parents is what makes the difference between whether a child ultimately "makes it" as an adult, or not. The professional's help, though vital at each point, is transitory. No matter how well or poorly equipped we are to meet the ongoing demands, we bear the responsibility for orchestrating the help our child needs—and the care our child gets. It's a difficult job. We can't afford the relief and release of total objectivity. Too much is at stake—the quality of our child's present and future life. And we can't leave the problem at the office at the end of the day. Our home *is* our "office."

Our Worry Is Appropriate

Our task is made all the more difficult when we meet the professional, relative or friend who tells us with all good intention, "Stop worrying!" or, "You're worrying too much!"—which is another way of saying, "You're over-anxious." And this makes us worry all the more, because we know we haven't succeeded in communicating the urgency of our child's situation and need. When we're in a dialogue with a professional, this communication gap can have serious consequences.

Too often we hear of parents who try to bring a troublesome physical condition in their child to the attention of a pediatrician who dismisses it, saying "He'll outgrow it," only to be confirmed later when it may be more difficult (or too late) to correct it. How many times have we heard stories of parents trying to get help at school for a child whose performance is characterized as a "behavior problem" or "not trying hard enough"? The parents know from their observations at home how hard their child is trying; his "problem" behavior is a symptom, not a cause, of his frustration and failure. Then, upon testing, the child is discovered to have a perceptual handicap, petit mal epilepsy, or a visual or hearing disorder of some kind. When parents see that their child is in trouble, but that help is not forthcoming, you can bet they'll get anxious. When parents insist on bringing problems to the attention of professionals, are they "over-anxious"? Or properly concerned?

Our Concern Changes As Our Children Change

When our child's difficulties are recognized and supportive help is available, that doesn't automatically dispel all anxiety. Chronic conditions don't disappear with remediation, although they may become more manageable. Each new situation, each new stage of life, presents a forest of unknowns to be dealt with. A change of school or a new teacher, an infant in the family, a new child in the neighborhood—any of these events can be a special challenge to our children. Or, the change may be internal, generated by a new stage of development. The "Terrible Two's" are the "Terrible Two's," no matter what else the child is dealing with, or what his chronological age when he arrives at that stage. Adolescence is a head-holder for everyone. The difficult task of establishing a sense of identity is blurred further by disability.

As each new situation or development presents itself, the parent is again a pioneer, trying to hack out a new path, looking for a familiar trail. The fact that many of our children cope as well as they do is a tribute to their inner strength and resources, *and ours*. The fact that many fail, or feel that they do, is a sad commentary on the lack of ready outside support and resourceful help. We know our children can "make it" when given the opportunity to do so.

How Others View Our Concern

It is curious that others look askance at our concern and special effort in behalf of our children. When there's a new story about a child trapped down a well or requiring blood donations, total strangers will respond and offer help. These people are applauded for their concern and generosity. And so they should be. They are responding to a recognized need. However, when a parent makes a similarly dedicated effort in behalf of her own child whose needs *she* clearly recognizes, she's told "You're over-anxious. You're worrying too much." Who is more entitled to worry? A complete stranger or a parent?

Sometimes, these discouraging assessments can be completely deflating. Often, they inhibit us from persevering with our efforts. We may feel intimidated, foolish, or guilty. One of the reasons we're put on the defensive is because of the social stigma attached to the terms "over-anxious," "anxious" or even "worried." Somehow, if one is visibly anxious about something, it is all too often seen as a sign that one must be "neurotic" and therefore incompetant. Who wants to be considered incompetent precisely when she is trying to enlist help for her child? *The last thing we should do is to stop trying.*

What is Anxiety?

Let's stop and take a good look at this nasty term *anxiety*. This is hard to do because anxiety is a shifty word. In clinical terms, it has to do with fear that seems "unrealistic." For instance, some people treat a sneeze as if it were pneumonia, or a momentary pain as if it were a symptom of cancer. But we can dispense with the clinical phenomenon, because what we're talking about here is entirely different—namely, proper concern with the problems which encumber our children. This is something very realistic.

In everyday usage, anxiety means fear or apprehension. As we all know, when a child is in difficulty, whether the difficulty is considered "minimal" or severe, there is due cause for apprehension. There is no such thing as a "minimal" disability if it's a condition which interferes with a child's normal development and threatens his future. Parents have no choice. We worry about it, whether it's a heart condition or stuttering, an emotional disturbance or poor coordination, autism or a hearing impairment.

Invisible Heroism

What about the advice to "Stop worrying!"? This is about the most outlandish combination of words I can think of in this context. One might as well tell a movie audience to stop worrying about the heroine tied to the railroad tracks with a locomotive coming around a blind curve. As long as a problem remains unresolved, one for which we feel a responsibility, it's human nature to be in a state of *active concern.* And when the problem involves our own child who has special difficulties, we worry. We'll stop worrying when we know our children are secure. It's that simple. Moreover, it's a waste of energy to worry about the fact that we're worrying. So, most of the time we respond. Our anxiety doesn't overwhelm us—although it has that potential. Instead, our anxiety makes us alert and ready to continue. It's one thing to summon energies and resources in a crisis situation and to take action—a man rescues a child from an icy lake and becomes a hero. But it also takes courage, resourcefulness and devoted determination to be an everyday hero or heroine. And this invisible heroism is what goes on in families with children with special needs. These rescue operations in the home are usually not matters of high drama, but of tedious dailiness. It may mean preparation of a special diet, every meal, every day. It may mean giving medication several times a day. It may mean giving medication several times a day, every day. Or giving a patient answer to an impatient child. Or giving the same answer or showing the same process for the 800th time to an uncomprehending child. It means long waits in a doctor's office or clinic to see a physician for a few brief minutes. Or conferences with teachers, principals, athletic coaches, camp directors or therapists many times during the year. It means trying to re-establish sme equilibrium in a family put off-center by the time and attention absorbed by the child with the greater needs.

This kind of effort goes on every day of every week of every year. There are no headlines or medals. But this kind of heroism is as vital to our child's well-being as his being rescued from an icy lake. Because as we all well know, without proper and sufficient ongoing support, our children do drown. They drown in their own mistrust of themselves and others, in their sense of failure and frustration, or in a condition which (if allowed to) envelops and suffocates their individuality.

We get worn down by the unending demands and pressures. The very fact that these responsibilities are tedious, repetitive and undramatic, however essential, makes us bored and irritated with carrying them out. Then, on top of everything else, we start to worry that we don't love our child enough. Such worry confuses the issue. We're entitled to notice and resent the internal bruises we suffer from the anxiety that bangs around inside, and the aches from the ongoing chores. But this is distinct from the love for our child and the commitment to him which keeps us at our tasks.

We're In This Battle Together

Perhaps one of the most difficult aspects of living with a child whose problems are not easily resolved is the inevitable sense of isolation. You're aware that to the world at large, you look as if you're doing perfectly ordinary things—going shopping, taking care of work in an office. But your thoughts and feelings are really elsewhere—on an invisible battlefield fighting an undeclared war that only you can see, hear and feel. In a "real" war situation, at least everyone is aware of the same dangers and appreciates the stress each is experiencing. How do we answer the casual conversation-opener "What's new?" Not knowing how to begin to explain, we find ourselves answering "Oh, nothing much." The fact is, we're all in the same battle together—the ongoing struggle to do the best we can for our children under difficult circumstances. The message in all this is "Trust yourself!" Because of your close bond with your children, because you have been alerted by your concern to act on their behalf, because you know them "subjectively," you do a job for your children which no one else can do. Fellow parents, you're okay!

EFFECTS OF A HANDICAPPED BROTHER OR SISTER ON SIBLINGS

Recognizing the added stress of a handicapped family member as well as the power of the family as a socializing agent, Stanhope and Bell (1981) remind us that educators and mental health professionals are increasingly involving both parents and siblings in the treatment of children with special needs. One school of thought is that brothers and sisters of the mentally retarded are "forgotten children," and counseling these children is a completely new field for professionals. Much of the current literature about the family of the handicapped child now includes the impact on normal siblings. Seligman (1983) offers the following viewpoint on sibling impact:

From an empirical point of view, the question of whether normal siblings are not affected, helped, or harmed by the presence of a handicapped brother or sister is largely unanswerable. Even in exceptional families where a child experiences emotional difficulties, it is virtually impossible to ascertain which factors have contributed to the situation. The emotional climate in some families is so stressful and unstable that sibling maladjustment is predictable based solely on family dynamics irrespective of the presence of a handicapped child. (p. 529)

Seligman also notes that a number of isolated factors contribute to sibling maladjustment. Table 7.2 lists the factors cited by Seligman.

TABLE 7.2   *Factors contributing to sibling maladjustment*

Factor	Seligman's Comment
Responsibility	The extent to which a sibling may be held responsible for a handicapped brother or sister bears a strong relationship to the perception and feeling children, adolescents, and adults have about their handicapped siblings and parents.
Catching the disability	In the wake of a disability, young children may be concerned about "catching" the disability. Anxiety about this is heightened when siblings learn that their handicapped brother's or sister's disability was caused by a disease like rubella or meningitis.
Anger and guilt	Siblings of handicapped children may experience anger in larger doses than siblings of normal brothers and sisters. Whether siblings harbor or openly express their feelings of anger and resentment depends on a complex arrangement of factors.
Communication	Lack of communication within a family over a child's disabling condition may contribute to the loneliness normal siblings experience. Siblings may sense that certain topics are taboo and that "ugly" feelings are to remain hidden.
Parental attitudes	There is some evidence that normal siblings are affected by their parents' attitudes toward the handicapped child. The degree of open communication about the afflicted child in families seems to be an excellent barometer of parental attitudes.

Siblings are becoming increasingly involved in the treatment of children with special needs.

Wasserman (1983) observes that unfortunately there is little professional literature that focuses on the relationship between retarded and nonretarded siblings. In reviewing the studies that do exist, however, he has identified four specific concerns that have been expressed by sibling groups:

1. *The need for information*—there was frequently a startling lack of information about the handicap, its manifestations, and its consequences.
2. *The need to understand and work through emotional reactions*—while many siblings struggle with fears, anxiety, and guilt, the emotional reactions of the siblings studied are inconsistent.
3. *Self-identity and roles*—the development of a separate identity from a mentally retarded sibling seems, based on Grossman's (1972) and Schreiber and Feeley's (1965) work, to be very important to normal siblings. Role identification is also a problem. For example, what is a normal sibling's role with respect to a mentally retarded sibling?

4. *The need for effective coping strategies*—the siblings frequently expressed the need for strategies to cope with their relationship with their mentally retarded brothers and sisters. Because of the importance of these concerns, Wasserman proposes counseling services of two types—direct and indirect. In the first type, a counselor works directly with siblings of the mentally retarded. The second type involves counseling siblings indirectly through the parents.

Hardman, Drew, and Egan (1984) offer an insightful view of sibling relationships.

> Siblings who learn that they have an exceptional brother or sister are frequently encumbered with many kinds of concerns. Such questions as "Why did this happen?" "What am I going to say to my friends?" and "Am I going to have to take care of him all of my life?" are common. Like their parents, siblings want to know and understand as much as they can about the condition of the impaired sibling. They want to know how they should respond and how their lives might be different as a result of this event. If these concerns can be adequately addressed, the prognosis for positive sibling involvement with the impaired brother or sister is much better. (p. 435)

According to Schwartz (1984), it is also important to understand that siblings of the exceptional child, as well as others, often take their cues from parental behavior and attitudes. Siblings may accept or reject the "special person" depending on their parents' attitude; they may certainly be resentful of parental overindulgence of the exceptional child. Schwartz concludes that realistic acceptance of and participation in caring for the handicapped child creates a happier and more productive family situation.

When reviewing literature from 1950 to the present, Schreiber (1984) found only five articles dealing specifically with social work practice with normal siblings of a mentally retarded child. In all five articles, the purpose was to help the normal sibling deal with an assumed difficulty arising from the presence of a retarded child in the family. Schreiber made two relevant points for *all* helpers who work with siblings and the family of mentally retarded or handicapped persons:

1. The articles as a whole draw the attention of the profession to a neglected area of practice. All of them demonstrate the attributes of a specialized practice and reflect the need for the worker to be able to deal with both basic and special needs of individuals and families.
2. The encouraging results of the practice efforts discussed in these articles suggest some areas for further inquiry. The greatest need is for long-term studies that offer greater understanding of the processes of childhood, adolescence, and adulthood that affect sibling and family interactions. Such studies would help to draw attention to the many kinds of interactions within families, and to decide when intervention would be most appropriate. Variables to be considered include socioeconomic status, race and ethnicity, family life-styles, childrearing patterns, and different kinds

of handicapping and stress-producing conditions. The number of siblings in a family, the age differences among them, and the kinds of alliances they build are other factors that need to be studied. The major focus of practice and research efforts should be on the ways that different kinds of siblings develop in different family environments.

CHAPTER SUMMARY

A counselor who works directly with parents of exceptional children should understand the dynamics of family relationships. Establishing effective parent/professional relationships depends on your ability and efforts to understand how the family copes with sudden unexpected disappointment—the presence of a handicapped child in the family. Helpers should be able (as best they can) to understand the impact a disabled or handicapped child has on his or her family, including the child's normal siblings.

Counselors should be aware of the possibilities of *the extended family,* a term frequently used to describe other family members such as grandparents, brothers and sisters of parents, or other close relatives. These relatives may become part of a resource network that can offer support, comfort, and understanding to the parents of a handicapped child. Beyond the extended family, there is a growing network of people who share traumatic experiences with others who will experience or have experienced the same thing. Networking, then, is the process of linking people to each other as resources—assisting, supporting, and helping others find the services and information they need. In many instances, parents want to talk to other parents who have coped with similar difficulties. A mother of a handicapped child describes the togetherness networking provides:

> If you think about a family and what it is, you realize that it's not just flesh and blood, but the fact that over the years, you have all shared something, and that is what makes you united. You don't even have to talk about these experiences. They are there. In our case, we have a sense of family because we share with each other something that is unknown to other people who do not have a child who is handicapped. You don't even have to talk about it, but when I am in a group of people with handicapped children, there is something that is unspoken between us which each of us knows and feels. (Witherspoon, 1980, p. 1-B)

ACTIVITIES, EXERCISES, AND IDEAS FOR REFLECTION AND DISCUSSION

1. Should brothers and sisters have responsibilities in caring for their handicapped siblings at home? At school?
2. Do you agree or disagree with the following statement: As with all children, a handicapped child's most important asset is the support and nurturance of his or her family. Explain.

3. Will some types of families, such as single parent families, teenage parents, poor families, or those without extended family or friends, find it more difficult to cope with a handicapped child than other kinds of families? Why?
4. Families differ significantly in their ethnic, racial, and religious backgrounds as well as economic status. How might these factors affect the family of a handicapped child?
5. As counselors, how can we help siblings develop greater maturity, tolerance, patience, and sense of responsibility toward their mentally retarded brother or sister?
6. Interview a brother or sister of a handicapped child. Find out their most notable concerns, frustrations, and adjustments.
7. Interview the mother and/or father of a handicapped child about their primary concerns and reactions to the child; what impact did the child make on the entire family?
8. How can counselors and helpers best prepare themselves to understand the impact and dynamics of a handicapped child on the family?

REFERENCES

Berdine, W. H., & Blackhurst, A. E. (1985). *An introduction to special education* (2nd ed.). Boston: Little, Brown.

Brammer, L. M. (1979). *The helping relationship: Process and skills* (2nd ed.). Englewood Cliffs, NJ: Prentice-Hall.

Crnic, K. A., Friedrich, W. N., & Greenberg, M. T. (1983). Adaptation of families with mentally retarded children: A model of stress, coping, and family ecology. *American Journal of Mental Deficiency, 88* (2), 125–138.

Dodson, L. S., & Kurpius, D. (1977). *Family counseling: A systems approach.* Muncie, IN: Accelerated Development.

Ehlers, W. H., Krishef, C. H., & Prothero, J. C. (1977). *An introduction to mental retardation: A programmed text.* Columbus, OH: Charles E. Merrill.

Gallagher, J. J., Beckman, P., & Cross, A. H. (1983). Families of handicapped children: Sources of stress and its amelioration. *Exceptional children, 50,* 10–19.

Grossman, F. (1972). *Brothers and sisters of retarded children.* Syracuse, NY: Syracuse University Press.

Hardman, M. L., Drew, C. J., & Egan, M. W. (1984). *Human exceptionality: Society, school, and family.* Boston: Allyn & Bacon.

Harra, V. (1975). Stop worrying? Nonsense! *The Exceptional Parent, 5,* 12–15.

Heward, W. L., & Orlansky, M. D. (1984). *Exceptional children* (2nd ed.). Columbus, OH: Charles E. Merrill.

Holmes, T., & Rahe, R. (1967). The social readjustment rating scale. *Journal of Psychomatic Research, 2,* 216–218.

Hosey, C. (1973). Yes, our child is still with us. *Children Today, 2,* 14–17, 36.

Kneedler, R. D., Hallahan, D. P., & Kauffman, J. M. (1984). *Special education for today.* Englewood Cliffs, NJ: Prentice-Hall.

Lombana, J. H., & Lombana, A. E. (1982). The home-school partnership: A model for counselors. *The Personnel and Guidance Journal, 61,* 35–39.

Robinson, N. M., & Robinson, H. B. (1976). *The mentally retarded child* (2nd ed.). New York: McGraw-Hill.

Schiamberg, L. B. (1985). *Human development* (2nd ed.). New York: Macmillan.

Schleifer, M. J. (1982). All our problems started when Jill was born. *The Exceptional Parent, 12*(1), 41–46.

Schreiber, M. (1984). Normal siblings of retarded persons. *Social Casework: The Journal of Contemporary Social Work, 65*(7), 420–427.

Schreiber, M., & Feeley, M. (1965). Normal adolescent siblings of the mentally retarded: Some beginnings in guided group education. (*Association for the Help of Retarded Children.* Publication No. 19). New York: Association for the Help of Retarded Children.

Schwartz, L. L. (1984). *Exceptional students in the mainstream.* Belmont, CA: Wadsworth.

Seligman, M. (1983). Sources of psychological disturbances among siblings of handicapped children. *The Personnel and Guidance Journal, 61*(9), 529–531.

Smith, S. L. (1984, April). Working with "difficult" parents of preschool children. Paper presented at Council for Exceptional Children Annual Convention, Washington, DC.

Stanhope, L., & Bell, R. O. (1981). Parents and families. In J. M. Kauffman & D. P. Hallahan (Eds.), *Handbook of special education.* Englewood Cliffs, NJ: Prentice-Hall.

Suran, B. G., & Rizzo, J. V. (1983). *Special children: An integrative approach* (2nd ed.). Glenview, IL: Scott, Foresman.

Wasserman, R. (1983). Identifying the counseling needs of the siblings of mentally retarded children. *The Personnel and Guidance Journal, 61*(10), 622–627.

Witherspoon, R. (1980, November 20). Easing grief of parents. *The Atlanta Constitution,* p. 1-B.

SELECTED REFERENCES FOR FURTHER READING AND STUDY

Blackard, M. K., & Barsch, E. T. (1982). Parents' and professionals' perceptions of the handicapped child's impact on the family. *Journal of the Association for the Severely Handicapped, 7*(2), 62–69.

Breshlaw, N., Weitzman, M., & Messenger, K. (1981). Psychologic functioning of siblings of disabled children. *Pediatrics, 61,* 344–353.

Bricker, D., & Casuso, V. (1979). Family involvement: A critical component of early intervention. *Exceptional Children, 46,* 108–116.

Friedrich, W. N., & Friedrich, W. L. (1981). Comparison of psychosocial assets of parents with a handicapped child and their normal controls. *American Journal of Mental Deficiency, 85,* 551–553.

Ogden, R. (1984). Parenting in the mainstream. *The Volta Review, 86*(5), 29–39.

Pfouts, J. (1976). The sibling relationships: A forgotten dimension. *Social Work, 21,* 200–204.

Powell, T. H., & Ogle, P. A. (1984). *Brothers and sisters—A special part of exceptional families.* Baltimore: Brookes.

Power, P. W. (1985, March–April). Family coping behaviors in chronic illness. *Rehabilitation Literature, 46*(3–4), 78–83.

Trevino, F. (1979, October). Siblings of the handicapped: Identifying those at risk. *Social Casework,* 488–493.

Tingey-Michaelis, C. (1983). *Handicapped infants and children: A handbook for parents and professionals.* Baltimore: University Park Press.

Wright, L. (1976). Chronic grief: The anguish of being an exceptional parent. *Exceptional Children, 23,* 160–169.

8 Counseling Parents of Mildly and Moderately Handicapped Children

After mastering the material in this chapter, you should be able to

1. Distinguish between mild, moderate, severe, and profound handicapping conditions.

2. Define a mild handicapping condition.

3. Define a moderate handicapping condition.

4. Understand the basis, rationale, and purpose of the teacher-helper parent conference.

5. Identify counseling goals for parents of mildly and moderately retarded children.

6. Understand how counseling goals may be intellectual, emotional, and behavioral in nature.

7. Define the crisis intervention method and identify factors that contribute to a return of equilibrium.

8. Describe and illustrate how the Carkhuff model may be used to counsel parents of handicapped children.

The counseling relationship, through its supportiveness, offers encouragement, comfort, and reassurance until natural processes of change, intraindividual or environmental, bring relief.
—Richard E. Pearson

All too frequently, professionals and parents assume that they hold the same values regarding what is desirable for the retarded individual. Yet, the values held by parents and the professional may be incompatible, leading to conflicts regarding program objectives and long-range goals.
—Philip Roos

DEFINING MILD AND MODERATE HANDICAPPING CONDITIONS

This chapter presents a definition and approach to both mild and moderate handicapping conditions; however, let us first examine this issue more specifically by defining mental retardation. The American Association on Mental Deficiency (AAMD) developed a common classification system of the mentally retarded. According to Hallahan and Kauffman (1982), since most professionals classify the retarded according to the severity of their problems, the most useful system based on severity is that of the AAMD. The terms used by the AAMD (mild, moderate, severe, and profound retardation) do not negatively stereotype the mentally retarded. The terms also describe the functioning of the child. Table 8.1 shows the relationship between the AAMD's classifications and intelligence test scores.

Heward and Orlansky (1984) agree that the AAMD classification system is the most widely used by diagnosticians; however, they note that because the skills and abilities of mentally retarded children vary, classification must be done carefully. Classifying a child as severely retarded solely on the basis of an IQ score could limit the child's access to programs for higher functioning children.

Hardman, Drew, and Egan (1984) discuss children with mild learning disorders and their place in the classroom.

TABLE 8.1 *AAMD levels and the corresponding intelligence test scores*

AAMD Level	IQ Range
Mild	50–55 to 70
Moderate	35–40 to 50–55
Severe	20–25 to 35–40
Profound	below 20–25

Individuals with mild learning and behavior disorders have been described as casualties of an educational system that has been unable to meet their academic or social needs. These students have traditionally been classified as having borderline mental retardation, mild behavior disorders, and specific learning disabilities. The more informal (unofficial) labels include slow learner, discipline problem, or poorly motivated student. The causes of mild learning and behavior disorders are generally unknown, but these problems are closely associated with diverse cultural backgrounds, socioeconomic differences, or poor teaching. The traditional categories have emphasized the discrepant characteristics of these students even when actual performance in the classroom suggests a considerable overlap from category to category in both academic and behavioral skills. (p. 111)

Heward and Orlansky (1984) note that mildly retarded children are often referred to by educators as educable mentally retarded (EMR).

Hardman, Drew, and Egan define a child with a moderate learning or behavior disorder as an individual who exhibits intellectual, academic, and/or social-interpersonal deficiences that range between two and three standard deviations from the norm. At this level, the individual will need substantial treatment and perhaps modified environmental accommodations. Heward and Orlansky note that moderately retarded children are sometimes referred to by educators as trainable mentally retarded (TMR). Typically, they will not benefit from traditional schooling. Instead, they will need a specialized training program that concentrates on self-care, communication, and social skills. Cartwright, Cartwright, and Ward (1984) indicate that of all mentally retarded persons, the mildly retarded are the largest subgroup, representing 85 to 87 percent of the total retarded population. The moderately retarded make up about 6 to 10 percent of the mentally retarded population.

COUNSELING STRATEGIES AND INTERVENTIONS

Vander Zanden and Pace (1984) point out that most parent counseling strategies fall into three categories: (1) informational programs to provide parents with facts about their child's condition, (2) psychotherapeutic programs to help parents deal with and understand their own problems and those of their children, and (3) parent training programs to help parents develop effective child management and teaching skills. Although all three strategies benefit parents, it is certain that most parents need basic essential information about their child's condition. At this point, we can identify and examine one of the most frequently used means of providing this information—the teacher-helper parent conference.

Lombana and Lombana (1982) devised a model of home-school collaboration that illustrates some important parent activities and the time and skill necessary for each. This model is presented in Figure 8.1. Lombana

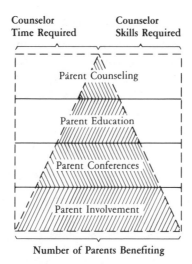

FIGURE 8.1 *Home-school partnership model*

and Lombana note that the bottom section of the triangle represents the number of parents who want to feel a part of the school. The next section represents parents who need productive conferences with counselors, teachers, and other personnel. The third level depicts parent education programs, or programs that teach parents more effective ways to discipline and communicate with their children. The top of the triangle represents the needs of the smallest number of parents—counseling. Lombana and Lombana also point out the importance of the two inverted triangles on either side. These illustrate the relationship between parental needs and counselor expertise and time. As we can see from the diagram, the relationship is inverse—the activities needed by the fewest parents are the most demanding of counselors in terms of time and skill.

Klein (1979) makes this point:

> A parents-school conference should be a productive, worthwhile experience for all involved. However, it is not easy. Merely placing parents and educators and/or professionals in the same room to discuss a child does not automatically make that experience fruitful. Unless such meetings are thoughtfully planned and carried out, they can be frustrating, time-consuming exercises in futility. Many educators (as well as parents) find themselves participating in such meetings with no specific training or experience about how to properly conduct such meetings. Everyone's lack of experience in communicating together adds to the fact that developing and carrying out an educational program for any child is a complicated task. The educational planning itself can result in conference participants feeling insecure, nervous, or on-the-spot feelings that influence their behavior in the conference itself. (p. E19)

Goals of the Helping Relationship

It would be helpful at this point to identify the goals or expected outcomes of the parent-school relationship. The advice of Heward, Dardig, and Rossett (1979) is especially helpful in this regard. According to them, a productive parent-professional relationship provides parents with

- [ ] greater understanding of the needs of their child and the objectives of the teacher.
- [ ] information on their rights and responsibilities as parents of an exceptional child.
- [ ] specific information about their child's school program and how they can become involved.
- [ ] specific ways to extend the positive effects of school programming into the home.
- [ ] increased skills in helping their child learn functional behaviors that are appropriate for the home environment.
- [ ] access to additional important resources (current and future) for their child. (p. 226)

In order to achieve these goals, Heward and Orlanski (1984) stress preparation as the key to effective parent-teacher conferences. To ensure that your meetings with parents are successful, preparation and planning are vital. One of the best ways to prepare is to develop an agenda or outline for each meeting. A sample outline is presented in Figure 8.2.

Practical Suggestions for Effective Parent Conferences

A parent conference may be defined as a short-term (often one meeting) purposeful exchange of meanings and ideas between a helper and parents for obtaining data, conveying information, or providing release and support. The following suggestions are offered to you to help improve your parent conferences. These are perhaps obvious and simple. It is because they *are* so basic that we tend to omit, forget, or overlook their importance. Observing and using these suggestions can be far-reaching in benefiting a helping relationship.

1. The parent as an individual
   Remember that every parent is an individual, with his own concerns and ideas about his child, the school, teachers, and the world. At any given moment, the way a parent sees things represents reality to them at that point and time.
2. Decide in advance what is to be discussed during the parent conference
   Assemble a folder of the child's work and jot down a checklist of the various problems.
3. Unless you ask for permission or explain your purpose, don't take notes while talking with parents
   They may feel intimidated and afraid to speak.

FIGURE 8.2 *Parent-teacher conference outline*

Conference Outline

Date _____   Time _____

Student's Name _____

Parent's Name(s) _____

Teacher's Name _____

Other Staff Present _____

Objectives for Conference:

Student's Strengths:

Area(s) Where Improvement Is Needed:

Questions to Ask Parents:

Parent's Responses/Comments:

Examples of Student's Work/Interactions:

Current Programs and Strategies Used by Teacher:

Suggestions for Parents:

Suggestions from Parents:

Follow-up Activities:
  Parents:

  Teacher:

Date Called for Follow-up and Outcome:

SOURCE: W. L. Heward, J. C. Dardig, and A. Rossett, *Working with parents of handicapped children*. Columbus, OH: Charles E. Merrill Publishing Company, 1979, p. 233. Used with permission.

4. Begin and end the conference with a positive and encouraging comment about the child

   Many parents report they have never been contacted by a teacher or counselor except for negative information.

5. Don't rush the interview

   It will probably take time for parents to relax and reveal what they are really concerned about.

6. Listen with enthusiasm

   Parents should be encouraged to do the talking, telling, and suggestion making. Give parents a chance to "sound off," especially when they are upset or angry. After they have let off steam, you will find it easier to discuss the problem calmly. Control your facial expressions of disapproval or anger.

7. Be willing to agree with parents whenever possible

   When the answer must be "no," take your time in saying it softly, without a trace of hostility. Communication becomes impossible in the midst of anger and recrimination.

8. Explain so that others can understand

   All too often when communicating verbally with parents, we assume understanding where it does not exist. Remember that obvious things are often the most difficult to perceive.

9. Use the simplest and clearest words you find to explain what you and their child do in school

   Gear your talk to the parents' interests and don't talk down to parents. They are not children and resent being treated as such. Whether well-educated or not, a parent may be embarrassed to admit not knowing a term the counselor uses with familiarity such as speaking glibly of "self-actualization" or "cognitive development."

10. Examine your own emotional reaction to criticism

    Do you dislike or feel threatened by people who give you new ideas, or who disagree with you? If so, you may be getting this message across in subtle, unspoken ways.

11. Don't let comments about other children creep into the conversation

    Avoid making comparisons with the child's brothers and sisters or members of his peer group.

12. Provide the parents with at least one action step—one thing they can do at home to help their child overcome a particular problem you've been discussing

    Help them understand that their child's success in school must be a joint project of home and school. Specific information often minimizes the hopeless-helpless feeling of futility and anxiety.

13. At the close of a conference summarize and jointly plan for the next conference

    At the close of the conference, parents should feel that something positive was accomplished and that future plans have been outlined. You may want to plan more frequent meetings for parents who seem to need a great deal of help.

14. Don't forget the follow-up

The first step is to write down the gist of what was discussed. These notes should be carefully reviewed and considered when planning the next conference. (National School Public Relations Association, 1968, pp. 21–22*)

Telford and Sawrey (1981) contend that the goals of counseling are essentially the same no matter who is being counseled. Although the methods, techniques, and types of information may vary, the purposes of counseling remain constant. These goals, according to Telford and Sawrey, are intellectual, emotional, and behavioral ones. In the intellectual realm, the parents need diagnostic information about the child's exceptionality as well as a prognosis for the future. The emotional component centers on the counselor's concern for the parents' fears, anxieties, and possible feelings of guilt and shame. The behavioral goal is that parents will develop modified behavior and specific plans for the family and the handicapped child. Telford and Sawrey comment that

The goals of counseling for parents of exceptional children are considerably more modest than those of psychotherapy. Counseling is not intended to change the personality of the counselee. It is intended to help reasonably well-integrated people understand and deal more adequately with the problems growing out of the presence of the deviant child in the family. Work with families of handicapped children is closer to social work than psychotherapy. It is more concerned with environmental manipulation and the handling of practical problems than with the personalities of the family members. (pp. 179–180)

Neisworth and Smith (1978) view counseling goals as (1) assisting people in dealing more effectively with their present situation, (2) helping individuals cope with immediate problems and function adequately in appropriate roles, (3) educating parents about intellectual competence and its influence on a child's daily performance and long-term development, (4) providing parents with assistance in handling daily behavior problems and family concerns and, (5) helping parents understand emotional concerns so that they will be able to find solutions and make decisions.

As you help parents of the handicapped to understand the day-to-day practical aspects of living with their child, you should keep in mind some general considerations. For example, Jordan (1972) suggested the following ten commandments for counselors:

1. Be honest in your appraisal of the situation and explain it without unnecessary delay.

2. Deal with both parents, since they are a natural unit.

---

*NOTE. From "Working with Parents: A Guide for Classroom Teachers and Other Educators," Washington, DC: National School Public Relations Association, 1968.

3. Be precise, but do not be unnecessarily technical in your explanation.
4. Point out who must be responsible ultimately.
5. Help the parents grasp the issues.
6. Keep in mind the referral agencies that can be of assistance.
7. Avoid precipitating ego-defensive reactions in the parents.
8. Do not expect too much too soon from the parents.
9. Allow parents their quota of concern and uncertainty.
10. Try to crystallize positive attitudes at the onset by using good counseling techniques. (p. 127)

Smith and Neisworth (1975) point out that sometimes professionals—whether teacher, physician, or psychologist—inadvertently reinforce the parents' denial of the damaged child. They stress what a great disservice this is to the parents and conclude:

> The only truly helpful approach is an honest presentation of reality, even though this reality may be extremely painful and threatening. One task of helping parents of exceptional children is to facilitate a realistic perception of conditions as they are, and the first principle of such help must be absolute honesty. (p. 184)

Robinson and Robinson (1976) enumerate some specific ways that counselors can help parents face reality issues:

☐ First, they can serve as sounding board and ally.
☐ Second, they can serve as teacher, if necessary, or at least see to it that the parents receive help in acquiring management techniques which for retarded children must be made explicitly a part of child-rearing practices.
☐ Third, counselors can make certain that parents are in touch with appropriate community services, not only those which presently exist but those which are in the making.
☐ Fourth, counselors can strongly encourage parents to make contact with local parents' groups.
☐ Fifth, counselors can, by virtue of their continuing relationship, assure the parents that they need not make decisions prematurely, that bridges need not be crossed until rivers are reached. (pp. 423–424)

What suggestions or counseling goals might a parent propose to a professional? Gorham (1975) speaks from the parent's point of view and offers these suggestions to professionals:

☐ Let the parent be involved every step of the way.
☐ Make a realistic management plan part of the assessment outcome.
☐ Inform yourself about community resources.
☐ Write your reports in clear and understandable language.
☐ Give copies of the reports to parents.
☐ Be sure the parent understands that there is no such thing as a one-shot, final, and unchanging diagnosis.

☐ Help the parent to think of life with this child in the same terms as life with his other children.

☐ Be sure that the parent understands his child's abilities and assets as well as his disabilities and deficiencies.

☐ Warn the parent about service insufficiencies. Equip him with advice on how to make his way through the system of "helping" services. Warn him that they are not always helpful. (pp. 523–524)

The stress a handicapped child places on a family can be great. Blake (1976) comments on the psychological strain a retarded individual puts on parents:

> For the family of a retarded child, the situation is more complicated and more hazardous. The particular handicaps of the child, the slowness of his development, the necessity of special arrangements for his physical care, training and companionship, and the adjustments which must be made in the family's expectations for the future combine to create pressure on the parents which tends to disrupt the normal family equilibrium. (p. 49)

A Crisis Intervention Method

Hoff (1984) points out that parents of developmentally disabled or handicapped children can experience crisis at many different times, such as

☐ When the child is born.

☐ When the child enters and does not succeed in a normal classroom.

☐ When the child develops behavior problems peculiar to his or her handicap.

☐ When the child becomes an adult and requires the same care as a child.

☐ When the child becomes an intolerable burden and parents lack the resources to care for him or her.

☐ When it is necessary to institutionalize the child.

☐ When institutionalization is indicated and parents cannot go through with it out of misplaced guilt and a sense of total responsibility.

☐ When the child is rejected by society and parents are reminded once again of their failure to perform as expected. (pp. 315–316)

What can a helper do to help ease a family's stress? Aguilera and Messick (1978) have developed a systematic, short-term, problem-solving approach to crisis intervention that focuses on solving the immediate problem. They believe that whenever a stressful event occurs, there are certain balancing factors that can bring about a return to equilibrium. These factors are

1. Realistic perception of the event
   If the event is perceived realistically, there will be recognition of the relationship between the event and feelings of stress. In other words, what does the event mean to the individual? How is it going to affect his future?
2. Available situational supports
   By nature, man is social and dependent upon others in his environment

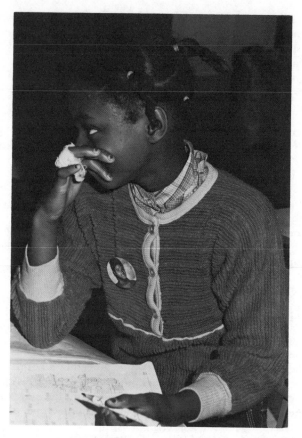

Parents of handicapped children can experience crisis at many different times, including when the child enters a regular class and does not succeed.

to supply him with reflected appraisals of his own intrinsic and extrinsic values. Situational supports mean those persons who are available in the environment who can be depended upon to help solve the problem.

3. Adequate coping mechanisms
   These are described as tension-reducing mechanisms and coping methods people use to relieve their tension and anxiety when faced with a problem. (pp. 70–71)

When the usual problem-solving techniques do not resolve the problems associated with having a handicapped child in the family, disequilibrium may result. Aguilera and Messick (1978) believe that the individual must either solve the problem or adapt to its presence. Leaving the problem unsolved leads to inner tension, signs of anxiety, disorganization of function, and a protracted period of emotional upset. Some parents will find solutions more easily than others; nevertheless, a professional helper must use skills, logic, and background knowledge to help parents define the problem and find a solution.

THE CARKHUFF MODEL OF HELPING

A particularly useful model of helping was designed by Robert R. Carkhuff (1983). According to this model, there are distinct phases of helping between the helpee (client or parent) and helper (counselor or therapist). Figure 8.3 allows you to visualize these relationships.

To appreciate the usefulness of Carkhuff's model, we need to understand the terminology. According to Carkhuff, *attending* is a necessary precondition of helping. Attending skills allow the helper to see and hear the helpee. *Involving* is also a prehelping phase. Helpees become involved by preparing themselves physically, emotionally, and intellectually. *Responding* provides the basis for the helping process. It involves responding to content, feelings, and meanings. *Exploring* involves helpees analyzing their experiences and diagnosing themselves according to those experiences. *Personalizing* is the critical helping phase in which the counselor leads the helpee in taking responsibility for personal problems. *Understanding* requires the helpee to develop and personalize goals. *Initialing* involves defining goals, developing programs, designing schedules, and reinforcing and individualizing steps. *Acting* emphasizes two phases: defining goals and developing programs.

Four basic counseling strategies were discussed earlier in Chapter Five. In working with parents of exceptional children, you are encouraged to review, study, and practice these strategies. Regardless of the particular strategy you choose, you should understand the critical importance of using an appropriate therapy technique for each individual. Clients (including parents) vary in their problems, their concerns, and their particular history of the person-environment transaction (Ivey & Simek-Downing, 1980). The

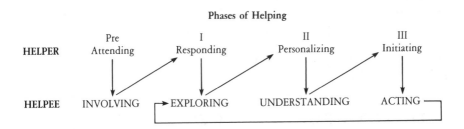

Phases of Helping

FIGURE 8.3 The Carkhuff model for helping

importance of choosing the right technique is emphasized by Walker and Shea (1980) when they state that

> The parents of a child with a problem are first and foremost human beings, and like all human beings, they react as individuals to the problems of loved ones. A particular parent's reaction is in large part determined by that individual's personal characteristics, life experiences, education and training, expectations, socioeconomic circumstances, and a variety of other variables. The parent's reaction is influenced by the characteristics of the child and the specific problem and, to some degree, by the educator's reaction to the problem. (p. 102)

CHAPTER SUMMARY

Parents of mildly and moderately handicapped children are often confronted with a variety of problems and concerns that are beyond the child-rearing responsibilities faced by parents of nonhandicapped children. As these needs and problems develop, parents often seek ways to identify, discuss, and resolve these problems. You may have the opportunity to assist these parents in overcoming their frustrations, tensions, and anxieties resulting from their beliefs and attitudes toward their handicapped child.

Because of the nature of mild and moderate handicapping conditions, parents will usually need information about their child, the nature and degree of the handicap, educational planning, and future prognosis. Don't assume that all parental problems or concerns are emotional. As a helper, your job may be only providing these parents with useful information to help them effectively cope with personal and practical day-to-day situations. With these parents, be particularly mindful of *the law of readiness.* Edward L. Thorndike and other theorists discovered principles of behavior that explained how learning takes place. The law of readiness says that when someone is ready to act, doing so is rewarding, and not doing so is displeasing. You must remember, then, that learning won't take place unless the person has a basic psychological need to learn. Parents of the handicapped possess a deep, innate capacity for psychological growth and personal development. As we work with parents, especially those reluctant, stubborn, or resistant to accepting information, we must develop our own capacity to wait for the "teachable moment." Only when parents have grasped the insight to change their behavior patterns can they adequately resolve their problems.

ACTIVITIES, EXERCISES, AND IDEAS FOR REFLECTION AND DISCUSSION

Note to the reader—Noticeably absent from this text are discussions of counseling principles that specifically relate to other defined areas of exceptionality, i.e., the speech impaired, the visually impaired, the hearing impaired, the physically handicapped and the child with behavioral disorders. There is no intent to ignore or slight these handicapping conditions. Because of limitations of space, only *general* counseling principles that are often applicable to other handicapping conditions were included. The following questions will, therefore, relate to those other areas in the hopes that you will at least be aware that you must be knowledgeable in your area of expertise or refrain from initiating a superficial or perhaps harmful relationship.

1. What are some specific counseling principles that are unique and applicable primarily or exclusively to the following handicaps: the visually disabled, the hearing impaired, the speech impaired, the physically handicapped, and the behavior disordered. An example might be your belief that being parents of the physically handicapped can place an additional financial burden on the family. A principle, therefore, might be to aid parents in securing financial relief or assistance. Cite other guiding principles of helping within each area. Support your viewpoints with research or studies.
2. The following is a list of frequently used terms associated with auditory impairments. Define these terms as if you had to explain their meaning to parents without using sophisticated technical jargon.

    decibels, otologist, speechreading, auditory training, oralism, manualism, fingerspelling, the simultaneous approach, audiometer, residual hearing, Rochester method

3. Parents whom you are counseling express concern about their visually impaired child's personal and social adjustment. What does research tell us we can share with these parents?
4. List agencies, diagnostic clinics, or other facilities in your community, county, city, or state that offer comprehensive professional services to strengthen the relationship between parents and the visually handicapped child and give parents the information and skills that would enable them to meet the child's special needs.
5. How would you explain to parents the difference between residential schools, day school, and special classes for deaf children? What are the advantages and disadvantages of each?
6. Why is it important for parents and relatives to realize that the child has limitations as well as potentials? In the counseling process, should the counselor emphasize the child's limitations, potentials, or give both equal consideration?
7. For an advanced research topic, trace the history of parent counseling.
8. Debate this statement: Teachers in training need as much preparation in working with parents and other professional personnel as they do in working with children.
9. Interview parents of children with physical handicaps. Identify past and future concerns that they have about their child. What unique problems do parents of the physically handicapped face when compared with other handicapping conditions?
10. Discuss the viewpoint that a physical disability is not an objective thing in a person, but a social value judgment.
11. List civic clubs or other organizations in your community that assist parents of physically handicapped children. What is the nature of their service?
12. You are counseling with the parents of a severely physically handicapped child. One parent says, "But I have my own life to lead." What implication may be

drawn from this statement? How would (could) you respond to such a statement? List and discuss some appropriate responses. List and discuss some inappropriate responses. What other factors need to be considered?

13. Invite a staff member from an organization such as the United Cerebral Palsy Association to visit your class and discuss children who have physical handicaps. How extensive is their work in counseling with the parents? Do they have a parent-training program?

14. What methods or approaches can be used to counsel parents who admit there's a problem with their son's behavior and then proceed to blame someone else or themselves?

15. Do professional people too often forget that parents are people? Explain.

16. Do professionals frequently underestimate the expertise of the parent in being a parent of a child with a behavioral disorder?

17. Give some reasons why emotional disorders, particularly in children, are often difficult for parents to understand, recognize, and accept.

REFERENCES

Aguilera, D. C., & Messick, J. M. (1978). *Crisis intervention: Theory and methodology* (3rd ed.). St. Louis: C. V. Mosby.

Blake, K. A. (1976). *The mentally retarded: An educational psychology.* Englewood Cliffs, NJ: Prentice-Hall.

Carkhuff, R. R.(1983). *The art of helping.* Amherst, MA: Human Resource Development Press.

Cartwright, G. P., Cartwright, C. A., & Ward, M. E. (1984). *Educating special learners* (2nd ed.). Belmont, CA: Wadsworth.

Gorham, K. A. (1975). A lost generation of parents. *Exceptional children, 41,* 521–525.

Hallahan, D. P., & Kauffman, J. M. (1982). *Exceptional children: Introduction to special education* (2nd ed.). Englewood Cliffs, NJ: Prentice-Hall.

Hardman, M. L., Drew, C. J., & Egan, M. W. (1984). *Human exceptionality: Society, school, and family.* Boston: Allyn & Bacon.

Heward, W. L., Dardig, J. C., & Rossett, A. (1979). *Working with parents of handicapped children.* Columbus, OH: Charles E. Merrill.

Heward, W. L., & Orlansky, M. D. (1984). *Exceptional children* (2nd ed.). Columbus, OH: Charles E. Merrill.

Hoff, L. A. (1984). *People in crisis: Understanding and helping* (2nd ed.). Mendo Park, CA: Addison-Wesley.

Ivey, A. E., & Simek-Downing, L. (1980). *Counseling and psychotherapy: Skills, theories, and practice.* Englewood Cliffs, NJ: Prentice-Hall.

Jordon, T. E. (1972). *The mentally retarded.* Columbus, OH: Charles E. Merrill.

Klein, S. D. (1979). Parent-school conferences: Guidelines and objectives. *The Exceptional Parent, 9*(4), E19–E21.

Lombana, J. H., & Lombana, A. E. (1982). The home-school partnership: A model for counselors. *The Personnel and Guidance Journal, 61,* 35–39.

Neisworth, J. T., & Smith, R. M. (1978). *Retardation: Issues, assessment, and intervention.* New York: McGraw-Hill.

Polloway, E. A., Payne, J. S., Patton, J. R., & Payne, R. A. (1985). *Strategies for teaching retarded and special needs learners* (3rd ed.). Columbus, OH: Charles E. Merrill.

Robinson, N. M., & Robinson, H. B. (1976). *The mentally retarded child: A psychological approach.* New York: McGraw-Hill.

Smith, R. M., & Neisworth, J. T. (1975). *The exceptional child: A functional approach.* New York: McGraw-Hill.

Telford, C. W., & Sawrey, J. M. (1981). *The exceptional individual.* Englewood Cliffs, NJ: Prentice-Hall.

Vander Zanden, J. W., & Pace, A. J. (1984). *Educational psychology in theory and practice* (2nd ed.). New York: Random House.

Walker, J. E., & Shea, T. M. (1980). *Behavior management: A practical approach for educators.* St. Louis: C. V. Mosby.

SELECTED REFERENCES FOR FURTHER READING AND STUDY

Abrams, J. C., & Kaslow, R. (1977). Family systems and the learning disabled child: Intervention and treatment. *Journal of Learning Disabilities, 10,* 86–90.

Apolloni, T. (1984). Who'll help my disabled child when I'm gone? *Academic Therapy, 20,* 109–114.

Bray, N. M., Coleman, J. M., & Bracken, M. B. (1981). Critical events in parenting handicapped children. *Journal of the Division for Early Childhood, 3,* 26–33.

Featherstone, H. A. (1980). *A difference in the family.* New York: Basic Books.

Ferguson, D. L. (1984). Parent advocacy network. *The Exceptional Parent, 14*(2), 41–45.

Greer, B. G. (1975). On being the parent of a handicapped child. *Exceptional Children, 41*(8), 519.

Lonsdale, G. (1978). Family life with a handicapped child: The parents speak. *Child Care, Health and Development, 4,* 99–120.

Main, M. B., & Weston, D. R. (1981). Security of attachment to mother and father: Related to conflict behavior and the readiness to establish new relationships. *Child Development, 52,* 932–940.

Orlansky, M. D., & Heward, W. L. (1981). *Voices: Interviews with handicapped people.* Columbus, OH: Charles E. Merrill.

Pearlman, L., & Scott, K. A. (1981). *Raising the handicapped child.* Englewood Cliffs, NJ: Prentice-Hall.

Turnbull, A. P., & Turnbull, R. R. (1978). *Parents speak out: Views from the other side of the two-way mirror.* Columbus, OH: Charles E. Merrill.

Wilcoxon, S. A. (1985). Healthy family functioning: The other side of family pathology. *Journal of Counseling and Development, 63* (8), 495–499.

9 Counseling Parents of Severely and Profoundly Handicapped Children

After mastering the material in this chapter, you should be able to

1. Understand and define severe and profound handicapping conditions.

2. Describe some typical needs of parents of severely and profoundly handicapped children.

3. Discuss counseling problems or concerns unique to mental retardation.

4. Understand and discuss various stages of parental reactions that are typical of parents of handicapped children.

5. Defend or refute *acceptance* of the handicapped child as a realistic and attainable parental goal.

6. Briefly list and describe the purposes and advantages of genetic counseling.

7. Discuss institutionalization in terms of its purpose, general guidelines, and placement decisions.

8. Identify and discuss applicable counseling strategies when working with parents of severely and profoundly retarded children.

9. From the parent point of view, understand and appreciate the complex phenomena and trauma often associated with being parents of a severely or profoundly handicapped child.

Times have changed. There has been an increase in concern regarding the rights of all individuals, including minorities such as the severely handicapped. Advocates for the severely handicapped are becoming larger in number, more experienced, and consequently more effective.

—Donna H. Lehr and Fredda Brown

Since options include some that are heavily weighted with ethical, moral, and emotional implications, there are some strong currents of controversy about genetic testing and counseling. Each individual and couple will have to evaluate personal, family, religious, and cultural values.

—Dorothy Dolph Zeyen

---

*H*elping parents of severely and profoundly handicapped children to become aware of their concerns and the search for realistic solutions presents a challenge to any helper. For example, guilt is a common parental reaction to diagnosis of their severely or moderately handicapped child. Parents have a tendency to blame themselves for their child's handicapping condition. The parent may feel he or she has actually done something that caused the problem, or the parent may experience vague yet deep-seated guilt feelings that can cause a great deal of anguish and turmoil.

The ways parents handle guilt may take many directions, but the most common appear to be (a) to blame themselves (which takes its toll on their own adjustment), (b) to switch the blame to someone else (an unhealthy practice because parents end up finding fault with others, sometimes those who are treating the child), (c) to completely deny the existence or the seriousness of the handicap, (d) to begin to blame each other (taken to an extreme, the mother may wonder if the genetic defect came from the father's relatives, or her mother-in-law), and (e) to resort to "shopping behavior," making visits to a number of different professionals or clinics hoping to find a "cure" for their child's handicap.

In this context, let us now examine in greater detail some principles and ideas related to working with these parents.

DEFINING SEVERE AND PROFOUND HANDICAPPING CONDITIONS

In Chapter Eight, the AAMD classification system was used to make some broad comparisons and distinctions between mild, moderate, severe, and profound retardation. Severely and profoundly retarded children were said to experience a low level of functioning. Their education programming, then, is based on functional daily skills (Hallahan & Kauffman, 1982).

Expressing a similar yet broader perspective, Hardman, Drew, and Egan (1984) have noted the following:

> Persons with severe and profound disorders generally have multiple impairments that transcend the characteristics associated with a single disabling condition. The characteristics of people with mental retardation range from being able to develop skills that will facilitate independence within their environment, to being unable to take care of themselves at all. The severely and profoundly retarded exhibit serious deficiencies in cognitive development, physical development, and communication skills. In addition, greater intellectual deficiency tends to result in a higher incidence of compounding sensory dysfunction. (p. 175)

Cartwright, Cartwright, and Ward (1981) note that the severely retarded represent about 3.5 percent of all retarded persons, and the profoundly retarded (those who score below 20 on standardized intelligence tests) comprise about 1 percent of the entire range of retarded persons. They also point out that in contrast to mild retardation, severe retardation is usually diagnosed early in a child's life.

MEETING THE NEEDS OF PARENTS OF SEVERELY AND PROFOUNDLY HANDICAPPED CHILDREN

Dean (1975) made this observation of parent needs:

> Although parents of handicapped children differ in many ways, there are certain experiences they share in common. Among these are a lack of adequate emotional support; a lack of information on where to turn for appropriate educational services after diagnosis, evaluation, and presentation have occurred; and a lack of information on how to change laws, rules, and regulations which exclude handicapped children from needed services. These life experiences which are common to parents of any handicapped child are even more important to parents of severely handicapped children. The type and quality of professional help available and the amount and type of parental cooperation will ultimately determine the strength and direction of the helping relationship. (p. 527)

Gordon (1977) sums up parental needs:

> Parents need guidance, they need comfort, and they need to be periodically freed from their heavy burden and lonely burden of providing for a child whose care requires more than the usual amount of parenting and nurturing.

> The needs of the children are great; the needs of the family are even greater.

> The needs of the children are frequently met; the needs of the family are too seldom recognized or satisfied. (p. 61)

What specifically can you do as a helper to offer support and comfort to families of severely handicapped children? Gordon (1977) offers four suggestions:

1. They [parents] need service from the first moment their child is identified as exceptional—service delivered *to them* rather than service they have to seek, service organized *for them* rather than service that they have to mobilize for themselves.
2. Parents of handicapped children need other parents of handicapped children with whom to speak, if only to know, as one parent put it, "that other mothers can live [through this] and can survive with these awful burdens, and sometimes can even smile and laugh."
3. Parents need professionals who are sound academically, stable emotionally, and ready to face the situation with them, empathize with them, and translate for them a realistic picture of the handicapped child's current status, as well as projections that can be made, while admitting that there are some projections that cannot yet be made about the child's future development and potential.
4. Perhaps the greatest initial assistance that can be offered to parents is respect for their feelings of shock, fear, and anxiety. Parents need to express feelings, rather than merely listen to reassurances that everything will turn out all right. (p. 62–63)

Ehlers, Prothero, and Lagone (1982) suggest six action steps designed to help parents cope:

1. Help parents to be more objective about both their child and the child's handicap.
2. Help parents to predict their child's future behavior—what behaviors will the child outgrow and what behaviors can they expect to continue?
3. Help parents to assimilate ideas and techniques for various problem situations common to families of a retarded child.
4. Help parents (as well as the entire family) to see that the handicapped child has the same physical, sexual, recreational, and educational needs as they do.
5. Help parents to discover all the community resources available to them (e.g., clinics, evaluation centers, parents' groups, workshops, and educational institutions for the retarded).
6. Help parents to devise a method of keeping track of the handicapped person's progress toward the set goals and objectives. (pp. 350–351)

In discussing experiences unique to families of severely handicapped persons, Lyon and Preis (1983), identified three areas of significant impact on the family: psychological/emotional, financial, and practical/logistical. The psychological or emotional area concerns parental and family reactions to the birth of a handicapped child. These reactions will be discussed in greater detail later in this chapter. Lyon and Preis point out that many parents have difficulty paying for the numerous services needed for their children.

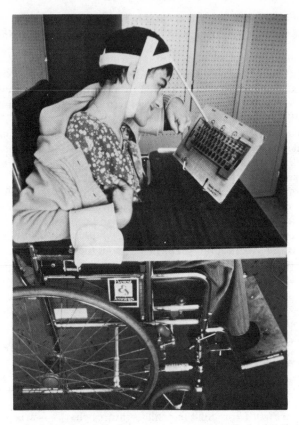

One of the counselor's goals is to help parents appreciate their child's potentialities and accept their child's limitations.

Finally, the practical side of meeting the needs of the handicapped child, maintaining satisfying marital relationships, fulfilling professional commitments, and the mundane concerns of daily living puts strain on a family. Complex family relationships are a major part of the child's adjustment. Farber (1968) comments that the role of the child in the family may be more important than the professional diagnosis of the child as a handicapped individual.

COUNSELING PROBLEMS UNIQUE TO MENTAL RETARDATION

To both the layman and professional, comprehending mental retardation is in many respects more perplexing and elusive than other types of handicapping conditions. Ross (1964) illustrates this by the following:

Even though the sighted person cannot possibly know how it feels to be blind, he can nevertheless imagine what it is like by walking blindfolded into a strange room. He can similarly imagine what is is like to be deaf or otherwise physically impaired. On the other hand, it is totally impossible to achieve any degree of empathy for the state of the mentally defective for we cannot suspend our higher mental processes or temporarily cancel everything we learned. Because of its nature, mental retardation offers some peculiar characteristics and problems which require enumeration. (p. 100)

The Diagnosis

The parents' most vulnerable time is when the child is first diagnosed. Parents usually are unable to face this problem realistically or even look at it constructively. They especially need help in handling their emotions and in planning for the child. Counseling these parents involves encouraging them to realistically assess the changes that will occur and to determine a proper course of direction. Stone (1948) suggested some guidelines for judging parental awareness. Even today these three levels can help the counselor determine parents' initial awareness and provide criteria for measuring their level of awareness.

Considerable awareness

1. The parent states that the child is retarded.
2. The parent recognizes the limitations of any treatment.
3. The parent requests information about suitable care and training, usually placement in an institution.

Partial awareness

1. The parent describes the symptoms of retardation with questions about the causes.
2. The parent hopes for improvement but fears that treatment will not be successful.
3. The parent questions his own ability to cope with the problems.
4. The worker evaluates him as having partial awareness of the child's real problem.

Minimal awareness

1. The parent refuses to recognize that certain characteristic behavior is abnormal.
2. The parent blames causes other than retardation for the symptoms.
3. The parent believes that treatment will produce a "normal" child. (p. 363)

Burton (1976) comments that the physician often fulfills the initial role of counselor. This counseling level is frequently inadequate, contributing to the crisis because the physician is unable to communicate effectively. Ehlers (1964) concludes that physicians have difficulty communicating the circumstances of retardation to families, frequently frightening and confusing the parents. Welch (1981) vividly illustrates this point.

> My baby was already a few minutes old and I had not yet held her. But I heard her crying, and as I turned my head I saw a crowd of people around an incubator. "What's wrong, what's wrong?" I continued to ask. I must have repeated that question several times before a woman came into view over my head and said, "Your baby is retarded." Then she disappeared.

> The trauma that I experienced immediately after my daughter's birth might have been lessened if the obstetrician, or anyone else in the room, had responded to me when I first asked about the baby. They did not have to instantly tell me that she was retarded. But someone should at least have said, "Give us one moment and we will be right with you" or "We will be right with you as soon as we complete the emergency procedures." (p. 525)

Welch makes an eloquent plea that professionals learn to be compassionate, thoughtful listeners and be able to respond to the emotional needs of the family, not just provide information. This is sound advice for all who counsel with parents of the severely and profoundly retarded.

Lee (1984) discusses new research that indicates another problem in the patient-doctor relationship—failing to communicate clearly. Boston University researchers questioned 800 women and doctors after they had met for genetic counseling sessions. The goal of the sessions was to educate patients about birth defects. The sessions lasted 40 to 60 minutes each, about three times longer than most doctor/patient consultations. The results of the Boston study indicated that only 16.7 percent of the doctors knew when the decision to have a child was the woman's main concern. Only 15.2 percent of the doctors knew when amniocentesis was the patient's primary concern. The results clearly show that doctors and patients just aren't communicating. Perhaps part of the problem is that patients don't ask the right questions out of fear or ignorance and, though doctors are trained to diagnose, they aren't trained to educate.

PARENTAL REACTIONS TO MENTAL RETARDATION

The first problem that many parents of mentally retarded children face is accepting the fact that *their* child is intellectually retarded. Our achievement-oriented society and the ambition of many parents to see their children lead happy, successful lives often compound the problem. Parents often see their children as extensions of themselves and are naturally bitterly disappointed to learn that their child has intellectual limitations. Acceptance is frequently cited as the first counseling goal, yet Roos (1977) challenges this assumption:

> Two popular objectives in counseling parents of the retarded are getting parents to accept mental retardation and lifting the depression which seems to be a

common parental reaction. Unfortunately, neither of these objectives is realistic. While parents may fully understand that their child is mentally retarded, it is unrealistic to expect them to accept this situation with blandness and equanimity; our society places too high a value on intelligence. (p. 73)

When their child's condition is diagnosed, parents of the severely and profoundly retarded may express their feelings in many ways. Wolfensberger (1967) cites only a few of the possible reactions:

Alarm, ambivalence, anger, anguish, anxiety, avoidance, bewilderment, bitterness, catastrophic reaction, confusion, death wishes, denial, depression, despair, disappointment, disbelief, disassociation, embarrassment, envy, fear, financial worries, grief, guilt, helplessness, identification, immobility, impulses to destroy the child, lethargy, mourning, over-identification, pain, projection, puzzlement, regret, rejection, remorse, self-blame, self-pity, shame, shock, sorrow, suicidal impulses, trauma, etc.

Stages of Parental Reaction

There has been an ever-increasing body of literature about parental stages of adjustment after learning their child has a handicapping condition. Heward and Orlansky (1984) state that

There is no question that the birth of a handicapped child or the discovery that a child has a disability is an intense and traumatic event. Parents can react in widely different ways, and most do go through an adjustment process trying to work their way through. But we see two problems with promoting the idea of "stages of adjustment." First, it is easy to assume that all parents must pass through a similar sequence of stages and that time is the most important variable in adjustment. Second, the stages parents are said to pass through have a distinct psychiatric flavor; professionals may mistakenly assume parents are maladjusted. Some educators seem to assume that all parents of handicapped children need counseling. (p. 432)

Despite this criticism, certain types of reactions are common and warrant additional discussion. None of these reactions is peculiar to parents in general or to the parents of defective children; they are common reactions to frustration and conflict. The average parent will display or experience these reactions to nondisabled children as a normal part of family life. It is helpful to the parents of handicapped children to be aware of the universality of their reaction (Telford & Sawrey, 1981).

Reviewing the literature on this subject suggests that parents tend to go through a series of stages after learning their child is handicapped. Hardman, Drew, and Egan (1984) note that the most predictable and common reaction to the birth of a child with a disorder is depression marked by grief or mourning. Burton (1976) claims that this depression is frequently compounded by a lack of information, or misinformation, and Wolfensberger

(1967) concluded that parents often felt guilty when the retardation was diagnosed at birth.

Mandell and Fiscus (1981) acknowledge the importance of grieving the loss of having a normal, healthy child. They suggest a five-stage process for both professionals and society to acknowledge. The stages are as follows:

1. Denial

   Parents often refuse to believe the existence of a handicap, the permanence of it, or its impact on the life of the entire family.

2. Guilt

   Parents' guilt is manifested in one of three ways. The least common is attaching the cause of the child's handicap to some specific past action. A second form of guilt is the belief that "bad things happen to bad people; therefore, I am bad." A third form—the most frequently found and the most difficult to deal with—is the belief that the impaired child is a just punishment for something the parent has done.

3. Depression

   Depression is anger turned inward. Parents punish themselves because they cannot do what they want to do—make the child nonhandicapped.

4. Anger

   Anger occurs on two levels. The first is often expressed as "Why me?" The other is usually unspoken and frequently is displaced onto the spouse, a sibling, or a professional. This silent anger is actually hatred for the handicapped child.

5. Bargaining

   The last stage is bargaining with science, with God, or with anyone to cure the child. It is a "last ditch" attempt by parents to change their circumstances.

Mandell and Fiscus emphasize that not all parents go through all stages—the intensity and duration of each stage varies from parent to parent.

A much earlier framework illustrating stages of parental reaction, again a five-step process, was proposed by Rosen (1955): (1) an awareness that a serious problem exists; (2) recognition of what the problem is; (3) a search for the cause; (4) a search for a solution; and (5) acceptance of the problem.

Blacher (1984) examined the existing literature for patterns or stages of parental adjustment to the birth of a child with handicaps. His purpose was to provide a brief overview of this literature and raise some practical questions to guide further research. Specifically, (a) How were the stages derived?, (b) Are the stages reliable indicators of parental adjustment?, and (c) Is there an alternative approach to the study of parental adjustment that might yield more useful information for people wishing to help parents of handicapped children? Blacher's detailed analysis presents views from both sides of the question of whether or not parents follow a sequence of adjustment, finally achieving acceptance. Blacher's conclusions and summary are worth our noting.

The question of whether sequential stages of parental adjustment to a handicapped child are clinically and scientifically derived fact, or an artifact of researchers' attempts to perpetuate ideas from the literature, remains to be determined. To date, the stages approach to understanding parental adjustment to a handicapped child has provided a useful heuristic. There remains the need for an instrument to be used by professionals who work with these parents (whether as parent trainers, counselors, school psychologists, or educational evaluators), to ascertain the parents' current level of awareness and adjustment and make practical programming and placement decisions accordingly. (p. 67)

PARENTS HAVE QUESTIONS

After diagnosis, the stress borne by parents of severely handicapped children leads to many questions. Feelings of inadequacy, shame, defensiveness, loss of self-respect, and increased ambivalence are typical parental reactions. The intensity of these reactions often leads the parents to ask more questions about the actual dimensions and severity of the child's disability.

Attwell and Clabby (1971) identified 231 specific questions that parents of mentally retarded children were likely to ask. We should again remember

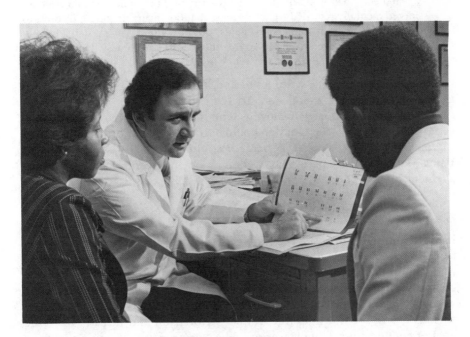

Genetic counseling can provide parents with reliable and valuable information.

that the specific nature of a parent's questions will always vary according to such variables as impact on the family, the degree of retardation, the parents' level of comprehension and understanding of their child's condition, and the ability to cope with their unexpected, ongoing burden. A representative sampling of these questions follows:

- [ ] What is the cause of our child's retardation?
- [ ] How severely retarded is he (she)?
- [ ] Why did this have to happen to us?
- [ ] Is it safe to have another child?
- [ ] Does the genetic background of one parent contribute more to the retardation of a child than that of the other person?
- [ ] Can mental retardation be "cured"?
- [ ] I cannot help but pity my child. Is this wrong?
- [ ] If our retarded child lives at home, will it affect our normal child adversely?
- [ ] How shall we explain him (or her) to our normal children?
- [ ] How shall we explain him (or her) to our relatives, friends, and neighbors?
- [ ] Should we belong to a parent organization? What are the advantages of belonging to a parent group? (pp. 15–87)

In looking at what the future holds for families of the severely retarded, McLeod (1985) makes the following comment:

> When a child has an IQ of 70 or below—the point at which people are considered mentally retarded—parents must abandon many dreams and adjust to their child's severely limited prospects. But how limited must such a life be? Must their child live forever in an institution or, if at home, be permanently dependent on the family or the state? (p. 42)

McLeod states that "attitudes toward the abilities of people with mental retardation have changed—quietly but profoundly" (p. 44). She quotes the Association for Retarded Citizens who now estimate that about 75 percent of mentally retarded children could become self-supporting adults with the proper training. Ten to 15 percent could be partially self-supporting. Using McLeod's information, helpers may be able to offer hope, encouragement, and support to parents of the severely retarded.

GENETIC COUNSELING

Heward and Orlansky (1984) define genetic counseling as a discussion between a specially trained medical counselor and prospective parents about the possibilities of giving birth to a handicapped child. Genetic counseling can provide parents with valuable, reliable information and can determine whether or not their child will be born with a chromosomal abnormality such as Down's syndrome. According to Hoemann and Briga (1981), the goal of genetic counseling is to provide accurate information to clients so that they can make an informed decision about having children.

A medical procedure called *amniocentesis* (am-nee-oh-sen-teé-sus) is a frequently used prenatal diagnosis that is especially useful to parents who have already given birth to a child with a chromosomal abnormality, or when the mother falls within a high-risk group. Beeson and Douglas (1983) note that amniocentesis is also appropriate for pregnancies in families with a history of diagnosable genetic disease such as Tay Sachs disease, alpho-thalassemia, sickle-cell anemia, and many inborn errors of metabolism. In fact, approximately 30 specific genetic disorders can be identified prior to birth.

Amniocentesis is performed during the second trimester of pregnancy (16–18 weeks from the first day of the last menstrual period). Amniocentesis is about a 10- to 15-minute outpatient procedure that involves extracting a sample of fluid from the amniotic sac surrounding the fetus. The fluid, which contains fetal cells, is then analyzed for chromosomal abnormalities.

A relatively new and promising procedure for detecting chromosomal abnormalities is now being tested in the United States, since amniocentesis cannot be performed before the 16th week of pregnancy (Begley, 1984). Another two or three weeks are needed for tests, leaving the mother little time to consider a second-trimester abortion if the fetus is abnormal. The new technique, called chorionic villus biopsy, provides an alternative. This procedure, performed in the 10th week of pregnancy, uses extra-embryonic tissue that is genetically identical to the fetus' cells. The tissue can then be analyzed for the extra chromosome typical of Down's Syndrome, probed with DNA to identify sickle-cell anemia, or ground up to test for Tay Sachs. We are on the threshold of new advances in technology, biology, and medicine that will expand our scope of knowledge and understanding of genetic counseling.

INSTITUTIONALIZATION/ DEINSTITUTIONALIZATION

The professional helper should be prepared to discuss institutionalization (the separation of child and family) to the parents. Robinson and Robinson (1976) comment on four factors making institutionalization a likelihood.

1. Level of retardation
   Institutions are being utilized for the most retarded segments of the population.
2. Ethnic background and economic status
   Within each IQ category, children in residential facilities tend to belong to the economically and socially least adequate families.

3. Behavioral problems
   The incidence of behavior problems is seen as an important factor leading to placement.
4. Family characteristics
   Signs of stress and maladjustment have been found in families who seek placement for their children. (pp. 436–438)

To help parents resolve this traumatic problem, Gearheart and Litton (1975) offer some logical guidelines. They suggest that institutionalization is needed when (a) vital educational, medical, or behavioral controls are unattainable at home, (b) the emotional and/or physical welfare of the family is seriously threatened, and (c) the child is a proven threat to self or society. Gearheart and Litton warn against institutional placement based on diagnostic labels and suggest that placement outside the home be on a trial basis.

Voelker (1975) remarks that there is no stock answer to the question of placing the child outside the home because of the complexity and many variables of each situation. He believes it is important to consider if there are community resources to assist the parents and the child, if the family can accept and successfully integrate the handicapped child into its structure, if the financial income of the family is sufficient to provide adequately for the handicapped child as well as other members of the family, and if the severity of the child's handicap will make permanent care and supervision inevitable.

Batshaw and Perret (1981) propose the following guidelines for institutionalization:

First, institutionalization should be viewed as a last resort to be considered only after less restrictive environments have failed. Conversely, institutionalization should not be ruled out as a possibility for the child with severe multiple handicaps.
Second, the decision should be a joint one involving both parents and professionals caring for the child. This eases the burden on everyone.
Third, if at all possible, the parents should continue to be involved with the child, visiting him and taking him home on weekends.
Finally, the need for institutionalization should be reviewed by all concerned at regular intervals and a less restrictive environment chosen should this become appropriate. (p. 361)

Institutionalization in the United States has had a controversial history. According to Blatt and Kaplan (1966), during the 1960s institutions were exposed as abusive environments that dehumanized both residents and staff. Kneedler, Hallahan, and Kauffman (1984) note that this justified criticism sparked a movement toward deinstitutionalization—moving the handicapped from large institutions to smaller community houses. This movement is still emphasized today for the severely and profoundly retarded.

Heward and Orlansky (1984) comment that "Fortunately, no new large state institutions for the retarded are presently on the drawing boards, and a variety of alternative residential placements are coming into reality" (p. 89). These alternatives to large institutions include regional facilities, day care centers, group homes, apartment living, outpatient clinics, foster care, and even adoptive services for the handicapped.

Regardless of the type and quality of the facility, the decision to place a child outside the home is a difficult, agonizing experience for the parents of the handicapped child.

Gross (1980) says this about making such a decision:

> I felt all alone with the questions that were in my head. On the one hand, how could I reject my own flesh and blood? What if Saul didn't get proper care? How would I know if he did not? I had read enough books and seen enough doctors to know that Saul would fare much better at home. How was I ever going to live with such guilt?

> On the other hand, was I prepared to care for a sickly child? Would I be willing to give up my numerous activities and interests for a perpetual toddler? Was it fair to David, or any other children I might have, to bring Saul home? What about my marriage—could it stand the strain? Could I? (p. L14)

Blaska (1984) says this about the difficult decision to institutionalize:

> It became apparent to us that we could no longer meet David's needs at home. If we were going to provide the best possible environment for our son where he could develop to his maximum capacity, it was time for him to leave home.

> Although intellectually the decision was made, the thought of packing his things and knowing he would never live with us again was almost more than I could endure. During the two weeks following our decision, I cried every time I thought of David leaving. Since David did not know yet of our plans and would not understand my tears, I would seek refuge in the locked bathroom. I tried to be strong. (p. 52)

COUNSELING STRATEGIES

Parents of a handicapped child will normally find themselves bombarded with advice and suggestions from friends, relatives, educators, psychologists, and medical doctors. To effectively help these parents, remember that

1. under no circumstances should you pretend to fully understand what the parents are experiencing. You can, of course, be sensitive and empathic toward these parents; however, unless you have personally experienced their situation, be honest with parents. We don't understand because we can't.
2. Within your capabilities, you can and should offer appropriate and meaningful information, comfort, and support to parents of severely and profoundly handicapped children.

A study by Fairfield (1983) suggests that counseling parents of handicapped children challenges the counselor to determine the attitudes, feelings, reactions, and concerns of the parents to maximize parental coping. Fairfield's summary of her study should be noted:

> In order to facilitate the family's adjustment to having a child with a genetic disease, the counselor needs to be able to understand clearly the true feelings of parents regarding their handicapped child. Pinpointing parental concerns permits the counselor to predict future difficulties for individual families and makes it possible to intervene appropriately and to prevent such problems from occurring. The present study suggests that soliciting and interpreting early recollections from the parents of a genetically disabled child can aid the counselor in a clinical setting to:
>
> 1. Distinguish between apparent coping and real coping.
> 2. Determine the most critical concern of the parents.
> 3. Uncover feelings that lie beneath a parent's denial of the child's condition.
> 4. Reveal hidden guilt of a parent.
> 5. Predict parental overprotectiveness of a child.

It is a challenge to the counselor to determine parental attitudes, feelings, reactions and concerns.

6. Clarify parental expectations and fears regarding the hereditability of the child's condition.

7. Encourage positive parental coping. (pp. 411, 415)

Seligman and Seligman (1980) stress the value of parental attitudes and feelings and offer the following practical suggestions:

> When considering a particular family situation, often the most useful vantage point is that of the parent. It would be extremely beneficial if professionals would value the parents' perspective about a particular child and family. It is necessary for the professional to view parental perceptions as adding to the information they already have, instead of considering them contradictory. Professionals who base their evaluations on the information received from other professionals, their own observations, the child, and the parents are in the strongest position to be helpful. (p. S13)

In a discussion of parents and families of persons with severe mental retardation, Fredericks (1985) comments:

☐ One of the major factors that seems to influence initial parental reactions to a child with severe mental retardation is the manner in which the information is passed to the parents by the professional who makes the diagnosis. (p. 144)

☐ Parents are involved with professionals throughout the child's life and the parent-professional relationship is always one of reciprocity; sometimes the relationship creates profitable tension and other times critical stress. (p. 148)

☐ Although today most parent-professional interactions are occurring at the preschool and school levels, there is another group of parents for whom professionals need to exhibit a deep sensitivity. Many parents of adults who are severely retarded and who have never been institutionalized are tired, somewhat discouraged, and disappointed. (p. 147)

☐ The need for better communication and better understanding between professional and parent can lessen the long range impact of having a handicapped child on parents and families. A supportive professional environment can lessen stresses and sadnesses which parents carry with them as they strive to help their severely retarded child function more normally in the environment. (p. 147)

COUNSELING INTERVENTION

Trout (1983) stresses the importance of carefully studying families of handicapped children over time "to understand how—or whether—the baby is finally integrated, and how long-term developmental and psychiatric outcome relates to early social and experimenal variables." He adds that

> In the meantime, we surely know enough to turn our educational, pediatric, psychological, and family medical attentions in some helpful directions. We can give parents and siblings clear and concise diagnostic, prognostic, and

etiological information. We can organize contact with a reliably available support system, in the hospital, for every family delivering a baby in trouble. The system could include a perinatal coach, a group of other parents of sick and handicapped babies, or just a family down the street with a similarly diagnosed child. We can offer families time to grieve, and we can support them in that experience largely by the time we offer and by what we do not say. We can understand and tolerate ambivalence without being shocked by it, and setting aside our need to wrap up major issues for families with a trite phrase ("It will be better later." "This is just a test of your strength, and you'll be fine." "Of course you don't hate her—you're just tired.") We can understand the dynamics of parental sabotage of our educational and medical interventions. We may find that our patience with such parental uncooperativeness is increased when we attempt to learn how it has been for the family, and the chances for the success of our work with the baby will be increased thereby. (pp. 346–347)

Opirhory and Peters (1982) believe early counseling helps parents adjust and accept the total situation and gives a positive outlook for future rehabilitation. Trust and confidence are important as well.

The parents have the right to know that their anxiety is normal. They may feel that their baby is still fragile. They may doubt their own competence in adequately caring for their child. With adequate reassurance and teaching from the counselor or other health professionals, the parents will come to trust themselves because of their counselor's confidence in them. The parents must receive continual support and reinforcement from the counselor as well as information regarding possible feelings and concerns that they may experience once their infant is home. In this way, the counselor has provided comprehensive and holistic care to the family of a less than perfect newborn and has facilitated their adjustment to and unconditional acceptance of their infant. (p. 454)

The personal account of Patty McGill Smith (1984),* a parent of a handicapped child, may help you to look at counseling parents on two levels: (1) from the parent viewpoint, particularly noting feelings and attitudes, and (2) from the helper's viewpoint, who may be called on to offer counseling to other parents who need support and understanding.

If you have recently learned that your child is developmentally delayed or has a handicapping condition, which either is or is not completely defined, this message may be for you. It is written from the personal perspective of a parent who has shared this experience and all that goes with it.

When parents learn about any difficulty or problem in their child's development, this information comes as a tremendous blow. The day my child was diagnosed as having a handicap, I was devastated—and so confused that I recall little else about those first days other than the heartbreak.

---

*Adapted from Patty McGill Smith, "You are not alone: For parents when they learn that their child has a handicap," March, 1984, *National Information Center for Handicapped Children and Youth*.

Many things can be done to help a parent through this period of trauma. That is what this paper is all about. In order to talk about some of the good things that can happen to alleviate the anxiety, let us first take a look at some of the common reactions that occur.

On learning that their child may have a handicap, most parents react in ways that have been shared by all parents before them who have also been faced with this disappointment and with this enormous challenge:

1. Denial
   "This cannot be happening to me, to my child, to our family."
2. Anger
   May be directed toward the medical personnel who were involved in providing the information about the child's problem. Early on, it seems that the anger is so intense that it touches almost anyone.
3. Feelings of grief and inexplicable loss
4. Fear
   People often fear the unknown more than they fear the known. Having the complete diagnosis and future prospects can be easier than uncertainty. Parents fear that the child's condition will be the very worst that it possibly could be. There is also fear of society's rejection, fears about how brothers and sisters will be affected, questions as to whether there will be any more brothers and sisters in this family, and concerns about whether the husband or wife will love this child. These fears can almost immobilize some parents.
5. Guilt
   Guilt and concern about whether the parents themselves have caused the problem: "Did I do something to cause this? Am I being punished for having done this? Did I take care of myself when I was pregnant? Did my wife take good care of herself when she was pregnant?" Much self-reproach and remorse can stem from questioning the causes of the handicap.
6. Confusion
   As a result of not fully understanding what is happening and what will happen, confusion reveals itself in sleeplessness, inability to make decisions, and mental overload. In the midst of such a trauma, information can seem garbled and distorted. You want to find out what it is all about, yet it seems that you cannot make sense of all the information you are receiving.
7. Powerlessness
   You cannot change the fact that your child is handicapped, yet parents want to feel competent and capable of handling their own life situations. It is extremely hard to be forced to rely on the judgments, opinions, and recommendations of others.
8. Disappointment
   That a child is not perfect poses a threat to many parents' egos and a challenge to their value system.
9. Rejection
   Rejection can be directed toward the child or toward the medical

personnel or toward other family members. One of the more serious forms of rejection, and not that uncommon, is a "death wish" for the child—a feeling that many parents report at their deepest points of depression.

Not all parents go through every one of these stages, but it is important for parents to identify with all of the potentially troublesome feelings that can arise so that they will know that *they are not alone.* There are many constructive actions that you can take immediately, and there are many sources of help, communication, and reassurance.

Seek the assistance of another parent

My first recommendation is to try to find another parent of a handicapped child, preferably one who has chosen to be a parent helper, and seek his or her assistance. The National Information Center for Handicapped Children and Youth has listings of parent groups that will reach out and help you.

Talk with your mate

Over the years, I have discovered that many parents don't communicate their feelings regarding the problems their children have. One spouse is often concerned about not being a source of strength for the other mate. The more couples can communicate at difficult times like these, the greater their collective strength.

Rely on positive sources in your life

One positive source of strength and wisdom might be your minister, priest, or rabbi. Another might be a good friend or a counselor. Go to those who have been a strength before in your life. Find the new sources that you need now.

Take one day at a time

Fears of the future can immobilize one. Living with the reality of the day which is at hand is made more manageable if we throw out the "what if's" and "what then's" of the future. Good things continue to happen each day. Take time to "smell the roses."

Learn the terminology

When you are introduced to new terminology, you should not be hesitant to ask what it means. Whenever someone uses a word that you don't understand, stop the conversation for a minute and ask the person to explain the meaning.

Seek information

Some parents seek virtually "tons" of information; others are not so persistent. The important thing is that you request *accurate* information. You should not be afraid to ask questions, because asking questions will be your first step in beginning to understand more about your child.

Do not be intimidated

Many parents feel inadequate in the presence of people from the medical or educational professions because of their credentials. Do not be intimidated by the educational backgrounds of these and other personnel who may be involved in treating or helping your child. You do not have to apologize for wanting to know what is occurring. Remember, this is your child, and the situation has a profound effect on your life and on your child's future.

Do not be afraid to show emotion

So many parents, especially dads, repress their emotions because they believe it to be a sign of weakness to let people know how badly they are feeling. The strongest fathers of handicapped children whom I know are not afraid to show their emotions.

Learn to deal with bitterness and anger

Ultimately, bitterness and anger will hurt you a great deal more than they will affect those toward whom the anger is directed. It is very valuable to be able to recognize your anger and then let go of it. Life is better when you are feeling positive. You will be better equipped to meet these new challenges when bitter feelings are no longer draining your energies and initiative.

Adopt a grateful attitude

It is hard to remain angry when one is grateful. Sometimes, when everything seems to be going wrong, it is difficult to find a cause for gratitude. However, in the scheme of things, if you look around and count your blessings, perhaps positive feelings can overtake the more negative ones.

Maintain a positive outlook

A positive attitude will be one of your genuinely valuable tools for dealing with problems. There is truly always a positive side to whatever is occurring. For example, when my child was found to be handicapped, one of the other things pointed out to me was that she was (and still is) a very healthy child.

Keep in touch with reality

To stay in touch with reality is to accept life the way it is. To stay in touch with reality is also to recognize that there are some things that we can change and other things that we cannot change.

Remember that time is on your side

Time heals many wounds. This does not mean that living with and raising a child who has problems will be easy, but it is fair to say that, as time passes, a great deal can be done to alleviate the problem.

Find programs for your child

Even for those living in isolated areas of our country, assistance is available to help you with whatever problems you are having. While finding programs for your handicapped child, keep in mind that programs are also available for the rest of your family, too.

Take care of yourself

In times of stress, each person reacts in his or her own way. A few universal recommendations may help: get sufficient rest; eat as well as you can; take time for yourself; reach out to others for emotional support.

Avoid pity

Self-pity, the experience of pity from others, or pity for your child are actually disabling. Pity is not what is needed. Empathy, which is the ability to feel *with* another person, is the attitude to be encouraged.

Avoid judgments

During this period, parents may become judgmental about the way people are reacting toward them or toward their child. Others may sometimes react inappropriately, but you need not use too much energy in being concerned over those who are not able to respond in ways that you might prefer.

Keep daily routines as normal as possible

My mother once told me, "When a problem arises and you don't know what to do, then do whatever it was that you were going to do anyway." Practicing this habit seems to produce some normalcy and consistency when life becomes hectic.

Remember that this is your child

This person is your child, first and foremost. Granted, your child's development may be different from that of other children, but this does not make your child less valuable, less human, less important, or less in need of your love and parenting. Love and enjoy your child. The child comes first; the handicapping condition is second. If you can relax and take the positive steps just outlined, one at a time, you will do the best you can, your child will benefit, and you can look forward to the future with hope.

Recognize that you are not alone

The feeling of isolation at the time of diagnosis is almost a universal feeling among parents. You can diminish these feelings by recognizing that they have been experienced by many, many others, that understanding and constructive help are available to you and your child, and that you are not alone.

CHAPTER SUMMARY

This chapter has provided a basis and rationale for counselors as they work with parents of severely and profoundly handicapped children. The emotional reactions to the diagnosis of a handicapped child form the foundation of this chapter. You should remember that it does little good (and possibly irreparable harm) to focus on the cause of the handicap or to allow one member of the family to place blame on another family member.

A handicapped child typically places parents and the family under stress at different points in their lives. The diagnosis is usually the first stressful occasion. Parents often pass through a typical sequence of reactions such as shock, denial, sadness, fear, anger, and finally adaptation or the restoration of equilibrium. Helpers should not conclude that all parents go through the same stages. These are emotions and reactions that parents may or may not experience in sequential order or at all. Parental reactions and stages are complex interactions among and between family members that find expression in feelings, attitudes, and beliefs.

Caring and knowledgeable professionals can help parents meet the basic and fundamental needs of providing and caring for their handicapped child. Present a description of what can be done for their child immediately, what services are available now, and what may be needed in the future. You are not limited to providing practical information—providing parents with psychological support and understanding is just as vital. To accomplish this task, recognize the parents as individuals with their own set of needs and feelings. Respect parents' feelings, offer support and psychological comfort, and be flexible in that each situation is unique.

ACTIVITIES, EXERCISES, AND IDEAS FOR REFLECTION AND DISCUSSION

1. As a helper, how might you respond to the following situations assuming that a child has been diagnosed as severely or profoundly retarded or handicapped? What dominant themes or ideas would likely be stressed?
   a. The parents blame themselves for their child's condition.
   b. The parents believe God is responsible for their child's condition.
   c. The parents feel that they have "let others down," especially the immediate family and significant others.
   d. The parents dwell on and continue to search for the cause of their child's condition.
   e. As a form of denial, the parents continue to search for a cure for their child. (This is often referred to as *shopping behavior.*)
   f. The parents are reluctant (or afraid) to discuss their feelings with you or any other helper.
   g. The parents convey to you that they feel helpless and that their situation looks hopeless.
   h. The parents say to you, "You just don't know what we're going through, you haven't been there!"
   i. The parents (who live in a very small community) say that they have read about "support systems" that can offer understanding and information from other sources.
   j. The parents express doubts about their ability to lead normal, productive, and rewarding lives.
2. Of the following responses, choose *one* that would help the most to bring about parental acceptance of their severely handicapped child's behavior?
   a. "No one is perfect."
   b. "There is room for everyone in a democracy."
   c. "We all have a contribution to make to society."
   d. "Everyone has weaknesses."
   e. "If we all work together, the child will have a successful life."
   f. None of the above. If so, why?

g. Your response _____

_____

3. When working with parents of severely and profoundly handicapped children, is it important for professionals to be able to recognize individual differences among families and to be flexible in helping mothers, fathers, and siblings? Why or why not?

REFERENCES

Attwell, A. A., & Clabby, D. A. (1971). *The retarded child: Answers to questions parents ask.* Los Angeles: Western Psychological Services.

Batshaw, M. L., & Perret, Y. M. (1981). *Children with handicaps: A medical primer.* Baltimore: Paul H. Brookes.

Beeson, D., & Douglas, R. (1983). Prenatal diagnosis of fetal disorders. *Birth: Issues in Prenatal Care and Education, 10*(4), 227–232.

Begley, S. (March 5, 1984). The genetic counselors. *Newsweek,* p. 69.

Blacher, J. (1984). Sequential stages of parental adjustment to the birth of a child with handicaps. *Mental Retardation, 22*(2), 55–68.

Blake, K. A. (1976). *The mentally retarded: An educational psychology.* Englewood Cliffs, NJ: Prentice-Hall.

Blaska, J. K. (1984). When it's time to go. *Exceptional Parent, 14*(2), 51–53.

Blatt, B., & Kaplan, F. (1966). *Christmas in purgatory: A photographic essay on mental retardation.* Boston: Allyn & Bacon.

Burton, T. A. (1976). *The trainable mentally retarded.* Columbus, OH: Charles E. Merrill.

Cartwright, G. P., Cartwright, C. A., & Ward, M. E. (1981). *Educating special learners.* Belmont, CA: Wadsworth.

Dean, D. (1975). Closer look: A parent information service. *Exceptional Children, 41,* 527–530.

Ehlers, W. H. (1964). The moderately and severely retarded child: Maternal perceptions of retardation and subsequent seeking and using services rendered by a community agency. *American Journal of Mental Deficiency, 68,* 660–667.

Ehlers, W. H., Prothero, J. C., Lagone, J. (1982). *Mental retardation and other developmental disabilities: A programmed instruction* (3rd ed.). Columbus, OH: Charles E. Merrill.

Fairfield, B. (1983). Parents coping with a genetically handicapped child: Use of early recollections. *Exceptional Children, 49*(5), 411–415.

Farber, B. (1968). *Mental retardation: Its social context and social consequences.* Boston: Houghton Mifflin.

Fredericks, B. (1985). Parents/families of persons with severe mental retardation. In D. Bricker & J. Filler (Eds.), *Severe Mental Retardation: From Theory to Practice* (pp. 142–160). Reston, VA: Division on Mental Retardation of the Council for Exceptional Children.

Gearheart, B. R., & Litton, F. W. (1975). *The trainable retarded: A foundations approach.* St. Louis: C. V. Mosby.

Gordon, R. (1977). Special needs of multi-handicapped children under six and their families: One opinion. In E. Sontag (Ed.), *Educational programming for the severely and profoundly handicapped.* Division of Mental Retardation, The Council for Exceptional Children, pp. 61–71.

Gross, C. C. (1980). We chose to place our baby. *Exceptional Parent, 10*(2), L13–L15.

Hallahan, D. P., & Kauffman, J. M. (1982). *Exceptional children: Introduction to special education.* Englewood Cliffs, NJ: Prentice-Hall.

Hardman, M. L., Drew, C. J., & Egan, M. W. (1984). *Human exceptionality: Society, school, and family.* Boston: Allyn & Bacon.

Heward, W. L., & Orlansky, M.D. (1984). *Exceptional children* (2nd ed.). Columbus, OH: Charles E. Merrill.

Hoemann, H. W., & Briga, J. I. (1981). Hearing impairments. In J. M. Kauffman and D. P. Hallahan (Eds.), *Handbook of Special Education* (pp. 222–247). Englewood Cliffs, NJ: Prentice-Hall.

Kneedler, R. D., Hallahan, D. P., & Kauffman, J. M. (1984). *Special education for today.* Englewood Cliffs, NJ: Prentice-Hall.

Lee, F. (October 5, 1984). Doctors, patients: Can we talk? *USA TODAY*, p. 1D.

Lyon, S., & Preis, A. (1983). Working with families of severely handicapped persons. In M. Seligman (Ed.), *The Family With a Handicapped Child: Understanding and Treatment* (pp. 203–222). New York: Grune & Stratton.

McLeod, B. (March, 1985). Real work for real pay. *Psychology Today, 19*(3), 42–50.

Mandell, C. J., & Fiscus, E. (1981). *Understanding exceptional people.* St. Paul: West.

Opirhory, G., & Peters, G. A. (1982). Counseling intervention strategies for families with less than the perfect born. *Personnel and Guidance Journal, 60*(8), 451–455.

Robinson, N. M., & Robinson, H. B. (1976). *The mentally retarded child* (2nd ed.). New York: McGraw-Hill.

Roos, P. (1977). A parent's view of what public education should accomplish. In E. Sontag (Ed.), *Educational programming for the severely and profoundly handicapped* (pp. 72–83). Division of Mental Retardation, The Council for Exceptional Children.

Rosen, L. (1955). Selected aspects in the development of the mother's understanding of her mentally retarded child. *American Journal of Mental Deficiency, 59,* 522.

Ross, A. O. (1984). *The exceptional child in the family.* New York: Grune & Stratton.

Seligman, M., & Seligman, P. A. (1980). The professional's dilemma: Learning to work with parents. *Exceptional Parent, 10*(5), S11–S13.

Smith, P. M. (March, 1984). You are not alone: For parents when they learn that their child has a handicap. *National Information Center for Handicapped Children and Youth.*

Stone, M. M. (1948). Parental attitudes to retardation. *American Journal of Mental Deficiency, 53,* 363.

Telford, C. W., & Sawrey, J. M. (1981). *The exceptional individual* (4th ed.). Englewood Cliffs, NJ: Prentice-Hall.

Trout, M. D. (1983). Birth of a sick or handicapped infant: Impact on the family. *Child Welfare, 62*(4), 337–348.

Voelker, P. H. (1975). Organization, administration, and supervision of special education programs. In W. M. Cruickshank & G. O. Johnson (Eds.) *Education of exceptional children and youth* (pp. 659–691). Englewood Cliffs, NJ: Prentice-Hall.

Welch, O. M. (1981). I know how it feels: A plea for compassionate counseling. *The Exceptional Parent, 11,* S25–S26.

Wofensberger, W. (1967). Counseling parents of the retarded. In A. A. Baumeister (Ed.). *Mental retardation: Appraisal, education, and rehabilitation* (p. 330). Chicago: Aldine.

SELECTED REFERENCES FOR FURTHER READING AND STUDY

Adix, R., Adix, M., & Rosenthal, D. (1984). A conversation with parents of a handicapped child. *Remedial and Special Education (RASE), 5*(5), 37–42.

Cone, J. D., Delawyer, D. D., & Wolfe, V. V. (1985). Assessing parent participation: The parent/family involvement index. *Exceptional Children, 51*(5), 417–424.

Conyne, R. K. (1983). Two critical issues in primary prevention: What it is and how to do it. *Personnel and Guidance Journal, 61*(6), 331–340.

Crnic, K. A., Fredrich, W. N., & Greenberg, M. T. (1983). Adaptation of families with mentally retarded children: A model of stress, coping, and family ecology. *American Journal of Mental Deficiency, 88*(2), 125–138.

Duff, R. (1981). Counseling families and deciding care of severely defective children: A way of coping with medical Vietnam. *Pediatrics, 67,* 315–320.

Fost, N. (1981). Counseling families who have a child with a severe congenital abnormality. *Pediatrics, 67,* 321–324.

Fowle, C. M. (1968). The effect of the severely mentally retarded child on his family. *American Journal of Mental Deficiency, 73,* 468–473.

German, M. L., & Maisto, A. A. (1982). The relationship of a perceived family support system to the institutional placement of mentally retarded children. *Education and Training of the Mentally Retarded, 17,* 17–23.

Greenberg, M. T. (1983). Family stress and child competence: The effects of early intervention for families with deaf infants. *American Annals of the Deaf, 128*(3), 407–417.

Heikkinen, C. A. (1979). Counseling for personal loss. *Personnel and Guidance Journal, 58,* 46–49.

Meyen, E. L. (Ed.). (1984). *Mental retardation: Topics of today—Issues of tomorrow.* Reston, VA: The Division on Mental Retardation of the Council for Exceptional Children.

Sandler, A., Coren, A., & Thurman, S. K. (1983). A training program for parents of handicapped preschool children: Effects upon mother, father and child. *Exceptional Children, 49*(4), 355–358.

Switzky, H. M., Haywood, H. C. & Rotatori, A. F. (1982). Who are the severely and profoundly mentally retarded? *Education and Training of the Mentally Retarded, 17*(4), 268–272.

Tawney, J. W., & Smith, J. (1981). An analysis of the forum: Issues in education of the severely and profoundly retarded. *Exceptional Children, 48*, 5–18.

Tausig, M. (1985). Factors in family decision-making about placement for developmentally disabled individuals. *American Journal of Mental Deficiency, 89*(4), 352–361.

Turnbull, A. P., & Turnbull, H. R. (1982). Parent involvement in the education of handicapped children: A critique. *Mental Retardation, 20*, 115–122.

Wrenn, C. G. (1979). Caring for others when they need you most. *Humanist Educator, 18*, 98–106.

PART THREE

Our final chapter, Chapter Ten, focuses on viable and meaningful ways that teachers, counselors, administrators, and other helpers can assist parents whose children are uniquely gifted and talented. The gifted child is exceptional because he or she differs from the norm in significant ways, including, but not limited to, higher mental abilities. It would be a serious oversight to not include fundamental principals and procedures for helping parents of gifted children. In fact, the gifted child can be a source of problems and frustrations, especially when parents do not understand giftedness.

Because of their gifts and potential for positive growth and development, the gifted are unique among the exceptional child population. In spite of obstacles, the gifted often gain some self-satisfying measure of success in many of their tasks and endeavors. Because they often have an ability to endure and survive, educators and parents too frequently ignore gifted children and their pleas for understanding and support. There is no justification for the failure of anyone to recognize, respect, encourage, and facilitate the many skills and abilities of our gifted children and youth. Failure to help gifted children reach their full potential is a personal and societal tragedy. Chapter Ten has two primary objectives: (1) to help you gain additional insight into the nature and characteristics of the gifted child and to recognize their contributions, and (2) to identify and discuss meaningful ways that professionals can assist and counsel parents as they seek to more fully understand and nurture their child's giftedness.

10 Counseling Parents of Gifted, Talented, and Creative Children

After mastering the material in this chapter, you should be able to

1. Define and explain the following terms and concepts:

Giftedness	Talented
Marland definition of giftedness	Creative
Renzulli definition of giftedness	Divergent
Clark definition of giftedness	thinking

2. Explain why it is important to establish helping relationships with parents of gifted, talented, and creative children.

3. Compare and contrast definitions of giftedness.

4. Understand the intellectual characteristics of the gifted.

5. Describe characteristics of the talented and creative child.

6. Identify and describe appropriate techniques or strategies used in counseling parents of intellectually gifted children.

America's position in the world may have been reasonably secure with only a few exceptionally well-trained men and women. It is no longer.

—*A Nation at Risk*

Creative minds, the world's greatest source of social change and human welfare, are considered to be the rarest and most valuable of human characteristics.

—Gertrude Hildreth

---

*S*chool-related programs and services for the gifted are now commonplace throughout the United States, but the vital role of parental support for the gifted has received scant attention. A popular—though mistaken—notion is that "the cream will rise to the top," i.e. nothing out of the ordinary needs to be done to develop a child's gifts and talents. Marland (1972) said that we are being stripped of the comfortable notion that a bright mind will make its own way; intellectual and creative talent *cannot* survive educational neglect and apathy. A large number of gifted children do not make it on their own. Bridges (1979) notes this is chiefly because of a lack of adult interest, support, and stimulation.

Zorman (1983) presents evidence that implies the importance of the parents' role in helping gifted children reach their emotional and intellectual potential. Parents may not know how to handle their gifted child's needs, however. Zorman questions whether parents can perform their role effectively on their own, or whether they need special guidance.

Colangelo and Zaffrann (1979) believe that counselors can effectively encourage parent involvement, and conclude by saying that the question is not *if* parents should be involved in gifted and talented programs, but rather *to what degree.*

WHY COUNSEL PARENTS OF GIFTED CHILDREN?

The case for building and maintaining effective helping relationships with parents of the gifted is both strong and compelling. According to Swaby (1983),

> the education of gifted children is receiving a great deal of national attention and interest. Not only are local school systems making significant strides in providing appropriate programs for gifted children, but many parents are also becoming sensitive to the concept of giftedness and are anxious to find out whether or not their children fit into the category of the gifted. (p. 141)

Gifted children are a precious natural resource for a society desperately in need of creativity and inventiveness.

Aside from the parent's own expressed interest, helping parents appreciate and understand their child's giftedness is important for two other reasons: (1) the possible loss to society, and (2) the possible loss and damage to the individual child when denied the opportunity to use gifts and talents toward individual development and self-fulfillment. The loss to society involves not only budding Einsteins and Madam Curies, but youngsters with an extraordinary capacity for leadership, creative and productive thinking, and excellence in the visual and performing arts. Because of their unusual talents and intellectual ability, these children and youth will continue to shape and mold our future. The gifted are a precious natural resource—educators and parents simply cannot afford to overlook the potential of a gifted mind in a society that desperately needs creativity and inventiveness.

Besides the loss to society, possibly tragic consequences may occur when the gifted child is denied the guidance, support, and understanding so vital in developing and using individual gifts and talents. Children's talents may be squandered if they are not constantly and appropriately challenged to make constructive use of these gifts and talents. Blackhurst and Berdine (1981) observe that if we believe education should help all students develop to their full potential, we have yet another reason to provide special programs for the gifted. It would be unfair to deny these children the opportunity to become all they are capable of being. The strength and beauty of giftedness lies in helping these children and youth find meaning and purpose in their lives. Seventeen-year-old Paul R. Wetzel wrote a poem about his goals and dreams:

The Future and My Contribution

The future spreads before me over the horizon,
Waiting to be explored and tested in all directions,
   The sky spreads before a young bird.

I am so optimistic that I may be unrealistic
Holding down the surging feeling of idealism,
   Stopping
      just short of
becoming quixotic.

My contribution of the future will be
the meeting of the challenge.
I am willing to contribute my talents, and purpose
To this certain destiny of man.

My contribution may be small, unknown;
Fleeting in the immensity of the world.
It may be commendable; benefiting the community.
It may be eminent; valuable to the entire nation.
It may be profound.

  Whatever my contribution is,
  If the future is better for at least one person
  With the simpleness of smile
  Or the brilliance of ideal.

  Then my challenge is met,
  My goal achieved,
My life fulfilled.

Paul R. Wetzel
Age 17
Gull Lake High School
Richland, Michigan

WHY INVOLVE AND COMMUNICATE WITH PARENTS?

Karnes (1976) lists five practical reasons why educators should communicate with and build effective working relationships with parents of gifted and talented youth.

1. The importance of early identification of the talented and gifted child is stressed throughout the literature. The parent with knowledge about the initial indicators of rapid development is in a strategic position to observe behavior suggestive of exceptional talents and gifts.
2. The parent is in a better position than anyone else to provide the rich, exciting, and stimulating environment in which the very young thrive prior to reaching school age.
3. Parents who become knowledgeable about the distinguishing characteristics and growth patterns of the talented and gifted can become excellent resource people when actively involved in educational programs for children who possess exceptionally high aptitudes.
4. Knowledgeable parents of the talented and gifted can become very influential leaders in promoting legislative and financial support for improved educational opportunities for their children.
5. Many parents of talented and gifted children pursue a wide range of interesting careers and are thus in a position to demonstrate career models and assist in increasing alternatives about which children learn as they develop. (p. 6)

Finally, helpers should reach out and communicate with these parents simply because they know more about their child than anyone else and will teach them longer than anyone else. As soon as a child is identified as gifted, counseling should be made available in the school or at home. From their experience in working with parents of gifted children, Colangelo and Dettmann (1983) report that these parents are usually highly motivated to contribute to the education of their children. Educators should capitalize on this motivation. Congdon (1979) stresses the importance of parental involvement by stating that

> when we discuss gifted or talented children we tend to concentrate on the subject of how to identify them, which is important, and how to provide for their formal education, which is also important. But in the past, too little stress has been given to the subject of advising, influencing, and supporting the parents of these children. Ultimately, this may well be the crucial factor in their future happiness and success. (pp. 348–349)

WHAT CONSTITUTES GIFTEDNESS?

It is somewhat difficult to pinpoint an exact defintion of giftedness. Carter and Kontos (1982) point out this problem by stating that

> many in the field of gifted education treat the concept of giftedness as something tangible, a trait that is easily observed. On the contrary, giftedness is a highly abstract concept, or construct, created by scholars to summarize the common characteristics of a select group of people. Unfortunately, there is wide disagreement over the set of characteristics that define the construct of giftedness. Yet individuals use the same term to refer to a different set of characteristics. This practice has led to much confusion about the nature and identification of giftedness. (p. 17)

In spite of the lack of agreement about what constitutes giftedness, to assist parents you need to know as much as possible about the nature and general characteristics of giftedness. Developing a definition of giftedness is important; it usually determines who will be admitted to programs and what educational approaches will be used. As Kauffman and Hallahan (1981) observe, the definition of the term *gifted* in the United States has evolved from a focus on intellectual ability (measured by intelligence tests) to a focus on not only general intellectual abilities, but specific abilities and talents as well. More recent definitions of giftedness have included a much broader range of talents and abilities. In this chapter, we will discuss three representative definitions of giftedness.

The Marland or "Federal" Definition

One way to illustrate giftedness is by examining a significant piece of federal legislation, Public Law 91–230 (1970), often called the "Marland Report" after S. P. Marland, the U.S. Commissioner of Education at that time. PL 91–230 directed a comprehensive study to determine if special programs are necessary to meet the needs of gifted and talented children. Among other directives, PL 91–230 stated that the Commissioner of Education shall define "gifted and talented" for purposes of Federal education programs. The advisory panel of gifted education authorities arrived at a definition that illustrates the expanding concept of giftedness. The definition established by the advisory panel reads as follows:

> Gifted and talented children are those identified by professionally qualified persons who by virtue of outstanding abilities, are capable of high performance. These are children who require differentiated education programs and/or services beyond those normally provided by the regular school program in order to realize their contribution to self and society. (Marland, p. 2)

Children capable of high performance include those with demonstrated achievement and/or potential ability in any or all of the following areas:

1. General intellectual ability
2. Specific academic aptitude
3. Creative or productive thinking
4. Leadership ability
5. Visual and performing arts
6. Psychomotor ability. (Marland, p. 2)

Note that the 1970 report of the U.S. Commissioner of Education states that a conservative estimate of gifted and talented elementary and secondary school children ranges between 1.5 and 2.5 million children out of 51.6 million. The gifted, therefore, constitute a sizeable portion of our exceptional child population.

The impact of this report is significant—a number of states and local school systems have adopted either this definition or a very similar one as the basis for identification, placement, and educational programming (Karnes and Collins, 1977).

The most recent definition used in federal law was the result of the Gifted and Talented Children's Act of 1978 (PL 95–561, Section 902) that defined the gifted as follows:

> Gifted and talented children means children and wherever applicable, youth, who are identified at the preschool, elementary, or secondary level as possessing demonstrated or potential abilities that give evidence of high performance capabilities in areas such as intellectual, creative, specific academic, or leadership ability, or in the performing and visual arts, and who by reason thereof, require services or activities not ordinarily provided by the school.

Kauffman and Hallahan (1981) mention that this 1978 federal legislation modified the definition slightly by eliminating psychomotor ability as an area of talent, clearly specifying the need for early identification, and emphasizing the need for differential programming.

The Renzulli Definition

Another definition of giftedness has been developed by Joseph S. Renzulli. Because of some major problems he saw with the U.S. Office of Education definition, Renzulli (1978) researched creative/productive people and found that persons who have achieved recognition because of their unique accomplishments and creative contributions possess a relatively well-defined set of three interlocking traits. These traits are above average, though not necessarily superior, general ability; task commitment; and creativity. Renzulli emphasizes that each trait is of equal weight; it is the interaction among the three clusters or traits that is the necessary ingredient for creative/productive accomplishment. Renzulli concluded his reexamination of giftedness by stating his own definition:

> Giftedness consists of an interaction among three basic clusters of human traits—these clusters being above average general abilities, high levels of task commitment, and high levels of creativity. Gifted and talented children are those possessing or capable of developing this composite set of traits and applying them to any potentially valuable area of human performance. Children who manifest or are capable of developing an interaction among the three clusters require a wide variety of educational opportunities and services that are not ordinarily provided through regular instructional programs. (p. 261)

The Clark Definition

Citing new research in brain/mind function, Clark (1983) suggests a different definition for giftedness. Intelligence can no longer be confined to cognitive function, but must include all the functions of the brain and their efficient and integrated use. Clark offers the following definition of giftedness:

> Giftedness is a biologically rooted concept, a label for a high level of intelligence that results from the advanced and accelerated integration of functions within the brain, including physical sensing, emotions, cognition, and intuition. Such advanced and accelerated function may be expressed through abilities such as those involved in cognition, creativity, academic aptitude, leadership, or the visual and performing arts. Therefore, with this definition of intelligence, gifted individuals are those who are performing, or who show promise of performing, at high levels of intelligence. Because of such advanced or accelerated development, these individuals require services or activities not ordinarily provided by the schools in order to develop their capability more fully. (p. 6)

Examining the Marland, Renzulli, and Clark definitions of giftedness illustrates the complexity of the problem. Each definition (and any other broad definition) covers a wide range of abilities and traits; however, helpers who counsel parents of the gifted need an in-depth understanding of all these definitions.

INTELLECTUAL (COGNITIVE) CHARACTERISTICS OF THE GIFTED

Lists of characteristics of gifted children abound in the literature. One of the most useful and recent listings was developed by Clark (1983). These cognitive characteristics consist of the following:

☐ Extraordinary quantity of information: unusual retentiveness
☐ Advanced comprehension
☐ Unusually varied interests and curiosity
☐ High level of language development
☐ High level of verbal ability
☐ Unusual capacity for processing information
☐ Accelerated pace of thought processes
☐ Flexible thought processes
☐ Comprehensive synthesis
☐ Early ability to delay closure
☐ Heightened capacity for seeing unusual and diverse relationships
☐ Ability to generate original ideas and solutions
☐ Early differential patterns for thought processing (e.g., thinking in alternatives, abstract terms, sensing consequences, making generalizations)
☐ Early ability to use and form conceptual frameworks
☐ An evaluative approach to themselves and others
☐ Persistent goal-directed behavior (p. 195)

After analyzing the learning style preferences of the gifted, Griggs (1984) suggests six characteristics associated with gifted and talented students: independent (self-learners), internally controlled, persistent, perceptually strong, nonconforming, and highly motivated. A knowledge of general characteristics can be helpful to those who counsel the gifted because, as Griggs states, "the counselor's role as a consultant to teachers and parents can support the student's independence and help adults deal effectively with patterns of self-reliance" (p. 429).

THE TALENTED AND CREATIVE CHILD

To provide a complete discussion of giftedness, we should also mention those children who are talented and creative. The term *talented* is often used to denote a special ability or aptitude in areas such as art, music, drama, or athletics. Blackhurst and Berdine (1981) stress the distinction between *giftedness* and *talent* by saying that although may talented children have high general intelligence, others show only average intellectual or creative ability. Blackhurst and Berdine also suggest that children with special talent in one area may need extra guidance to stimulate interest in other subjects and areas.

HELPING PARENTS TO RECOGNIZE AND ENCOURAGE THE DEVELOPMENT OF TALENT AND CREATIVITY

Havinghurst (1957) suggests that only about half of the most able 20 percent of gifted children actually develop their abilities to a point where they make an important contribution to society. Why doesn't the other half develop their talents more fully? Perhaps it is because those with under-developed talent are persons whose environments have been least favorable to producing high-level ability. Children from low-status families often fail to develop their abilities because of a lack of opportunity and stimulation. Of course, this may also hold true for families from upper socioeconomic levels. The quality of life at home, the nature of parent guidance and controls, as well as life in the neighborhood all influence the gifted child's intellectual, social, and emotional development. The parents set the example for the young child's growth and responsibilities more than any other influence. You as a counselor must offer parents concrete suggestions to encourage an optimum home environment. Many traditional failings of the gifted child are due largely to poor guidance and management; this can be counteracted by taking certain precautions in home training. In many instances, parents are overprotective or overanxious, and the counselor must help them overcome their undue concern so that the child can gain more confidence. The child who has understanding and supportive parents working with teachers is more likely to reach goals and make a contribution to self and society.

Creativity, in contrast to talent, has been called "the highest expression of giftedness" and is a very special condition, attitude, or state of being that is difficult to define (Clark, 1983). Citing the earlier works of J. P. Guilford, Torrance (1965) states that creative thinking refers to such abilities as fluency (large number of ideas), flexibility (variety of different approaches or categories of ideas), originality (unusual, off-the-beaten-track ideas), elaboration (well-developed and detailed ideas), sensitivity to defects and problems, and redefinition (perceiving in a way different from the usual, established, or intended way or use.) Parke (1985) comments that "Research studies indicate that factors commonly associated with creativity, such as fluency, flexibility, originality, and elaboration, can be encouraged, contrary to the once popular belief that either you have it or you don't. Over the past thirty years, studies have consistently shown that training has a measurable positive effect on creative production" (p. 378).

Torrance (1970) defines creativity in a broader sense by referring to it as becoming sensitive to or aware of problems, deficiencies, gaps in knowledge, missing elements, and disharmonies; bringing existing information together in new relationships, defining the difficulty of identifying the missing elements, searching for solutions, making guesses, or formulating hypotheses about the problems or deficiencies; testing and retesting them; and finally, communicating the results.

Divergent thinking has been called the keystone to creativity. It may be described as using knowledge in new ways to produce new solutions. Creative thinking requires the individual to supply new formulations or new hypotheses and imagine the possible consequences of untried solutions. By contrast, convergent thinking is recalling the already learned information and fitting it to new situations in a more or less mechanical way. Kirk and Gallagher (1983) suggest that two high-level thinking processes, divergent production and evaluation, are important for educators of the gifted because they are not often measured in standard intelligence tests. Table 3.1 illustrates how different thinking processes can be encouraged by different types of questions asked in a discussion of "Hamlet."

TABLE 3.1 *Questions to encourage different types of thinking processes*

Operation	Example
Memory	Whom did Hamlet kill by mistake?
Convergent thinking	Explain why Hamlet rejected Ophelia.
Divergent thinking	Name some other ways Hamlet might have accomplished his goals.
Evaluative thinking	Was Hamlet justified in killing his uncle?

SOURCE: From *Teaching the gifted child,* 2nd ed. (p. 238) by J. Gallagher, 1975, Boston: Allyn & Bacon.

Using his research on the background and traits of high and low achievers, Williams (1982) stresses that creativity development at home and in school depends on attempts made in both places to enhance such human potential. Williams offers some specific suggestions for parents and teachers to help develop more highly functioning, creative individuals for later life:

1. Both home and school should be responsive and expressive places for children. Stretch and expand places where their becoming more creative has a chance to burst forth.
2. The home and school both should encourage self-resourcefulness. Demand and expect children to do things, to produce things on their own.
3. Parents and teachers alike should recognize, respect, and give emotional support to children for questions, and unusual thinking that displays their attitudes and feelings. Listen very carefully to children's ideas and thoughts.
4. Adults rearing children at home and teachers guiding children in school must expect and allow for comfortable regression in growth patterns. Teach them to accept mistakes, but capitalize upon them; to laugh at themselves, turning humor into serious productions.
5. Both teachers and parents should provide balance between interpersonal and intrapersonal experiences for children. There must be times when they should join others.
6. Well-defined standards of discipline and conduct must persist both at home and in school. There should be only a few rules both at home and in school, but those that exist must be well-defined, understood, and seldom infringed upon.
7. Home as well as school must recognize differences between ability and performance. There should not be criticism nor negative feedback which deflates or discourages a child regardless of his or her ability.
8. Parents and teachers must trust children. Making decisions and having choices to do what is reasonable in a responsible way must be given to all children. Trust can best be built by noticing positive ways children operate in spite of all the obstacles they face. (pp. 2–6)

ISSUES AND CONCERNS IN COUNSELING PARENTS OF INTELLECTUALLY GIFTED CHILDREN

So far we have dealt almost exclusively with assisting parents of talented and creative children, but we should also explore some of the significant issues in counseling parents of the intellectually gifted child. From this point on in the discussion, *the gifted* will refer to those children and youth with achievement or potential in general intellectual ability.

Telford and Sawrey (1972) discuss some of the issues that parents of gifted children may face. They state:

> The parents of the gifted need help in understanding the extent and nature of their child's superiority. They often require assistance in accepting the fact of the child's status without excessive anxiety or pride. They need to be aware

of the possibilities and dangers of exploiting the child's cleverness on the one hand, and of neglecting or rejecting him on the other. Rejection and favoritism, either of the gifted child or of his less gifted siblings, are always possibilities. Sometimes the superior child is favored because he can be exploited for parental glory, and his less favored siblings are neglected; less often, he may be neglected because his parents believe that he can look out for himself and therefore needs less than the others. Sometimes neglect of the superior child results from parental attempts to somehow compensate the more normal siblings for their lack of giftedness. (p. 120)

Congdon (1979) has identified several issues that he feels are important in helping parents of gifted children. These are summarized in Table 10.2.

TABLE 10.2 *Summary of Congdon's principles of helping parents of gifted children*

Issue/Concern	Parents Role and Comment
Early identification	The parents' role is crucial; early formative years will lay the foundations for future development.
Discourage over-reaction	Above all, parents should refrain from changing their whole attitude toward the child.
Reassurance	Parents of a gifted child often need reassurance. They may be convinced that they themselves are inferior to the child and will be unable to cope.
Responsibility to the child	Parents need to realize their responsibility towards their child. A happy and settled home environment means more to the gifted child than any other single factor.
Respect for the child	Respect is essential for every child, but it is particularly important when trying to understand the gifted.
Avoiding over-concentration on the gifted child	Parents should avoid over-concentrating on their gifted child to the exclusion of siblings. Make an equal number of comments about the non-gifted child.
Avoid pressuring the gifted child	The best preparation for adulthood is to have lived fully as a child. There are times when children want to play and act like other children and they should be allowed to do so.
Time and space for the gifted child	There is no better investment than to put time aside for the gifted child, but it

(TABLE 10.2,   continued)

Issue/Concern	Parents Role and Comment
Time and space for the gifted child	should be made clear that there are periods during the day when patience is required of the child.
Language development	It is important that parents talk *with* rather than *to* the child. Encourage the child's curiosity and respond to questions.
Variability within the group	Although gifted children as a group have many common characteristics, parents should be aware of the high degree of variability they can exhibit.
Parental interest in school	It is essential that parents take an interest in the child's school whether or not the child is gifted.
Sexual stereotyping	The most tragic loss in an educational system may be that of gifted girls.

Parents have tremendous influence regarding their gifted child's social, emotional, and intellectual development. It is important that parents understand the nature, needs, and characteristics of their gifted children to develop their child's self-concept and to open communication within the family. Coleman (1982) notes that parenting a gifted child is similar to parenting a child of average intelligence, but added stress appears when trying to accept a creative child's unique value system, to cope with school discipline problems arising from the child's boredom, and to let the child decide on and map his or her own future. It is within these problem areas that you can help parents of the gifted the most.

Colangelo and Dettmann (1983) have summarized a review of parents and families of gifted children as follows:

1. There is a great need to do more experimental research and to replicate studies concerning parent and gifted child interaction.
2. Parents can play an important role in the identification and educational development of their gifted children.
3. Parents, in general, are confused about their own gifted children. This confusion results from being unprepared to raise an "exceptional" child and from having insufficient knowledge on the nature of giftedness and creativity.
4. Parents are uncertain about their role with the schools. It seems the most promising practices occurred when parents became more active partners with the school.
5. Characteristics of achievement and creativity seem to be related to specific characteristics of parents and the home environment.

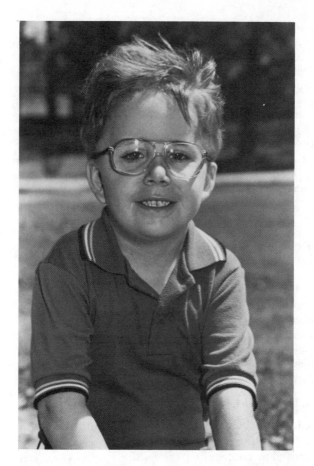

Parents must understand their responsibilities to their gifted children.

6. Gifted children pose challenges and problems to parents that are different from those of other children. Our review indicated that educators are not always aware of these possibilities and have not provided parents specific direction for dealing with them. (p. 26)

In an article entitled "Our Gifted and Talented: What Are Their Needs and What Can We Do?", Weiner (1981) stresses the idea that talent must be preserved and nurtured:

Studies of gifted children continually indicate that this group has problems that require assistance. A gifted child, like any other, can founder in a morass of failure, frustration, and maladjustment. He or she can be left rudderless, restless, and unfulfilled, his or her great gifts lost to society. How many millions of persons in the eons of time must have shown great promise? How pitifully few of these found fulfillment! How many of this group survived because of the intervention of an interested concerned person? Marconi's mother found her son space in the attic to work with his wires and contrivances when his rigid, intolerant father, having failed to force him into a military life, wrote him off as a failure. Churchill's English master imbued him with a love of language and the magic of words when he had been excused from Latin and Greek because he was a dullard. Einstein's uncle aroused his interest in mathematics, after he had nearly flunked in elementary school, by teaching him mathematical games and puzzles. The headmaster of Handel's small town school got him musical instruction despite his father's vehement objection to his son's having piano lessons.

Consider the children we have examined here. Who will intervene on behalf of Eric, whose social adjustment is so poor it has ostracized him from peers and teachers? Who will help Matt, who cannot withstand the continued pressure from his father to become his prototype? What about Jim, whose teacher turned him away from mathematics in the second grade when she punished him for taking his book home in the fall of the year and working out all the problems over the weekend? What will become of Karen, brilliant, musically talented, who despises her teachers as being stupid and weeps in agonized frustration because she has no friends?

These findings unmistakably refute the myth that gifted children not only have no problems but can make it on their own. There is also the ample evidence that many eminent persons and their gifts would have been lost to use without the supportive intervention of a concerned mentor. Parents and teachers are in a logical position to provide mentorships when needed by gifted children and thus assure self-fulfillment and societal enrichment. (p. 30)

CHAPTER SUMMARY

Gifted children need the attention that any child needs, but they are also entitled to educational experiences that will recognize and nurture their unique potential to contribute to self and society. As we strive toward this goal, parents and educators have a distinct responsibility to create an environment that will best guide, direct, and help the gifted child fulfill the highest possible levels of intellectual, emotional, and social growth. Those who counsel parents of the gifted must not only be knowledgeable of the nature and characteristics of giftedness, they must share these insights to assist parents to face the special challenges in bringing up their gifted offspring. In particular, parents must be helped to understand giftedness so that their child's intellectual development matches or his or her abilities.

The role of the counselor may be to provide the parents with short-term and direct information when they ask questions such as, "How can I go about getting my child admitted to school early? How do I explain giftedness to my child in order to make him feel more comfortable about being gifted?" Counseling may be more complex when the parent asks if a gifted child has a different way of learning than other children or if the parent wants to help the child find the best possible style of learning.

Regardless of the question or concern, the helper's responsibility is to provide information or suggest appropriate action steps to parents. They in turn will be well-informed and can adopt effective parenting practices to guide and direct their gifted child's total development. With proper help and guidance, parents can create favorable conditions and can model behavior and attitudes that will stimulate curiosity, exploration, experimentation, questioning, and self-directed learning to create a foundation for nurturing the child's intellectual and creative growth.

Colangelo and Zaffrann (1979) suggest five specific ways that counselors and helpers can assist parents of gifted children. As you review their list, think about your own qualifications, competencies, and counseling skills.

☐ Provide *understanding* to parents who may feel bewildered, frustrated, guilty, or threatened about raising a gifted child.

☐ Provide *information* about common characteristics of gifted children; about available programs, materials, and facilities; or about referral sources.

☐ Provide *advocacy, action, and support* for parent and family programs in schools.

☐ Help *initiate* parents' groups that can meet for information, for action, or simply for exchanging perceptions and feelings.

☐ Share *information* with the parents about their children, and facilitate family communication *by* the family *about* the family. (pp. 393–394)

Finally, Feldhusen and Kroll (1985) comment:

The United States is faced with a variety of economic, political, and social crises which seem to call for new insights, creative problem solving, and new talent. To ignore or neglect the educational needs of the gifted student is not only shortsighted but also undermines the development of this country's most precious natural resources. (p. 252)

ACTIVITIES, EXERCISES, AND IDEAS FOR REFLECTION AND DISCUSSION

1. Survey your school system to determine services provided for gifted children. Are they adequate? What types of services *should* be provided?
2. Interview the parents of a gifted child. What types of problems, concerns, and special challenges did or does their gifted child present to them? Was counseling available if and when they needed it?
3. Write or contact the Association for the Gifted (TAG) of the Council for Exceptional Children (CEC) and the National Association for Gifted Children (NAGC) for information about their purposes, goals, membership, and meetings. What are the similarities and differences in these organizations? How might parents of a gifted child profit from membership in these organizations?

4. How would you go about initiating and organizing a parent group dedicated to the understanding, advancement, and appropriate educational programming of gifted children?
5. Discuss differences in the way a counselor would work with parents of the gifted child as opposed to working with parents of handicapped children. Are the counseling skills and processes essentially the same? If not, how do they differ?
6. Why is it important for parents not to exaggerate their child's superiority or make him unduly conscious of it? What course of action can they take in this respect?
7. How might the counselor assist parents to listen to their gifted child with more insight and understanding?
8. It has been said that the gifted are, in fact, our most handicapped population because of the lack of available services and programs. Do you agree or disagree? What reasons can you offer to support your view?
9. Do you have a broad or narrow view of what constitutes giftedness? How might your own personal definition affect a counseling relationship with parents?
10. (a) You have been asked to present a program to a group of parents of gifted children and your talk is entitled, "Understanding and Nurturing Your Child's Giftedness." What specific issues, topics, or points would you focus on and discuss with this parent group? Is there one point or idea that you would emphasize? Why?
    (b) At the conclusion of your presentation, one parent angrily says, "I'm opposed to the idea of giftedness and gifted programs because they are not democratic and they encourage an elitist concept by giving special treatment to a select few." How would you respond to this accusation?

REFERENCES

Blackhurst, E. A., & Berdine, W. H. (1981). *An introduction to special education.* Boston: Little, Brown.

Bridges, S. A. (1979). The gifted child in the family. In J. J. Gallagher (Ed.), *Gifted children: Reaching their potential* (pp. 333–346). Jerusalem, Israel: Kollek & Son.

Carter, K. R., & Kontos, S. (1982). An application of cognitive-developmental theory to the identification of gifted children. *Roeper Review, 5*(2), 17–20.

Clark, B. (1983). *Growing up gifted* (2nd ed.). Columbus, OH: Charles E. Merrill.

Colangelo, N., & Dettman, D. F. (1983). A review of research on parents and families of gifted children. *Exceptional Children, 50,* 20–27.

Colangelo, N., & Zaffrann, R. T. (Eds.). (1979). *New voices in counseling the gifted.* Dubuque, IA: Kendall/Hunt.

Coleman, D. (1982, March/April). Parenting the gifted: Is this a job for superparent? *G/C/T, 22,* 47–50.

Congdon, P. J. (1979). Helping parents of gifted children. In J. J. Gallagher (Ed.), *Gifted children: Reaching their potential* (pp. 347–363). Jerusalem, Israel: Kollek & Son.

Feldhusen, J. F., & Kroll, M. D. (1985). Parent perceptions of gifted children's educational needs. *Roeper Review, 7*(4), 249–252.

Griggs, S. A. (1984). Counseling the gifted based on learning styles. *Exceptional Children, 50*(5), 429–432.

Havinghurst, R. H. (1957). Conditions favorable and detrimental to the development of talent. *School Review, 65*(1), 20–26.

Karnes, F. A. (1976). For and about parents. *Talents and Gifts: The Official Journal of the Association for the Gifted, 18,* 8.

Karnes, F. A., & Collins, E. (1977). Teacher certification in gifted education: A national survey. *Gifted Child Quarterly, 21,* 204–207.

Kauffman, J. M., & Hallahan, D. P. (Eds.). (1981). *Handbook of special education.* Englewood Cliffs, NJ: Prentice-Hall.

Kirk, S. A., & Gallagher, J. J. (1983). *Educating exceptional children.* Boston: Houghton Mifflin.

Marland, S. P. (1972). *Education of the gifted and talented: Report to the Congress of the United States by the U.S. Commissioner of Education.* Washington, D.C.: U.S. Government Printing Office.

Parke, B. N. (1985). Methods of creativity. In R. H. Swassing, *Teaching gifted children and adolescents* (pp. 376–401). Columbus, OH: Charles E. Merrill.

Renzulli, J. S. (1978). What makes giftedness? *Phi Delta Kappan, 60*(3), 180–184, 261.

Swaby, B. (1983). Questions parents ask about reading and the gifted. *Teaching Exceptional Children, 15*(3), 141–143.

Telford, C. W., & Sawrey, J. M. (1972). *The exceptional individual.* Englewood Cliffs, NJ: Prentice-Hall.

Torrance, E. P. (1965). *Gifted children in the classroom.* New York: MacMillan.

Torrance, E. P. (1970). *Encouraging creativity in the classroom.* (Dubuque, IA: Brown.

Weiner, A. (1981). Our gifted and talented: What are their needs and what can we do? In B. S. Miller & E. M. Price (Eds.). *The gifted child, the family, and the community* (pp. 27–31). New York: The American Association for Gifted Children: Walker.

Wetzel, P. R. (1981). The future and my contribution. In B. S. Miller & E. M. Price (Eds.), *The gifted child, the family, and the community* (pp. 188–189). New York: The American Association for Gifted Children: Walker.

Williams, F. E. (1982). Developing children's creativity at home and in the school. *G/C/T, 24,* 2–6.

Zorman, R.. (1982). Parents do make a difference. *Roeper Review, 5*(2), 41–43.

SELECTED REFERENCES FOR FURTHER READING AND STUDY

Alvino, J. (1981, November/December). Guidance for the gifted. *Instructor,* 64–66.

Anthony, S. (1982). Suggestions to 'turn on' bright children at home. *G/C/T, 25,* 22.

Ballering, L. D., & Koch, A. (1984). Family relations when a child is gifted. *Gifted Children Quarterly, 28*(3), 140–143.

Bloom, B. S. (1982). The role of gifts and markers in the development of talent. *Exceptional Children, 48*(6), *510–522.*

Chapey, G. D., & Trimarco, T. A. (1984). Participation of parents in programs for the gifted in New York City. *Journal for the Education of the Gifted, 7*(3), 178–191.

Colangelo, N., & Dettman, D. F. (1981). A conceptual model of four types of parent-school interactions. *Journal for the Education of the Gifted, 5*(2), 120–126.

Dettman, D. F., & Colangelo, N. (1980). A functional model for counseling parents of gifted students. *Gifted Child Quarterly, 24*(4), 158–161.

Goleman, D. (1980). 1,528 little geniuses and how they grew: The gifted children of the Terman study, 60 years later. *Psychology Today, 13*(9), 28–43.

Gogel, E. M., & McCumsey, J. (1983). What parents are saying. *G/C/T, 26,* 52–54.

Hayes, D. G., & Levitt, M. (1982). Stress: an inventory for parents. *G/C/T, 24,* 8–12.

Hunt, N. (1983). Creative parenting. *G/C/T, 28,* 30–31.

Johnson, T. F. (1985). Helping the gifted child adjust to the outside world. *G/C/T, 38,* 30–33.

Karnes, M. B. (1984). Special children . . . Special gifts. *Children Today, 13*(5), 18–23.

Karnes, M. B., Shwedel, A. M., & Lewis, G. F. (1983). Long-term effects of early programming for the gifted/talented handicapped. *Journal for the Education of the Gifted, 6*(4), 266–278.

Laibow, R. E. (1981). An open letter to parents of extremely gifted youngsters. *G/C/T, 17,* 23–25.

Lyon, H. C. (1980). Our most neglected natural resource. *Today's Education, 70*(1), 15GS–20GS.

Mathews, F. N. (1981). Effective communication with parents of the gifted and talented: Some suggestions for improvement. *Journal for the Education of the Gifted, 6*(3), 207–210.

Mathews, F. N. (1981). Influencing parents' attitudes toward gifted education. *Exceptional Children, 48*(2), 140–143.

Moore, N. D. (1982). The joys and challenges in raising a gifted child. *G/C/T, 25,* 8–11.

Roeper, A. (1982). How the gifted cope with their emotions. *Roeper Review, 5*(2), 21–23.

Ross, A., & Parker, M. (1980). Academic and social self-concepts of the academically gifted. *Exceptional Children, 47*(1), 6–11.

Schetky, D. H. (1981). The emotional and social development of the gifted child: Psychiatrist looks at giftedness. *G/C/T, 18,* 2–4.

Swayer, R. N. (1984). Advice for parents: Open doors, show love, relax. *Psychology Today, 18*(6), 36.

Whitmore, J. R. (1981). Gifted children with handicapping conditions. *Exceptional Children, 48*(2), 106–114.

Wolf, J. S., & Stephens, T. M. (1984). Training models for parents of the gifted. *Journal for the Education of the Gifted, 7*(2), 120–129.

SELECTED JOURNALS/NEWSLETTERS IN GIFTED EDUCATION

In particular situations you may need additional information about gifted, talented, and creative children. There are many national, regional, state, and local organizations that can be of assistance to you, as well as newsletters and journals. The following is a partial list of these:

G/C/T is a bi-monthly magazine for parents and teachers of Gifted, Creative, and Talented Children. For subscription information write:

G/C/T Publishing Co., Inc.
P.O. Box 6448
Mobile, AL 36660

The Gifted Children Newsletter, published monthly, is primarily intended for the parents of children with great promise. Write for information to:

Gifted Children Newsletter
P.O. Box 7200
Bergenfield, NJ 07621

The Roeper Review, published quarterly, focuses on the philosophical, moral, and academic issues that relate to the lives and experiences of the gifted and talented. It presents various positions and approaches relating to these issues and translates them into practice in the home, school, and community. For information write:

The Roeper Review
Roeper City and County School
P.O. Box 329
Bloomfield Hills, MI 48013

The National Association for Gifted Children (NAGC) seeks to further the education of the gifted and to enhance the child's potential creativity. Members receive *The Gifted Child Quarterly.* Write or contact:

The National Association for Gifted Children
5100 North Edgewood Drive
St. Paul, MN 55112

The American Association for Gifted Children (AAGC) is a nonprofit organization dedicated to encouraging the optimal development of gifted and talented children and youth, particularly through the family and community. For further information, write or contact:

The American Association for Gifted Children
15 Gramercy Park
New York, NY 10003

The Association for the Gifted (TAG) is a division of the Council for Exceptional Children whose members include teachers, administrators, and others interested in gifted and talented children. Their quarterly publication is entitled *Journal for the Education of the Gifted.* For further information, write or contact:

The Council for Exceptional Children
1920 Association Drive
Reston, VA 22091

Appendix A
Selected Publications and Journals
Related to Exceptional Persons

JOURNALS

For All Disabilities

CHILDREN TODAY. U. S. Department of Health and Human Services, Office of Human Development Services, Administration for Children, Youth, and Families, Children's Bureau. 6 issues a year, $14.00. (Send payment to the Superintendent of Documents, U.S. Government Printing Office, Washington, DC 20402.)

DISABLED USA. President's Committee on Employment of the Handicapped, Washington, DC 20210. Bimonthly, no charge.

EXCEPTIONAL CHILDREN. Council for Exceptional Children, 1920 Association Drive, Reston, VA 22091. 6 issues a year, $25.00, or with membership.

EXCEPTIONAL PARENT. Psy-Ed Corporation, 296 Boylston Street, Third Floor, Boston, MA 02116. 6 issues a year, $14.00.

FOCUS ON EXCEPTIONAL CHILDREN. Love Publishing Company, 1777 South Bellaire Street, Denver, CO 80222. 9 issues a year, $10.00.

JOURNAL OF REHABILITATION. National Rehabilitation Association, 633 South Washington Street, Alexandria, VA 22314. 4 issues a year, $20.00, or with membership.

REHABILITATION LITERATURE. Easter Seal Society, 2023 West Ogden Avenue, Chicago, IL 60612. 6 issues a year, $15.00.

TEACHING EXCEPTIONAL CHILDREN. Council for Exceptional Children, 1920 Association Drive, Reston, VA 22091. 4 issues a year, with membership.

UP FRONT. UPF, Inc., 90 Cherry Street, Box 19, Johnstown, PA 15907. 6 issues a year, $15.00; two years, $20.00.

For Autism

JOURNAL OF AUTISM AND DEVELOPMENTAL DISORDERS. Plenum Publishing Corporation, 233 Spring Street, New York, NY 10013. 4 issues a year, $25.00 for individuals.

For Hearing Handicaps

THE DEAF AMERICAN. National Association of the Deaf, 814 Thayer Avenue, Silver Spring, MD 20910. 8 issues a year, $10.00.

THE VOLTA REVIEW. Alexander Graham Bell Association for the Deaf, 3417 Volta Place, Northwest, Washington, DC 20007. 7 issues a year, $35.00 with membership.

For Learning Disabilities

ACADEMIC THERAPY. Academic Therapy Publications, Inc. 20 Commercial Boulevard, Novato, CA 94947. 5 issues a year, $9.00.

JOURNAL OF LEARNING DISABILITIES. The Professional Press, Inc. 101 East Ontario Street, Chicago, IL 60611. 10 issues a year, $24.00.

LEARNING DISABILITIES QUARTERLY. Council for Exceptional Children, 1920 Association Drive, Reston, VA 22091. 4 issues a year, $12.50, or with membership.

For Mental Retardation

AMERICAN JOURNAL OF MENTAL DEFICIENCY. American Association on Mental Deficiency, 5101 Wisconsin Avenue, Northwest, Washington, DC 20016. 6 issues a year, $20.00.

EDUCATION AND TRAINING OF THE MENTALLY RETARDED. Council for Exceptional Children, 1920 Association Drive, Reston, VA 22091. 4 issues a year, $16.00, or with membership.

JOURNAL FOR SPECIAL EDUCATORS. American Association of Special Educators, 179 Sierra Vista Lane, Valley Cottage, NY 10989. 4 issues a year, $15.00 with membership.

MENTAL RETARDATION. American Association on Mental Deficiency, 5101 Wisconsin Avenue, Northwest, Washington, DC 20016. 6 issues a year, $26.00, or with membership.

SHARING OUR CARING. Caring, Post Office Box 400, Milton, WA 98354. 5 issues a year, $10.00.

For Physical Handicaps

ACCENT ON LIVING. Cheever Publishing, Inc., Post Office Box 700, Gillum Road and High Drive, Bloomington, IL 61701. 4 issues a year, $5.00.

For Visual Impairments

JOURNAL OF VISION IMPAIRMENT AND BLINDNESS. American Foundation for the Blind, 15 West 16th Street, New York, NY 10011. 10 issues a year, $15.00.

For Severe and Multiple Handicaps

JASH. The Association for the Severely Handicapped, 7010 Roosevelt Way Northeast, Seattle, WA 98115. 4 issues a year, $30.00, or with membership.

Appendix B
Selected Organizations
Serving Exceptional Children,
Youth, and Adults

In recent years, groups organized by parents of handicapped children and by disabled adults have been trailblazers in the movement to win full acceptance of people with handicaps as members of the human family. These organizations have grown strong through the determination of their members. Parents have helped other parents, adults with disabilities have joined together in advocacy, and all have worked to overcome obstacles of indifference and ignorance. By beaming the public spotlight on severe problems, working for reform and demanding that society respond, they have created a force that has scored remarkable victories—in legislation, in better services, in a more open and aware society.

This list of major national organizations is a source of information and advocacy for handicapped individuals. We urge you to get in touch with the groups that can be most helpful to you—whether you are a parent, a disabled person, a professional, or simply a person who can volunteer time and energy. New groups are coming to our attention all the time; if you cannot find what you need on this list, please contact us and we will try to refer you to an appropriate group.

Ask about chapters near your home. Write for their newsletters and other informative literature. Find out about their wide-ranging national, state, and local activities. Whatever your needs—whether services, reports on new research, resources to help a disabled person, information about vocational training, or the encouragement of others who have been through similar situations—see what these groups can tell you. With them, you can help raise awareness of the needs and potential of handicapped children and adults and work for a more responsive and open society.

Source: From *Closer look: A project of the Parents' Compaign for Handicapped Children and Youth,* Box 1492, Washington, DC 20013.

AUTISM

National Society for Autistic Children
1234 Massachusetts Avenue, N.W.
Suite 1017
Washington, DC 20005

CEREBRAL PALSY

United Cerebral Palsy Association
66 East 34th Street, 3rd Floor
New York, NY 10016

DEAF-BLIND

National Association of the Deaf-Blind
2703 Forest Oak Circle
Norman, OK 73071

National Deaf-Blind Program
Bureau of Education for the Handi-
capped
Room 4046, Donohoe Building
400 6th Street, S.W.
Washington, DC 20202

EMOTIONALLY DISTURBED

Mental Health Association, National
Headquarters
1800 North Kent Street
Arlington, VA 22209

The National Alliance for the Mentally
Ill
P.O. Box 1016
Evanston, IL 60204

EPILEPSY

Epilepsy Foundation of America
1828 L. Street, N.W., Suite 406
Washington, DC 20036

HEALTH IMPAIRMENTS

American Cancer Society
777 Third Avenue
New York, NY 10017

American Diabetes Association
600 Fifth Avenue
New York, NY 10020

American Heart Association
7320 Greenville Avenue
Dallas, TX 75231

American Lung Association
1740 Broadway
New York, NY 10019

Asthma and Allergy Foundation of
America
19 West 44th Street, Suite 702
New York, NY 10036

The Candlelighters Foundation
123 C Street, S.E.
Washington DC 20003

Cystic Fibrosis Foundation
3384 Peachtree Road, N.E.
Suite 875
Atlanta, GA 30326

Juvenile Diabetes Foundation
23 East 26th Street, 4th Floor
New York, NY 10010

Leukemia Society of America
800 Second Avenue
New York, NY 10017

National Association for Sickle Cell
Disease, Inc.
3460 Wilshire, Suite 1012
Los Angeles, CA 90010

National Hemophilia Foundation
19 West 34th Street
Room 1204
New York, NY 10001

National Kidney Foundation
Two Park Avenue
New York, NY 10016

National Neurofibromatosis Foundation
340 East 80th Street, #21–H
New York, NY 10021

National Tay Sachs Foundation and
Allied Diseases Association
122 East 42nd Street
New York, NY 10017

National Tuberous Sclerosis Association, Inc.
P.O. Box 159
Laguna Beach, CA 92652

United Ostomy Association
2001 W. Beverly Boulevard
Los Angeles, CA 90057

HEARING IMPAIRED

Alexander Graham Bell Association for the Deaf
3417 Volta Place, N.W.
Washington, DC 20007

National Association of the Deaf
814 Thayer Avenue
Silver Spring, MD 20910

LEARNING DISABILITIES

Association for Children and Adults with Learning Disabilities
4156 Library Road
Pittsburgh, PA 15234

The Orton Society, Inc.
8415 Bellona Lane
Suite 115
Towson, MD 21204

National Network of Learning Disabled Adults
P.O. Box 3130
Richardson, TX 75080

MENTAL RETARDATION

Association for Retarded Children
2709 Avenue E. East
P.O. Box 6109
Arlington, TX 76011

Down's Syndrome Congress
1640 W. Roosevelt Road
Room 156E
Chicago, IL 60608

PHYSICALLY HANDICAPPED

American Brittle Bone Society
Cherry Hill Plaza Suite LL-3
1415 East Marlton Pike
Cherry Hill, NJ 08034

Arthritis Foundation
3400 Peachtree Road, N.E.
Suite 1106
Atlanta, GA 30326

Human Growth Foundation
4930 West 77th Street
Minneapolis, MN 55435

Little People of America
P.O. Box 126
Owatonna, MN 55060

Muscular Dystrophy Association, Inc.
810 Seventh Avenue
New York, NY 10019

National Amputation Foundation
12–45 150th Street
Whitestone, NY 11357

The National Association of the Physically Handicapped, Inc.
76 Elm Street
London, OH 43140

National Multiple Sclerosis Society
205 East 42nd Street
New York, NY 10017

National Spinal Cord Injury Foundation
369 Elliot Street
Newton Upper Falls, MA 02164

Osteogenesis Imperfecta Foundation
632 Center Street
Van Wert, OH 45891

Spina Bifida Association of America
343 South Dearborn Street
Room 319
Chicago, IL 60604

Tourette Syndrome Association
40–08 Corporal Kennedy Street
Bayside, NY 11361

SPEECH IMPAIRMENTS

American Speech—Language—
Hearing Association
10801 Rockville Pike
Rockville, MD 20852

VISUAL IMPAIRMENTS

American Council of the Blind
1211 Connecticut Avenue, N.W.
Suite 506
Washington, DC 20036

American Council of the Blind
Parents
Rt. A Box 78
Franklin, LA 70538

American Foundation for the Blind
15 West 16th Street
New York, NY 10011

International Institute for Visually
Impaired 0–7, Inc.
1975 Rutgers Circle
East Lansing, MI 48823

National Association for Parents of
Visually Impaired
2011 Hardy Circle
Austin, TX 78757

National Association for Visually Handicapped
305 East 24th Street
New York, NY 10010

National Federation of the Blind
1800 Johnson Street
Baltimore, MD 21230

ALL DISABILITIES

American Coalition for Citizens with
Disabilities
1200 15th Street, N.W. Suite 201
Washington, DC 20005

The Association for the Severely Handicapped
1600 West Armory Way
Garden View Suite
Seattle, WA 98119

March of Dimes Birth Defect Foundation
1275 Mamaroneck Avenue
White Plains, NY 10605

National Easter Seal Society for Crippled Children and Adults
2023 W. Ogden Avenue
Chicago, IL 60612

Closer Look: National Information
Center for the Handicapped
Box 1492
Washington, DC 20009

Council for Exceptional Children
1920 Association Drive
Reston, VA 20091

National Center for Law and the Handicapped
1233 North Eddy Street
South Bend, IN 46817

National Committee for Citizens in Education
410 Wilde Lake Village Green
Columbia, MD 21044

Physical Education and Recreation for
the Handicapped: Information and
Research Utilization Center
1201 16th Street N.W.
Washington, DC 20036

President's Committee on Employment
of the Handicapped
Washington, DC 20210

Appendix C
Code of Ethics and Standards
for Professional Practice

Adopted by the CEC Delegate Assembly, April 1983

■ Standards of a profession are formally codified sets of beliefs. As such, they should be based upon universal ethical principles. In the standards that follow, special education professionals charge themselves with obligations to three parties: the exceptional student, the employer, and the profession. Ethical responsibilities in these three areas have been translated into eight principles which form the basis for all professional conduct. These eight principles comprise the *Code of Ethics* for special educators. They, in turn, have been translated into a set of minimum standards of conduct called *Standards for Professional Practice.* Taken together, the code of ethics and standards for practice provide guidelines for professional etiquette, for effective interpersonal behavior, for resolution of ethical issues, and for making professional judgments concerning what constitutes competent practice.

CEC CODE OF ETHICS

We declare the following principles to be the Code of Ethics for educators of exceptional persons. Members of the special education profession are responsible for upholding and advancing these principles. Members of The Council for Exceptional Children agree to judge by them in accordance with the spirit and provisions of this Code.

I. Special education professionals are committed to developing the highest educational and quality of life potential of exceptional individuals.

II. Special education professionals promote and maintain a high level of competence and integrity in practicing their profession.

III. Special education professionals engage in professional activities which benefit exceptional individuals, their families, other colleagues, students, or research subjects.

IV. Special education professionals exercise objective professional judgment in the practice of their profession.

V. Special education professionals strive to advance their knowledge and skills regarding the education of exceptional individuals.

VI. Special education professionals work within the standards and policies of their profession.

VII. Special education professionals seek to uphold and improve where necessary the laws, regulations, and policies governing the delivery of special education and related services and the practice of their profession.

VIII. Special education professionals do not condone or participate in unethical or illegal acts, nor violate professional standards adopted by the Delegate Assembly of CEC.

CEC STANDARDS FOR PROFESSIONAL PRACTICE

1. PROFESSIONALS IN RELATION TO EXCEPTIONAL PERSONS AND THEIR FAMILIES

1.1 Instructional Responsibilities

1.1.1 Special education personnel are committed to the application of professional expertise to ensure the provision of quality education for all exceptional individuals. Professionals strive to:

1.1.1.1 Identify and use instructional methods and curricula that are appropriate to their area of professional practice and effective in meeting the needs of exceptional persons.

1.1.1.2 Participate in the selection of and use appropriate instructional materials, equipment, supplies, and other resources needed in the effective practice of their profession.

1.1.1.3 Create safe and effective learning environments which contribute to fulfillment of needs, stimulation of learning and of self-concept.

1.1.1.4 Maintain class size and caseloads which are conducive to meeting the individual instructional needs of exceptional persons.

1.1.1.5 Use assessment instruments and procedures that do not discriminate against exceptional persons on the basis of race, color, creed, sex, national origin, age, political practices, family or social background, sexual orientation, or exceptionality.

1.1.1.6 Base grading, promotion, graduation, and/or movement out of the program on the individual goals and objectives for the exceptional individual.

1.1.1.7 Provide accurate program data to administrators, colleagues, and parents, based on efficient and objective record-keeping practices, for the purpose of decision making.

1.1.1.8 Maintain confidentiality of information except where information is released under specific conditions of written consent and statutory confidentiality requirements.

1.2 Management of Behavior

1.2.1 Special education professionals participate with other professionals and with parents in an interdisciplinary effort in the management of behavior. Professionals:

1.2.1.1 Apply only those disciplinary methods and behavioral procedures which they have been instructed to use and which do not undermine the dignity of the individual or the basic human rights of exceptional persons (such as corporal punishment).

1.2.1.2 Clearly specify the goals and objectives for behavior management practices in the exceptional person's Individualized Education Program.

1.2.1.3 Conform to policies, statutes, and rules established by state/provincial and local agencies relating to judicious application of disciplinary methods and behavioral procedures.

1.2.1.4 Take adequate measures to discourage, prevent, and intervene when a colleague's behavior is perceived as being detrimental to exceptional persons.

1.2.1.5 Refrain from aversive techniques unless repeated trials of other methods have failed and then only after consultation with parents and appropriate agency officials.

1.3 Support Procedures

1.3.1 Adequate instruction and supervision shall be provided to professionals before they are required to perform support services for which they have not been previously prepared.

1.3.2 Professionals may administer medication, where state/provincial policies do not preclude such action, if qualified to do so or if written instructions are on file which state the purpose of the medication, the conditions under which it may be administered, possible side effects, the physician's name and phone number, and the professional liability if a mistake is made. The professional will not be required to administer medication.

1.3.3 Professionals note and report to those concerned whenever changes in behavior occur in conjunction with the administration of medication or at any other time.

1.4 Parent Relationships

1.4.1 Professionals seek to develop relationships with parents based on mutual respect for their roles in achieving benefits for the exceptional person. Special education professionals:

1.4.1.1 Develop effective communication with parents, avoiding technical terminology, using the primary language of the home, and other modes of communication when appropriate.

1.4.1.2 Seek and use parents' knowledge and expertise in planning, conducting, and evaluating special education and related services for exceptional persons.

1.4.1.3 Maintain communications between parents and professionals with appropriate respect for privacy and confidentiality.

1.4.1.4 Extend opportunities for parent education, utilizing accurate information and professional methods.

1.4.1.5 Inform parents of the educational rights of their children and of any proposed or actual practices which violate those rights.

1.4.1.6 Recognize and respect cultural diversities which exist in some families with exceptional persons.

1.4.1.7 Recognize that the relationship of home and community environmental conditions affects the behavior and outlook of the exceptional person.

1.5 Advocacy

1.5.1 Special education professionals serve as advocates for exceptional persons by speaking, writing, and acting in a variety of situations on their behalf. Professionals:

1.5.1.1 Continually seek to improve government provisions for the education of exceptional persons while ensuring that public statements by professionals as individuals are not construed to represent official policy statements of the agency by which they are employed.

1.5.1.2 Work cooperatively with and encourage other professionals to improve the provision of special education and related services to exceptional persons.

1.5.1.3 Document and objectively report to their supervisors or administrators inadequacies in resources and promote appropriate corrective action.

1.5.1.4 Monitor for inappropriate placements in special education and intervene at the appropriate level to correct the condition when such inappropriate placements exist.

1.5.1.5 Follow local, state/provincial, and federal laws and regulations which mandate a free appropriate public education to exceptional students and the protection of the rights of exceptional persons to equal opportunities in our society.

2. PROFESSIONAL EMPLOYMENT

2.1 Certification and Qualification

2.1.1 Professionals ensure that only persons deemed qualified by having met state/provincial minimal standards are employed as teachers, administrators, and related-service providers for persons with exceptionalities.

2.2 Employment

2.2.1 Professionals do not discriminate in hiring on the basis of race, color, creed, sex, national origin, age, political practices, family or social background, sexual orientation, or exceptionality.

2.2.2 Professionals represent themselves in an ethical and legal manner in regard to their training and experience when seeking new employment.

2.2.3 Professionals give notice consistent with local education agency policies when intending to leave employment.

2.2.4 Professionals adhere to the conditions of a contract or terms of an appointment in the setting where they practice.

2.2.5 Professionals released from employment are entitled to a written explanation of the reasons for termination and to fair and impartial due process procedures.

2.2.6 Special education professionals share equitably the opportunities and benefits (salary, working conditions, facilities, and other resources) of other professionals in the school system.

2.2.7 Professionals seek assistance, including the services of other professionals, in instances where personal problems threaten to interfere with their job performance.

2.2.8 Professionals respond objectively when requested to evaluate applicants seeking employment.

2.2.9 Professionals have the right and responsibility to resolve professional problems by utilizing established procedures, including grievance procedures when appropriate.

2.3 Assignment and Role

2.3.1 Professionals should receive clear written communication of all duties and responsibilities, including those which are prescribed as conditions of their employment.

2.3.2 Professionals promote educational quality and intra- and interprofessional cooperation through active participation in the planning, policy development, management, and evaluation of the special education program and the education program at large so that programs remain responsive to the changing needs of exceptional persons.

2.3.3 Professionals practice only in areas of exceptionality, at age levels, and in program models for which they are prepared by reason of training and/or experience.

2.3.4 Adequate supervision of and support for special education professionals is provided by other professionals qualifed by reason of training and experience in the area of concern.

2.3.5 The administration and supervision of special education professionals provides for clear lines of accountability.

2.3.6 The unavailability of substitute teacher or support personnel, including aides, must not result in the denial of special education services to a greater degree than to that of other educational programs.

2.4 Professional Development

2.4.1 Special education professionals systematically advance their knowledge and skills in order to maintain a high level of competence and response to the changing needs of exceptional persons by pursuing a program of continuing education including but not limited to participation in such activities as inservice training, professional conferences/workshops, professional meetings, continuing education courses, and the reading of professional literature.

2.4.2 Professionals participate in the objective and systematic evaluation of themselves, colleagues, services, and programs for the purpose of continuous improvement of professional performance.

2.4.3 Professionals in administrative positions support and facilitate professional development.

3. PROFESSIONALS IN RELATION TO THE PROFESSION AND TO OTHER PROFESSIONALS

3.1 To the Profession

3.1.1 Special education professionals assume responsibility for participating in professional organizations and adherence to the standards and codes of ethics of those organizations.

3.1.2 Special education professionals have a responsibility to provide varied and exemplary supervised field experiences for persons in undergraduate and graduate preparation programs.

3.1.3 Special education professionals refrain from using professional relationships with students and parents for personal advantage.

3.1.4 Special education professionals take an active position in the regulation of the profession through use of appropriate procedures for bringing about changes.

3.1.5 Special education professionals initiate support and/or participate in research related to the education of exceptional persons with the aim of improving the quality of educational services, increasing the accountability of programs, and generally benefiting exceptional persons. Professionals:

3.1.5.1 Adopt procedures that protect the rights and welfare of subjects participating in research.

3.1.5.2 Interpret and publish research results with accuracy and a high quality of scholarship.

3.1.5.3 Support a cessation of the use of any research procedure which may result in undesirable consequences for the participant.

3.1.5.4 Exercise all possible precautions to prevent misapplication or misuse of a research effort, by oneself or others.

3.2 To Other Professionals

3.2.1 Special education professionals function as members of interdisciplinary teams and the reputation of the profession resides with them. Professionals:

3.2.1.1 Recognize and acknowledge the competencies and expertise of members representing other disciplines as well as those of members in their own disciplines.

3.2.1.2 Strive to develop positive attitudes among other professionals toward exceptional persons, representing them with an objective regard for their possibilities and their limitations as persons in a democratic society.

3.2.1.3 Cooperate with other agencies involved in serving exceptional persons through such activities as the planning and coordination of information exchanges, service delivery, and evaluation and training, so that no duplication or loss in quality of services may occur.

3.2.1.4 Provide consultation and assistance, where appropriate, to both regular and special education as well as other school personnel serving exceptional persons.

3.2.1.5 Provide consultation and assistance, where appropriate, to professionals in nonschool settings serving exceptional persons.

3.2.1.6 Maintain effective interpersonal relations with colleagues and other professionals, helping them to develop and maintain positive and accurate perceptions about the special education profession.

Name Index

Subject Index